MW00466687

Feminist Post-Liberalism

Judith A. Baer

Feminist
Post-Liberalism

TEMPLE UNIVERSITY PRESS
Philadelphia • Rome • Tokyo

TEMPLE UNIVERSITY PRESS
Philadelphia, Pennsylvania 19122
tupress.temple.edu

Copyright © 2020 by Temple University—Of The Commonwealth System of Higher
  Education
All rights reserved
Published 2020

Library of Congress Cataloging-in-Publication Data

Names: Baer, Judith A., author.
Title: Feminist post-liberalism / Judith A. Baer.
Description: Philadelphia : Temple University Press, 2020. | Includes bibliographical
  references and index. | Summary: "Feminist Post-Liberalism argues that feminism and
  liberalism need each other, and that they can together better elucidate controversies in
  American politics, law, and women and politics. It develops a theory of feminist
  post-liberalism that is true to the principles of both ideologies"—Provided by publisher.
Identifiers: LCCN 2019011979 (print) | LCCN 2019980019 (ebook) | ISBN 9781439917282
  (paperback) | ISBN 9781439917275 (cloth) | ISBN 9781439917299 (ebook)
Subjects: LCSH: Feminism. | Liberalism. | Feminist theory. | Women—Political activity—
  United States. | Women—United States—Social conditions. | United States—Politics and
  government—21st century.
Classification: LCC HQ1155 .B34 2020 (print) | LCC HQ1155 (ebook) | DDC 305.42—dc23
LC record available at https://lccn.loc.gov/2019011979
LC ebook record available at https://lccn.loc.gov/2019980019

♾ The paper used in this publication meets the requirements of the American National
Standard for Information Sciences—Permanence of Paper for Printed Library Materials,
ANSI Z39.48-1992

Printed in the United States of America

9 8 7 6 5 4 3 2 1

To my teachers

Contents

Preface and Acknowledgments

In 2016, the Democrats nominated a woman for president. She had been a U.S. senator and secretary of state. The Republicans nominated an outsider who had never held public office. The Democrat triumphed in the debates. Polls predicted a Democratic victory. Surely a Democrat would fill the Supreme Court vacancy created by the death of Antonin Scalia. Mass incarceration and antichoice policies were in danger. Domestic violence, sexual assault, economic inequality, and climate change had become serious issues. Then came the general election.

Donald Trump defeated Hillary Rodham Clinton in the presidential race while the Republican Party kept control of House and Senate. Republicans made gains in state governments, reinforcing their control over legislative districting and enabling them to impose more voting restrictions. Trump's vilifying of Mexicans and Muslims, his ridicule of a disabled person, and his remarks about women that crossed the line from sexism into misogyny did not disqualify him. Clinton's negatives—her marriage to a former president, her use of a private email account while secretary of state, her well-paid speeches on Wall Street, the family foundation that accepted money from "rogue" states, or any combination of these factors—disqualified her. "American women have learned that even a buffoon with no experience in government and no history of public service is more likely to be elected president—so long as he has a penis, a television program, and a billion dollars (more or less)."[1] Enough voters in enough states preferred a misogynist to a woman. Enough people in enough states failed to vote at all, which helped elect the misogynist. "Even at this late date, too many people who call themselves liberals still can't bring themselves to vote for a woman."[2]

Did Clinton lose because she is a woman? There is no shortage of alternative explanations, most of which have evidence to support them. The worst-case scenario is conspiracy: Did the Russians, the Federal Bureau of Investigation, and/or other actors plot to swing the election to Trump? Evidence supports this explanation. A second explanation reasons from structure: Trump won because the electoral college system distributes power disproportionately to states with large populations and struggling economies. Clinton's three-million-vote majority indicates that a more democratic mode of election might have produced different results. An explanation from individual responsibility, a concept that liberals love too much,[3] suggests that Trump won because Clinton made mistakes, which she did.[4] We can expect to see Ph.D. dissertations weighing these factors and choosing among them for the rest of the twenty-first century. Questions about what civil rights law calls "but-for causation" are unanswerable; nobody knows if a male Democrat would have beaten Trump. But gender bias contributed to Clinton's defeat. Let facts be submitted to a candid world.

Hillary Clinton lost the presidency twice. In 2008, she lost the nomination to Barack Obama, partly because members of a powerful liberal Democratic family pledged their support to Barack Obama in January and campaigned for him until November. Caroline Kennedy, the late president's daughter, said, "I have never had a president who inspired me the way people tell me that my father inspired them. But for the first time, I believe I have found the man who could be that president—not just for me, but for a new generation of Americans."[5] Senator Ted Kennedy of Massachusetts endorsed "the candidate who inspires me, who inspires all of us, who can lift our vision and summon our hopes and renew our belief that the country's best days are still to come."[6] Kennedy acknowledged the influence of his niece. He was not the only American to look to the younger generation for guidance that year.

Caroline's sexism is obvious. If you look for a man, that is what you will find. The vocabulary of evaluation privileges the subjective—"inspires," "makes me say ah-ha!" "fits in better," and so on—and can mask bias. Ted telephoned the former president, not the candidate, to inform the Clintons of his decision.[7] By 2016, Ted Kennedy was dead, and Caroline's influence had waned.

This time, Clinton was the youngest of the three major candidates. She was sixty-nine; her rival for the nomination, Bernie Sanders, was seventy-four; Donald Trump was seventy. If you turned off the sound and watched Sanders and Trump on television, you saw two white-haired, red-faced white men working their jaw muscles. Who they were got in the way of what they said. Sanders's support for Heath Mello, a Democrat running for mayor of

Omaha who opposed abortion rights, confirmed feminists' suspicions that gender equality was not among his priorities.

"A woman, but not *this* woman" was a familiar refrain in 2016. But each woman candidate in her turn will become "this woman," with her own particular experiences that will get heightened scrutiny. Some voters were reluctant to see a former first family return to the White House. But, presently, all spouses of former presidents are female. For now, to oppose spouses of presidents is to discriminate against women. Children and siblings of prominent Americans have won high office. Disqualifying candidates on the basis of family connections now would eliminate women and minority hopefuls who take a familiar path to public office. Anyone nominated by a major party will have made mistakes, associated with the rich and powerful, and received benefits from someone somebody does not like. Clinton's negatives got more exposure than those of any presidential candidate in history. Women in traditionally male roles are used to this kind of treatment. More is expected of women than of men. Different things are expected of women than of men. Clinton's defeat was partly due to her gender. Liberal theory and practice contributed to that defeat. So did some feminist theory.[8]

Things have worsened since Trump took office. An alliance of conservatives, capitalists, and evangelical Christians has emerged, united by their commitment to or tolerance of the recriminalizing of abortion. Trump committed himself to appointing Supreme Court justices who will make a majority for overturning *Roe v. Wade*, thus returning the issue to state legislatures. People who disagree about important issues have joined in destroying a woman's right to choose. The Department of Education has made it easier for sexual predators to escape punishment. Federal benefits are at risk. Earth is in jeopardy, both from uncontrolled climate change and nuclear war.

Despair is easy. But the conservative-evangelical consensus is not as solid as it looks. Hillary Clinton won the popular vote with a majority about four times the size of Al Gore's in 2000. If the movement to abolish the Electoral College succeeds, Clinton and Gore will have accomplished more in defeat than some presidents do in victory. Trump won Texas, as expected, but his majority of 9 percent was well below Mitt Romney's majority in 2012. Democrats gained seats in both houses of Congress. The Me Too movement has imprisoned some predators and removed others from power. The results of the 2018 election are anyone's guess. The way forward is to understand the past and confront the future. This book is an effort to refute both conservative and radical critiques and to arrive at a feminist post-liberalism. I argue that feminism and liberalism need each other.

The first two chapters of this book introduce the reader to feminist post-liberalism and what I call imperative theory, derived from the imperative jurisprudence discussed in *Our Lives before the Law.*[9] Chapter 1 analyzes the development of feminist and antifeminist liberalism and feminist and radical antiliberalism from the eighteenth century to the present. Chapter 2 defines imperative theory in terms of the necessary tasks that all societies must accomplish and the tasks some people force other people to perform. My reading of anthropology and zoology convinced me that male supremacy is no more a product of "human nature," whatever that means, than it is of men's ability to subdue women.

Chapter 3 explores decisions from statutory and constitutional court cases to reinforce the point that liberalism as we know it cannot adequately protect women's interests. Like all judicial opinions, these decisions are primarily legal interpretations and only secondarily essays in political theory. They are at least as much the product of politics as of political ideologies. Their authors are constrained by institutional norms; they resolve only the issues before them rather than seeking an ideal conclusion. My justifications for using court opinions as examples of political theory rather than of legal doctrine are, first, that many opinions can stand on their own merits as theory; second, that many judicial scholars insist that court decisions are influenced primarily by the judges' ideologies;[10] and, third, that liberalism and constitutionalism have historically had a close relationship.[11] Chapter 4 approaches the subject of crime through a critical treatment of liberals' role in mass incarceration. Topics covered include the death penalty, Megan's Laws, and sexual assault. Chapter 5 focuses on feminist, liberal, and radical views on the conventional family and the creation of alternative structures.

If feminist and liberal theory can correct each other's characteristic errors, might the two ideologies also share characteristic errors? Chapters 6 and 7 address this possibility. An early version of Chapter 6 remarked, "'Liberal guilt,' separated from individual action, is a familiar phenomenon. Women's propensity to guilt feelings . . . is something feminists know only too well."[12] I argue that liberal guilt arises from recognition of privilege and commitment to equality, while feminist guilt is the result of women's disproportionate share of responsibility. But if the sources are different, the results are similar. Tolerance and self-examination are virtues, but within both feminist and liberal thought, these virtues have been carried to extremes. Robert Frost, hypothetically a liberal in one of his poems, describes himself as "so altruistically moral / I never take my own side in a quarrel."[13] Feminists have agonized over all sorts of questions that consume energy needed for action.

Chapter 7 raises an issue I had not considered before a panel discussant raised it in response to a presentation of the ideas in this book. Might an emphasis on gender equality, she asked, not reinforce gender binaries? A growing number of people who identify as bisexual, intersexual, and transgender dispute the notion that gender is a fixed dichotomy. Is gender equality the same as sex equality? I found myself confronting more general issues about binaries: How do they help, and how do they frustrate, human thought? The dangers lie not in binaries but in the hierarchies they encourage. Chapter 8 attempts to bring this twenty-year project on constructing feminist post-liberalism to something resembling a conclusion.

No scholar can write a book alone. I owe much to my fellow theorists in the political science department at Texas A&M University: Cary Nederman and Diego Von Vacano and our former colleagues Ed Portis and Lisa Ellis. Texas A&M University gave me a faculty development leave in the fall 2009 semester. My graduate assistants, Abhisekh Ghosh Moulick, Tyler Theel, and Reed Stevens, dealt with reference questions and the growing reference list. Versions of the first six chapters appeared, at least once, as papers at professional meetings; the comments and questions from fellow panelists and audience members helped me sharpen and clarify my arguments. Aaron Javsicas has guided the project at Temple University Press. The reviewers he selected produced extensive, thoughtful, and penetrating critiques that immeasurably improved the book. Wendy Jo Dymond and Rebecca Logan were the best copy editors any author could wish for.

I retired from Texas A&M University on May 31, 2018. My progress from pupil to scholar was made possible by the teachers who inspired me on my way. In elementary and high school, their learning and dedication fit me for opportunities they were denied. In college and graduate school, they were mentors and exemplars. Most of them have died. I dedicate this book to them, not to pay a debt but to acknowledge it.

Feminist Post-Liberalism

1

An Introduction to Feminist Post-liberalism

Modern Western feminism developed historically and logically from liberalism. A belief system that replaced faith with reason, divine right with popular sovereignty, hierarchy with equality, and obedience with self-assertion invited critical scrutiny of gender asymmetry. Less than fifty years after the English revolution, the English Bill of Rights, and the publication of John Locke's *Second Treatise on Government,* "Sophia, a person of quality" issued "A short and modest Vindication of the natural Right of the FAIR-SEX to a perfect Equality of Power, Dignity, and Esteem, with the Men."[1] Judith Sargent Murray published "On the Equality of the Sexes" a year after the U.S. Constitution was ratified. She attacked the entrenched pre-liberal opinion that women were intellectually inferior to men and attributed observable differences to women's lack of education.[2] Her essay invites comparison with Query 15 of Thomas Jefferson's *Notes on Virginia,* not to his credit.[3]

Mary Wollstonecraft, a British contemporary of Murray, was better known in her own time than Murray and Sophia were. Wollstonecraft was part of an intellectual circle whose members read one another's works. Her liberal roots are evident in the corpus of her work. *A Vindication of the Rights of Woman* appeared in 1792, two years after her *Vindication of the Rights of Men.* Sophia, Murray, and Wollstonecraft had the rare benefit of a classical education. Murray studied with her brother as he prepared for admission to Harvard. But Abigail Adams, who had little education, held similar views.

She advised her husband, John, to "remember the ladies" at the Second Continental Congress in 1776. He replied, "I cannot but laugh."[4]

Eighteenth-century France generated liberal defenses of male supremacy, liberal arguments for gender equality, and radical attacks on liberal feminism. Jean-Jacques Rousseau wrote, "The children's health depends in the first place on the mother's, and the early education of man is also in a woman's hands; his morals, his passions, his tastes, his pleasures, his happiness itself, depend on her. A woman's education must therefore be planned in relation to man. To be pleasing in his sight, to win his respect and love, to train him in childhood, to tend him in manhood, to counsel and console, to make his life pleasant and happy, these are the duties of woman for all time, and this is what she should be taught while she is young."[5] Rousseau grounded his antifeminism where most arguments against gender equality have been grounded: in women's childbearing capacity. Was this a reason or an excuse? When reduced to its essentials—"Because only members of Group A can perform a function necessary for society, Group A must be subordinate to Group B"—the argument based on reproductive capacity becomes ludicrous.

Wollstonecraft wrote partly in response to Rousseau. Her most original insight was her argument that forced ignorance and learned subservience made women unfit even for their assigned roles. She answered her rhetorical question, "And have women who have early imbibed a notion of passive obedience, sufficient character to manage a family or educate children?," firmly in the negative.[6]

The French Revolution stimulated feminist activism. The 1789 Declaration of Rights of Man and the Citizen was followed in 1790 by Nicolas de Condorcet's "On the Admission of Women to the Rights of Citizenship" and in 1791 by Olympe de Gouges's "Declaration of the Rights of Woman."[7] The fact that Gouges addressed her declaration to Marie Antoinette did not find favor in the proletarian revolt that followed the bourgeois one. Gouges was guillotined and Condorcet imprisoned because of their counterrevolutionary reputations, not because of their views on women. Jacobin women, anticipating Karl Marx, considered affordable bread more important than liberal rights. In 1792, a crowd of these women attacked and permanently disabled Theroigne de Mericourt, a prominent Girondin feminist.[8]

So, by 1800, liberal traditionalists, liberal feminists, and radicals had staked out positions. These positions survive in the twenty-first century. Conservatives such as Edmund Burke are still read and discussed.[9] Today's antifeminist women often identify with the Christian tradition, as did counterrevolutionary French women.[10] "Occupation: Housewife" in the 1950s went, and "total motherhood" now goes, at least as far as Rousseau did in finding autonomy incompatible with motherhood.[11] Radical thinkers, including many feminists, accused second-wave feminists of prioritizing liberal rights over economic fairness.[12] Neither feminism nor liberalism has been static. Classical liberalism has been supplemented, and, to some extent, replaced, by welfare liberalism. Feminists have responded to radical criticism by emphasizing class issues.

Back in the last century, I devoted much of *Our Lives before the Law* to feminist critiques of liberal theory. Here, I briefly reconsider what I wrote there. I then turn to liberal critiques of feminism and radical critiques of feminist liberalism. I argue that these critiques do not make convincing arguments for rejecting liberalism. Instead, I try to construct what I call a feminist post-liberalism: *not*, note, a liberal post-feminism.

Rights without Freedom: Gender Equality versus Male Supremacy

Feminism and liberalism are distinct but tangled philosophies. Each has challenged and influenced the other. But liberalism has coexisted with both feminism and male supremacy. Condorcet may have been the first male liberal feminist, but he was not the last. Jeremy Bentham supported women's suffrage, and John Stuart Mill opposed male supremacy.[13] Early feminist causes, such as securing the vote and protecting married women's property rights, sought to apply liberal principles to women. Women's struggle to win the "rights of men" lasted well into the twentieth century. The United Kingdom did not extend full voting rights to women until 1928. French women had to wait until the German occupation ended in 1944. French husbands and fathers did not lose their legal status as heads of households until 1970. Louisiana, the only state whose law was based on the Napoleonic Code, had a similar rule until 1981, when the Supreme Court struck it down.[14]

The "separate spheres" ideology—man as breadwinner, woman as homemaker—was entrenched in the United States by the time the Seneca Falls convention met in 1848. Opponents of first-wave feminism invoked gender stereotypes to defend the status quo. "The power of woman is her dependence, flowing from the consciousness of that weakness which God has given her for her protection," a Congregationalist minister declared.[15] Early activists, such as Elizabeth Cady Stanton, turned this rhetoric around, insisting that women's role in family life conferred their moral superiority to men and justified women's participation in public life.[16] Nineteenth-century feminists promoted women's financial independence so they would not have to marry unless they wanted to. But these feminists relied on women's domestic role to support their cause. Men defined the separate spheres. Women socialized women within their sphere. The "social feminists" of the Progressive Era and the "difference feminists" of the late twentieth century not only supported women's rights but also emphasized women's traditional roles.[17] In so doing, they reinforced, or at least failed to challenge, the social expectations of women. I am not blaming any of these activists for Donald Trump's victory. The early suffragists had to attract women to their cause; the advocates of protective labor legislation responded to working conditions that were particularly harmful to women; the difference feminists were valorizing women's traditional work.

Ironically, Stanton's emphasis on women's superior morality would come back to haunt her reputation. First-wave feminism grew out of the antislavery movement. Stanton and her contemporaries were committed to abolition. Frederick Douglass and other abolitionists supported women's suffrage before the Civil War. But when the Fifteenth Amendment came before Congress, Douglass declared, "This is the Negro's hour." He ignored the fact that extending the vote to women would double the Radical Republicans' political base. Stanton questioned "whether we had better stand aside and see 'Sambo' walk into the kingdom first."[18] Her racism intensified for the rest of her life. She made exactly the same error Douglass did; she limited the size of her group's potential constituency. What is interesting is the different judgments Douglas and Stanton received for their exclusionary politics. His omission of women has been considered pragmatic; her alliance with white supremacists is condemned as immoral.

The victories of first-wave feminism were absorbed into Western society without changing gender roles. The liberalism I grew up with after World War II either defended male supremacy or tacitly accepted it. The support for individual rights, equality, due process, the welfare state, the primacy of reason over emotion, and democracy coincided with the beliefs that wives should defer to their husbands, that motherhood was a full-time job, that women should reject ambition in favor of family life, and the like. Gender equality was not a liberal value.

These developments resonated with my own experience. Girls in the pre–Title IX cohort got the message that liberal principles did not quite apply to them, even as adults. Intelligence was important, but do not raise your hand every time you know the answer. We were encouraged to attract, to intuit, and to play dumb. The women I knew were either homemakers or spinster schoolteachers. Our futures seemed to be linked to children, whatever path we took.

Family and milieu introduced me to opinion. Education introduced me to theory. I read John Stuart Mill in high school, Erich Fromm in college, and David Riesman in graduate school.[19] I developed a concept of adulthood that entailed possessing the rights and liberties they discussed—and I could not wait. Mill and Riesman argued that this status applied to women as well as to men. But Fromm wrote a book called *Man for Himself*.[20] Paul Goodman declared in *Growing Up Absurd*, "The problems I want to discuss in this book belong primarily, in our society, to the boys: how to be useful and make something of oneself. A girl does not *have* to, she is not expected to, 'make something of herself.' Her career does not have to be self-justifying, for she will have children, which is absolutely self-justifying, like any other natural or creative act. With this background, it is less important, for instance, what job an average young woman works at till she is married."[21] Goodman reinforced a message I had already encountered: motherhood makes up for everything girls do not get to do. Fromm's and Goodman's books appeared in the 1940s and 1960s. By 1970, I was eager for a new feminist movement.

Because of that movement, Fromm and Goodman could not now get away with writing as they did. But we need look back no farther for examples of sexism than the historian, biographer, and public intellectual Arthur Schlesinger, Jr., who described himself as an "unrepentant and unreconstructed liberal and New Dealer."[22] His death in 2007 prompted the usual reminiscences and the publication of his edited journals.[23] The *Washington Post* recalled an occasion when liberalism's exemplar "pooh-poohed the fish-and-fowl on the menu as women's food. He told the waiter to bring him meat."[24] His journal stonewalled questions about the sexual behavior of prominent men. John and Robert Kennedy's connections to Marilyn Monroe posed "a question [he] d[id] not regard as legitimate." He sympathized with a Kennedy nephew charged with rape. Other comments included a remark about "Kitty Galbraith, dowdily dressed as if to show what she thought of handsome and stylish women," and the description of Madeleine Albright as "a third-rate woman, and not a nice one either."[25] His liberalism never forced him to reconsider his misogyny. Liberals who shared his views may well have voted for Trump.

Liberalism was holding its own among competing views in the 1950s and 1960s, when I became aware of ideas.[26] To many people, liberalism was not an ideology at all. The word *ideology* was more often preceded by *communist* or even *Nazi*. Liberalism was common sense; it was pragmatism. Barry Goldwater, the conservative who won the Republican nomination for president in 1964, was too much even for some members of his party. Many Americans perceived his resounding defeat by Lyndon Johnson, the return of Democratic majorities to the House and Senate, the war on poverty, and the passage of the Voting Rights Act of 1965 as decisive and permanent liberal victories. The Supreme Court's prompt validation of this law and its recognition of a right to privacy in *Griswold v. Connecticut* (1965) indicated that all three branches of government were on the same page.[27]

After 1965, liberalism had nowhere to go but down. The Vietnam War overrode the war on poverty and soured many Americans on government. The New Left, an outgrowth of the civil rights and antiwar movements, collapsed under the power of the forces arrayed against it. The Republicans had exiled their liberals by 1980. Liberals who stayed with the Democrats became neoliberals. They accommodated the fear of crime that had helped Richard Nixon become president by forming the Democratic Leadership Council and abandoning their opposition to the death penalty (see Chapter 4). Ronald Reagan in the 1980s and the Tea Party in the twenty-first century made Goldwater look like a liberal—and they won elections. Bill Clinton responded to a Republican takeover of Congress by reaffirming his commitment to "end welfare as we know it."[28]

Feminism, by contrast, had nowhere to go in 1965 but up. The publication of *The Feminine Mystique* two years earlier coincided with the report of the President's Commission on the Status of Women. This commission opposed the Equal Rights Amendment and supported women's labor legislation.[29] Still more reactionary was the document known as the Moynihan Report. Its author, Daniel Patrick Moynihan, was then assistant secretary of labor and later U.S. senator from New York. *The Negro Family: The Case for National Action* was published by the department in March 1965. Moynihan, then a liberal, found a "tangle of pathology" in African American households. He attributed this malfunction to a "matriarchal structure," evinced by the prevalence of the "female family head" (never the single-parent family).[30]

Moynihan did not blame racial inequality on matriarchy or on mothers who assumed responsibility rather than on men who abdicated it. But he regarded patriarchy as a necessary condition for racial equality: "Ours is a society which presumes male leadership in private and public affairs. The arrangements of society facilitate such leadership and reward it. A subculture, such as that of the Negro American, in which this is not the pattern, is placed at a distinct disadvantage."[31] Moynihan's prescription became conventional wisdom. Attitudes like these invited feminist resistance.

Moynihan made the same connection Rousseau had: children's welfare requires women's subordination to men. The Moynihan Report provoked accusations of racism and victim-blaming. But Nicholas Kristof, a columnist for the *New York Times*, marked the fiftieth anniversary of the report in "When Liberals Blew It." He wrote, "Scholars, fearful of being accused of racism, mostly avoided family structure and poverty." He bemoaned the effects of "father absence" but praised same-sex parents and avoided terms like *matriarchy* and *male leadership*.[32] He seemed unaware of Moynihan's male supremacist attitudes. The transition from "female family head" to "single-parent families" has been typical of commentators on the report.[33]

The revival of the feminist movement in the late 1960s was not met with joy by established interests. Feminist activists made enemies and still do. Feminist ideas received vehement criticism and still do. But the record of feminist accomplishments shows that being opposed and criticized is better than being ignored or ridiculed. The failure of the Equal Rights Amendment to win ratification proved a temporary setback.[34] There is a movement now, and it is taken seriously even by those who disparage it.

The twenty-first century has brought one unambiguous victory for feminists and liberals: the seismic change in public policy and public opinion toward homosexuality, in general, and same-sex marriage, in particular. Primary credit belongs to the pioneers who took the risks and bore the consequences of revealing their homosexuality. Feminists and liberals were late starters in this struggle. As these ideologies had long coexisted with racism, they coexisted with homophobia. The conventional liberal position was that homosexuality was a disease. The American Psychiatric Association did not remove it from its list of mental illnesses until 1973. The 1969 riots at the Stonewall Inn in New York City are often identified as the beginning of the gay liberation movement. That same year, Betty Friedan, the president of the National Organization for Women (NOW), identified lesbianism as a "lavender menace" threatening the feminist movement. Lesbians resisting the efforts of mainstream feminist organizations to exclude them appropriated this term.[35]

The gay liberation movement forced heterosexuals to acknowledge the sexual preferences of friends, relatives, and associates as more and more people came out. Heterosexuals learned that homosexuals were no more likely to exhibit psychopathology than they were. Feminists recognized contradictions between gender equality and rejection of lesbians. Liberals saw contradictions between homophobia and support for individual rights. Many perceived an economic advantage in acceptance as homosexuals became a reliable market.[36] Both feminists and liberals perceived the advantages of gaining new allies. When New York legalized same-sex marriage in 2011, NOW and the American Civil Liberties Union (ACLU) joined the celebration. Support for same-sex marriage increased from 27 percent in 1996 to 42 percent in 2004 to 57 percent in 2015.[37] The conventional conservative position, that homosexuality is an abominable and detestable crime against nature, is held by a shrinking minority. In 2013, 34 percent of Republicans, and even 32 percent of Tea Party members, supported same-sex marriage.[38] The Supreme Court's 2015 decision legalizing same-sex marriage was a decisive victory for homosexuals and their allies.[39]

Despite their reputations, both feminism and liberalism are healthy and energetic. They have responded to ethical and pragmatic challenges. They have changed themselves and helped change the world. They have made common cause. But feminism and liberalism do not always unite. A victory for one may be a defeat for the other. Consider, for example, the nationwide controversy over the proper response to pervasive sexual assault on college campuses. A magazine article in the summer of 2014 reports a widespread consensus that "school disciplinary boards have rarely done a very good job of handling these cases."[40] Investigations focus on the victim's behavior, invoke stereotypes about rape that are no longer allowed in criminal trials, and let the accused off lightly.

Liberal critics emphasize the rights of the accused. Some feminists argue that these cases belong in the criminal justice system, although it "has failed rape victims so consistently."[41] Others concentrate on reforming campus systems to make them more responsive to victims. When the defense to rape charges is consent, triers of fact choose between believing the accuser and believing the accused. False accusations have occurred. Liberals' concern for due process is legitimate. But feminists' concerns about the welfare of victims and the elimination of sexual assault are equally legitimate. These two groups are in conflict.[42]

Even when feminists and liberals agree, they may reach the same conclusions from contradictory premises. Both the ACLU and La Leche League International (LLLI) support a woman's right to breastfeed in public. The ACLU emphasizes individual rights, as it usually does. LLLI thinks people should do it; the ACLU thinks people should be allowed to do it. Not everyone identifies LLLI's principles as feminist. But breastfeeding advocates describe themselves and their cause as feminist and identify the interests of women with those of children.[43]

Women within Liberalism

The words *feminist* and *liberal* mean so many different things to the people who use them that these words require clarification. Definitions can sidetrack and even overwhelm discourse, but here they are necessary. I let the experts I discuss label themselves and let history label the dead experts. My concept of liberalism is post–New Deal welfare liberalism, not classical liberalism or libertarianism. The classical liberalism of eighteenth- and nineteenth-century feminists did not achieve equality. I am increasingly pessimistic about whether equality is compatible with capitalism. I also reject rational choice and populism. I do not accept the rational actor model as the basis for, or "the people want it" as a defense of, any policy. By feminism, I mean a commitment to actual, not just formal or legal, equality between women and men and between cisgender and transgender people and to policies and practices that further all women's interests. This equality demands the rejection of conventional gender roles. I reject the idea that women's interests are identical with any others, like those of men, children, families, the poor, or the environment.[44]

Most liberals and many feminists prioritize economic inequality over male supremacy as a source and cause of injustice. I refuse to make that choice. I see no reason to rank-order the two variables. Ending poverty is unlikely to end male dominance and vice versa. Both goals are as important in themselves as they are in relation to each other.

Male dominance is incompatible with liberalism's emphasis on reason. The commonest defense of male supremacy relies on women's ability to do something important that men cannot do. No defenses of sexism are intellectually tenable. Liberal feminist theory could posit that women counted as liberal subjects and proceed from there. But what sufficed as a basis for liberal feminism proved, at best, inadequate and, at worst, counterproductive for feminist liberalism.

Feminists Confront Liberalism

The idea of a possible connection between thinkers' particular standpoints and their ostensibly neutral ideas has informed scholarly analysis at least since Karl Mannheim began "unmasking" ideologies.[45] Feminist assertions that liberalism has an inherent male bias are similar, in structure if not in content, to Marxist critiques of liberalism. One need not accept Marx's theory of history or his commitment to revolution to recognize the truth of his statement that, under capitalism, "property is already done away with for nine tenths of the population"[46] or Lenin's observation that "the modern wage slaves, owing to the conditions of capitalist exploitation, are so much crushed by want and poverty that . . . in the ordinary peaceful course of events, the majority of the population is debarred from participating in social and political life."[47] Twentieth-century feminism recognized what nineteenth-century Marxism had: liberalism excluded some people while claiming inclusiveness and privileged some people while claiming neutrality. Feminist scholarship itself has been subjected to, and has learned from, minority critiques making similar points.[48]

"Virtually all" feminist scholars "acknowledge the vast debts of feminism to liberalism."[49] But feminists who agree on little else agree that liberalism is not enough for gender equality. Feminist critiques of liberalism have held that it "presumes that the family "is a just institution" (Susan Moller Okin) and presupposes a "sexual contract" that assigns inferior status to women (Carole Pateman).[50] Emphasizing individual rights "ignores *needs*" (Barbara

Katz Rothman) and "authorize[s] the male experience of the world" (Catharine MacKinnon).[51]

Feminist scholarship influenced by arguments such as these has influenced liberal discourse. The work of MacKinnon and Andrea Dworkin has made it difficult for liberals to presume that sex is consensual.[52] Neither the family nor the workplace is immune from feminist scrutiny. Martha Fineman has introduced the idea of a "caretaking" family to counter the traditional "sexual family," whose function is to establish fatherhood.[53] Joan Williams has challenged the notion of the "ideal worker," the employee with few or no home responsibilities.[54] Martha Nussbaum's and Amartya Sen's work on "capabilities" has produced theory that is both feminist and liberal.[55]

Some feminists go so far as to insist that liberalism and gender equality are incompatible. Feminist analysis has exposed what Zillah Eisenstein called the "patriarchal and individualist" roots of liberalism.[56] Robin West concludes that liberalism is "essentially and irretrievably masculine." Its "'separation thesis' about what it means to be a human being" is "patently untrue of women" because they are "actually or potentially materially connected to other human life. Men aren't."[57] The charge of male bias is plausible on its face. Liberalism is a belief system developed primarily by men who were the dominant group in society and whose lives were very different from the lives of women or children. Why would the ideology not incorporate the male view of the world and stress the interests of the dominant rather than those of the subordinate? Liberalism is, indeed, rooted in male supremacy. Liberalism is based on a notion of what it means to be a human being that characterizes men's lives. Liberal theory emerged and grew in contexts where women's labor allowed men to assert rights and to construct theories.

But liberalism authorizes *a*, not *the*, male experience of the world. Only a select few men got to have this experience. The majority of men earned their living through physical labor. Liberal theory works best for people who can live like liberal theorists. John Stuart Mill's defense of "the liberty of thought and discussion" and his focus on "the limits of the authority of society over the individual" appealed most to people like him: intellectuals who earn their living with their brains and have few or no domestic responsibilities.[58] Most people who fit this description were men, but most men did not fit this description. But the irrelevance of liberal values to the lives of many people does not make these values unimportant. Liberal concerns became more salient to more people when and if their lives improved.

The domestic servants who made the liberal lifestyle possible in the nineteenth century were replaced by labor-saving devices in the twentieth. As opportunities increased, more and more women were able to live like the men who had monopolized the theorizing. Women who started as graduate students and ended as academics, for instance, could approximate the liberal intellectual lifestyle—if they lived alone, among women, or in the egalitarian heterosexual partnerships that proved difficult to establish. But motherhood brought domestic duties down on the heads of middle-class professional women. Their equality with men was compromised, not by the fact that women bear children—the logical connection between women's work and their reproductive function is incomplete—but by the fact that the work must be done and by expectations that women do it.

Liberalism did not have much to offer in these situations, and much of what it did offer was counterproductive. A woman chose to marry or not, to have children or not, to breast- or bottle-feed. Once she made the choice, she accepted its consequences. A woman in an abusive relationship chose to stay or leave. To interfere was to violate the family's right to privacy.[59] (One need not reject the presumption of free will to perceive that choice is only of possible things.) Liberal theory sufficed only for the woman who could afford to hire out domestic responsibilities at the risk of exploiting other women. To the extent that a woman must choose between a profession and parenthood, she is that much less a liberal subject.

Character and Situation

Differences among feminists have been as important as differences between feminists and liberals. Early feminist victories extended liberal principles to women. First-wave feminists united in supporting these goals. But they were divided about whether freedom of contract should extend to women. "Equal opportunity" feminists, such as the members of the National Women's Party, insisted that with respect to labor, women should have the same freedom to make contracts with their employers that men had. But "social" or "relational" feminists supported special restrictions for women so that they could fulfill their obligations as wives and mothers.[60] Feminist critics of liberalism agreed that "women share some distinctive features that make male-centered theory wrong for them,"[61] but they disagreed about why and how this was true. Robin West identifies with "cultural feminists," for whom "the important difference between men and women is that women raise children and men don't."[62] Catharine MacKinnon labels these authors "difference" theorists, and I call them "character" theorists. This body of work is similar in structure to a philosophy that goes back at least to Plato: it reasons from a theory of human character to a theory of politics. So do Thomas Hobbes, John Locke, James Madison, and other liberal theorists. The feminist version substitutes *women* for the (implicit or explicit) *men* of early character theory.

West juxtaposes cultural feminists to "radical feminists," who hold that "the important difference between men and women is that women get fucked and men fuck."[63] MacKinnon practices the "dominance approach," whose guiding premise is "the difference is that men have power and women do not."[64] I call this type of feminism "situation" theory and jurisprudence, which asserts that "what makes law male is the fact that men use it to subordinate women."[65] Situation theory is similar in structure to Marxism: it substitutes male dominance for class struggle.

The dichotomy between cultural and radical feminism is not an either-or division. Organizing much of the work from the 1980s and 1990s on this basis is useful. Some influential scholarship falls outside these categories. Zillah Eisenstein, for example, is a radical feminist but not a situation theorist. She focuses not on women but on liberalism itself: "The demand for real equality of women with men, if taken to its logical conclusion, would dislodge the patriarchal structure necessary to a liberal society."[66] The dichotomy certainly does not apply to all contemporary feminist scholarship. Feminist theory may have exhausted the possibilities of the "difference debate" in the last thirty years.[67]

I have expressed a strong preference for situation theory over character theory. To summarize, I argued that the latter ascribed to nature gender differences imposed by society and reinforced conventional expectations that burden women.[68] I did not fully realize that character theory is inherently conservative. Its concepts of gender difference are pre-feminist, and it does not untangle theory from roles. Cultural feminism has not made a convincing case that liberalism is irretrievably masculine. But this is not the whole story for two reasons.

First, character theory and situation theory, like liberalism and Marxism, are examples of "grand theory." Each is what C. Wright Mills called "a systematic theory of 'the nature of man [sic] and society.'"[69] Later scholars have criticized grand theories for being abstract and for claiming an essentialism they do not have.[70] If grand theories are viewed not as truths but as methods, they are valuable even when they have flaws. One need not agree with Marx that history is about class struggle, or with Sigmund Freud that Eros and Thanatos drive human behavior, to use concepts such as "reserve army" or "the subconscious." Character feminism and situation feminism have similar strengths. Grand theories are more than ideas; they are also epistemologies and language games.[71]

Second, radical feminists' arguments that liberalism and gender equality are incompatible are no more persuasive than the cultural feminist versions are. Zillah Eisenstein has not made a convincing argument that liberalism is patriarchal and individualist or that individualism is something bad either.

If by "individualistic" Eisenstein means the "rugged individual" of Westerns and war stories, she is right: size and brawn are crucial, and most men surpass most women in these attributes.[72] But this is not what David Riesman meant or what individualism must mean. An individualist may also be a person resisting conformity, as feminists do. The statement I quote previously begs the question about the relationship between the liberal and the patriarchal. Eisenstein proceeds from the insight that liberalism is *rooted* in patriarchy to the conclusion that liberalism *entails* patriarchy.

"Ahead of Whatever's in Second Place": The Case for Reconciliation

I argue that feminism and liberalism need each other. How, with all the conflict and discontinuity, can I defend this position? First, an examination of pre-feminist critiques of liberalism and their intellectual descendants indicates that liberalism is far friendlier to gender equality than some of its adversaries. Second, the two ideologies can correct some, although not all, of each other's characteristic errors. Both feminism and liberalism must refuse to rank thinking over feeling, and vice versa. Liberalism focuses too narrowly on the individual, while feminism needs a dose of individualism. Liberalism's emphasis on rights and autonomy puts it in a good position to scrutinize the family. Although liberalism long assumed that the family is immune from critical scrutiny, it neither idealizes the institution, as many conservatives do, nor assumes with the radicals that what happens within the family is secondary to class oppression.

Liberalism offered more to a second-wave feminist scholar than the available ideologies of the traditional right and the radical left. Studying political science when and where all these ideologies made their presence felt, I discovered recurring patterns in my peers' responses to feminist challenges. Many conservatives endorsed conventional notions of natural differences between the sexes; some even questioned whether feminists really knew what they wanted. Radicals tended to trivialize gender issues and insist that class issues preempted them. Today, few, if any, conservatives want to confine women to traditional roles; they eagerly promote women candidates for public office. But radicals continue to assert that gender is secondary to class and that economic exploitation is more significant than male supremacy.

We know enough about proletarian revolution and communist systems to be pessimistic about them. Governments that deserved to be overthrown were, but their replacements combined repression with deprivation. The people of the USSR did not take long to perceive what the protagonist of Arthur Koestler's novel *Darkness at Noon* told his inquisitors: "Acting comprehensively in the interests of coming generations we have laid such terrible privations on the present one that its average length of life is shortened by a quarter."[73] In Cambodia, deprivation took the extreme form of genocide. The People's Republic of China told people that "suffering will make you a better Communist."[74] Conditions in North Korea were so dire for so long that people asked, "What can we expect from Kim Jong-Eun, when his father runs the country so badly that people are starving to death?"[75] Even Cuba, whose size and climate make scarcity improbable, forced privation and labor on its people with little compensation beyond the assurance that "you don't have to feel guilty" because you have nothing anybody else lacks.[76]

The Soviet Union collapsed, China rejected doctrinaire communism, and the future of North Korea and Cuba remains an unanswered question. The transfers of power from monarchs to elected officials that took place throughout Europe in the twentieth century were more successful in containing privilege than in establishing egalitarian societies.

Marxism's fate has been the reverse of what happened to liberalism and feminism: its theory has outlasted its practice. Franklin Delano Roosevelt's "a third of a nation ill-housed, ill-clad, and ill-nourished" echoed, consciously or not, Lenin's proletariat "crushed by want and poverty."[77] Marxist, radical, and socialist thought combined with hard times had a deep and lasting influence on the quiet transitions of the twentieth century. As these ideologies reshaped liberal practice, so, too, did they transform liberal theory. Classical "laissez-faire" liberalism has been supplemented, although not supplanted, by what I call "welfare liberalism."

To characterize welfare liberalism as a kind of "post-liberalism" would not be far-fetched. My goal here is to develop a feminist post-liberalism that is true to the principles of both ideologies. The success of socialist and radical theory in changing liberalism suggests that feminist theory has similar potential. We can look forward to a twenty-second century in which liberalism has become even more complex. Feminist post-liberalism may not persuade everyone in either the classical or welfare liberal camps, but it may force thinkers to reexamine, reground, or reject their own positions.

The case for a feminist post-liberalism becomes stronger when we review some pre-Marxist and pre-feminist critiques of liberal principles and the intellectual descendants of these critiques. Feminist theory cannot do without the principles of equality and autonomy; these principles are essential to any ideology committed to the equality of the sexes. Thomas Jefferson's statement that "all men are created equal," a self-evident truth for him, was "a great and dangerous error" to John C. Calhoun.[78] John Stuart Mill's defense of individual liberty in "self-regarding" actions was countered by James Fitzjames Stephen's defense of "persecution of the grosser forms of vice."[79] Neither of these nineteenth-century conservative arguments enjoys much favor now. The equality principle has long since become a "given" in democratic political discourse; the gap here is between theory and practice. The "law and morals" debate foundered as even conservative consensus about what constituted "vice" weakened in democratic societies. But this debate has morphed into concerns about family and community that threaten gender equality.

Patrick Devlin adapted Stephen's critique, insisting that the enforcement of moral principles may be necessary not to prevent vice but to preserve the "community of ideas" essential to the preservation of society. To the extent that those shared ideas include traditional gender roles, they are destructive to an egalitarian society. Devlin's own phraseology—"whether a man should be allowed to take more than one wife"—does not reassure on this point.[80] Sixty years later, Devlin's argument seems almost as quaint as Stephen's, but contemporary critics of liberalism continue exploring the connection between social cohesion and shared values. Michael Sandel's concern with liberals' lack of a shared concept of the good is compatible with Devlin's critique. Both authors emphasize "shared" rather than "good."[81] Charles Taylor and Alasdair MacIntyre suggest that liberalism essentially misunderstands human beings, perceiving them as autonomous individuals rather than as the creations of the communities to which they belong.[82] Whereas Robin West asserts that liberalism's "separation thesis" is true only for men, Devlin, Stephen, Sandel, Taylor, and MacIntyre, among others, posit a "connection thesis" for all human beings.[83]

The label "communitarian" has been applied to these theorists. Both Sandel and MacIntyre reject it. Self-styled communitarians, such as Mary Ann Glendon, criticize liberal discourse for mounting "strident talk about rights" while exhibiting "near-aphasia concerning responsibilities."[84] The call to subordinate one's own desires to the collective good evokes a reality all too familiar to women. I have argued that rights must be talked about because they are vulnerable, whereas responsibilities are givens that are disproportionately imposed on women.[85] Self-labeled defenders of the family emphasize not social programs that could improve the situation of many families but "family values" that often include traditional gender roles. If liberalism is inconsistent with feminism, these counter-liberal ideologies are hostile toward it. Whether or not liberalism is compatible with gender equality, it is not feminism's worst enemy.

Conclusion

No case for reconciliation can accept any variety of liberalism that now exists. But ideologies are dynamic, not static. They change, and are changed, in response to new ideas and to political and social change. Liberal priorities have become more relevant to women's lives as they move into formerly male roles. We have seen that liberal principles often are more supportive of gender equality than those of competing ideologies. Liberalism already includes classical liberalism, social liberalism, and neoliberalism. What would a feminist post-liberalism look like?

What do you get if you take the patriarchy out of the Moynihan Report? You get an argument that is no longer Moynihan's: that two-parent families are better than one-parent families. What's wrong with that? A lot if you conclude that the children of single parents should not exist, impose penalties on single parents, or forbid single-parent adoption. But suppose you mean that a family in which responsibility is divided between two adults is stronger than a family in which one adult is isolated in responsibility. Well, you may have to confront objections that three or more adults are better than two, but you now have an argument that is gender-neutral on its face. As applied, this argument fails on both feminist and liberal grounds. Since most single parents are mothers, the danger that even a neutral argument can lead to concentrating on family structure rather than on lack of opportunity and training, and on the failings of present mothers rather than absent fathers, is real. Liberals' emphasis on individual autonomy will reject the argument as a basis for public policy, accepting it (or not) as a guide to personal behavior.

Infant feeding is another issue on which both feminism and liberalism have failed. To privilege breastfeeding, like LLLI, goes too far; to support breastfeeding rights, like the ACLU, does not go far enough. The first choice rests on too narrow a definition of feminism, while the second reflects too formal a concept of liberalism. My criticism of these organizations does not discount the valuable work each has done, the ACLU by supporting rights and LLLI by public and private education and worldwide opposition to aggressive marketing of infant formula. Women must be free to breast- or bottle-feed as they choose, but all mothers of infants need concessions and accommodations for their choice to be truly free.

2

Imperative Theory and Feminist Post-liberalism

The last chapter of *Our Lives before the Law* calls for an "imperative" theory. I phrased its organizing question as "What can people and society not do without?"[1] My primary concern was gendered role expectations. I thought asking my question could lead to valuable insights. The inquiry proved formidable and frustrating. I delayed the project as long as I could. Framing tangential issues, reviewing literature, and applying my ideas to specific topics occupied my research agenda for several years and even produced a spin-off.[2] But eventually I turned to basic works in zoology and anthropology, fields I had not studied. Here, I discovered that my project was doomed from the start, because I was asking the wrong question. I could not not get where I wanted to go from where I started.

I knew I was not the first to ask such questions. Bronislaw Malinowski, a twentieth-century scholar who has been called the father of social anthropology, wrote:

> Man has, first and foremost, to satisfy all the needs of his organism. He has to create arrangements and carry out activities for feeding, heating, housing, clothing, or protection from cold, wind, and weather. He has to protect himself and organize for such protection against external enemies and dangers. . . . All these primary problems of human beings are solved for the individual by artifacts, organization into cooperative groups, and also by the development of knowledge, a sense of value and ethics. . . . [T]he basic needs . . .

can be linked up with the derivation of new cultural needs; . . . these new needs impose upon man and society a secondary type of determinism.[3]

Malinowski perceived that the distinction between needs and wants is difficult to draw and that wants also become imperatives: whether or not they must be satisfied, someone must satisfy them. (Abraham Maslow's hierarchy of "higher and lower needs" is a reversal of Malinowski's primary and secondary needs, but Maslow showed no familiarity with Malinowski's work.)[4] My exposure to anthropology suggested that my concept needed revision to include not only what you *must* do but also what people *make* you do. Imperative theory needs a concept of power.

Robert Redfield wrote, "Malinowski looks at the people, then looks back at the books, then looks again at the people. He does not, as some have done, look at the people, if at all, to find here what the books have told him he should find."[5] Many of those books propounded the theory misleadingly known as "social Darwinism." Herbert Spencer's *Social Statics* was published in 1851, eight years before *Origin of Species*. Darwin cited Spencer favorably in his later work, but the ideas of "natural selection" and "survival of the fittest" came from anthropology, not zoology.[6] Social Darwinism led easily to the idea that some groups had evolved further than others, an idea that led to racist pseudoscience. John Langdon Down, who in 1866 identified what he called Mongolism and we call Down Syndrome, "proposed that human evolution had gone from black people to Asians to white people, and that white people born with Mongolism were actually a throwback to their primitive Asian ancestors—a position then considered rather progressive insofar as it acknowledged evolution."[7] The notion that all groups would evolve into modern industrial societies lingers in the terminology of "developed," "developing," and "underdeveloped" countries that pervades political economy. Must Greece become more like Germany or leave the European Union?[8] If Greece did become more like Germany, how would that change affect the status of Greek women?

Malinowski found that primitive societies were complex. Their practices were functional for their societies, not a sign of low intelligence. Magic did not substitute for tending one's garden; it grew out of a gardener's recognition that "in spite of all his forethought and beyond all his efforts there are agencies and forces which one year bestow unwonted and unearned benefits of fertility . . . and another year again the same agencies bring ill luck and bad chance. . . . To control these agencies and these only he employs magic."[9] The rain usually comes soon enough after the rain dance to convince the tribe of its ritual's utility, and the performance brings collateral benefits such as cooperation and solidarity. Franz Boas, who was called the father of American or modern anthropology, insisted that "human culture does not always develop from the simple to the complex [but that] in many aspects two tendencies inter-cross,—one from the complex to the simple, the other from the simple to the complex."[10]

What Malinowski got right is as important as what he did not quite get. But the more I read, the more I suspected that Malinowski had oversimplified and overgeneralized. The needs are common, but different societies meet common needs in different ways. Yes, everybody needs food, but the need for food can be satisfied by hunting animals or gathering plants or fishing or some combination of these methods. Everybody needs water, but some groups have adequate access to it, while others have to find it.[11] Everybody needs protection from the elements, but some people fear monsoons, and others fear blizzards. Behavior, including the assignment of tasks, is at least as much a product of circumstances as of needs.

The concept of "human nature" is important in Malinowski's thought. He defines it as "the biological determinism which imposes on every civilization and on all individuals in it the carrying out of such bodily functions as breathing, sleep, rest, nutrition, excretion, and reproduction."[12] These functions are natural, but they are not exclusively human; animal species share them. The key word here is *biological*. Malinowski emphasizes "the fact that all human beings belong to an animal species,"[13] thereby making anthropology a subfield of zoology.

Charles Darwin wrote, "Man has also some few instincts in common, as that of self-preservation, sexual love, the love of the mother for her new-born offspring, the desire possessed by the latter to suck, and so forth. But man, perhaps, has somewhat fewer instincts than those possessed by the animals which come next to him in the series. The orang in the Eastern islands, and the chimpanzee in Africa, build platforms on which they sleep; and, as both species follow the same habit, it might be argued that this was due to instinct, but we cannot feel sure that it is not the result of both animals having similar wants, and possessing similar powers of reasoning."[14] When I was a child, an adult explained the difference between human and animal brains thus: "A cat can't go to a library and find out what another cat was thinking a thousand years ago." Apes cannot do that either. Maybe they do not have to. The species from which *Homo sapiens* evolved may have depended more on instinct than on intelligence.

Why, however, are the similarities between human beings and animals more important than the differences? We require conscious thought to do what instinct does for them. Cats and dogs know how to nurse their young; human mothers must learn. Cats know they must bury their excrement to conceal their presence from predators; human beings built outhouses and devised plumbing systems. Biological determinism explains more animal behavior than human behavior.[15]

Maybe there is no such thing as human nature. Would Thomas Hobbes have found "a perpetual and restless desire for power after power, that ceaseth only in death" in "all mankind" if he had lived among the Arapesh of New Guinea?[16] James Madison's *Federalist* 10 emphasized "the diversity of the faculties of men, from which the rights of property originate."[17] But Adam Smith reached the opposite conclusion: "The very different genius which appears to distinguish men of different professions, when grown up to maturity, is not upon many occasions so much the cause as the effect of the division of labour."[18] Is human nature, like the social contract theorists' "state of nature" and John Rawls's "veil of ignorance," a "what if?"—part of a heuristic technique?[19] If so, liberal theory, and the ancient theories that preceded it, need serious revision. But what we can do with a theory is as important as how true it is (see Chapter 1). The idea of human nature has been the foundation of some insightful work.[20] The heuristic value of studying human beings as if they were beasts is undeniable. So is its connection with gender difference and male supremacy.

Gender Roles, Male Supremacy, and Society

Gender roles predate *Homo sapiens*. Primates display them. Male supremacy may predate the need to defend it; obeying and imitating require less brain power than questioning does. Archeologists have found evidence of human activity as far back as 2.5 million years ago. Scholars agree that written language developed independently in two parts of the world: Mesopotamia in about 3200 B.C.E. and Mesoamerica about 600 B.C.E. Although gendered norms can be taught through oral communication within a society, these traditions are older than our ability to communicate across cultures. Gender roles were entrenched before they were explained, justified, or rationalized in ways that survive to the present. Defenses of them are either post hoc justifications or functional explanations like Malinowski's discussion of magic. Aristotle's defense of slavery and male dominance in book 1 of the *Politics* is not a blueprint for a new society any more than Rousseau's *Emile* is; both are rationalizations of the status quo.[21] Slavery was not natural; it was an institution.

Gender differences became, and remain, a site of controversy within zoology and anthropology. Franz Boas's students included the first two American women to become famous anthropologists. Both specialized in cross-cultural scholarship. Ruth Benedict's *Patterns of Culture* preferred cultural relativism to social Darwinist hierarchies. Cultural relativism, now styled as multiculturalism, has come back to frustrate gender equality. Multiculturalism has been the basis for the defense of practices such as bride kidnapping, female genital cutting, and honor killing. An edited book titled *Is Multiculturalism Bad for Women?* led inexorably to an affirmative answer.[22] But Benedict's relativism also rejected biological determinism: "The physical correlations that the biologist may provide in the future, . . . so far as they concern hereditary transmission of traits, cannot, at their best, cover all the facts as we know them."[23] Margaret Mead had "shared the general belief in our society that there was a natural sex-temperament which could at the most only be distorted or diverted from normal expression."[24] Her research in primitive societies, including the Arapesh, convinced her otherwise. *Sex and Temperament* found that in each society, the similarities between men's and women's characters were greater than the differences.[25] Unlike Benedict, Mead lived long enough to become a hero of second-wave feminism. But when her studies were published, they were criticized and even ridiculed. An entire review of *Sex and Temperament* read, "Margaret, have you found a culture yet where the men had the babies?"[26] No anthropologist found a culture in which women dominated men either. For Benedict, the generalization that "the adult prerogatives of men are more far reaching in any culture than women's" was a "social fact."[27] But that was all it was.

As late as the 1970s, to argue that male supremacy was natural, universal, and inevitable was quite the thing.[28] Desmond Morris theorized that male primates became hunters and females gatherers because "the females were too busy rearing the young to be able to play a major role in chasing and catching prey."[29] Lionel Tiger suspected that men would always dominate because "males are prone to bond, male bonds are prone to aggress, and . . . males more than females will incline to tough mastery of the environment."[30] Tiger's argument was at least original; it did not attribute male dominance to women's childbearing function.

Later zoologists and anthropologists have challenged these theories. None is received wisdom any longer.[31] Sarah Blaffer Hrdy wrote, "Anyone who even for a moment thinks that what is natural is necessarily desirable has only to remember that 90 percent of all species that ever evolved are now extinct— by natural processes."[32] While there is no record of a society where women dominate men, the degrees and kinds of male supremacy differ widely among societies. Men and women do not always live together. Aboriginal women in central Australia, for example, "spend most of their time and energy in all-women camps."[33] Some societies are matrilocal (married couples live near the wife's kin or clan) or matrilineal (descent is determined through the female line), while others are patrilineal or patrilocal; some even mix the two types.

Even if male supremacy were universal and inevitable, its details have not been. Even if scholars such as Morris and Tiger were right, the inevitability and necessity of gender roles and male dominance applied only to prehistoric times. Our brains are better developed now, and we have written languages. We need not accept male dominance; we can redistribute adult prerogatives. What happened in the past does not justify what happens now. To rely on "nature" or "instinct," to claim that anyone is "hard-wired" to want or do anything, is either to offer an excuse or to justify an expectation.

Everywhere, women bear children, and men do not. These are sex roles, based on physical differences, whereas gender roles are social constructions. Thinking about gender tends to start with reproductive function. For too long, it got stuck there. With all the ways in which males and females are similar, how did their different reproductive functions become so important? The logical connection between childbearing capacity and male dominance is tenuous. Reproduction is essential to all species: Why should the ability to do something necessary that men cannot do not confer status and privilege? One reason why not is that most men are physically stronger than most women in the same group. Driven by innate sexual urge, acquired desire to dominate, or some mixture of motives, a man can subdue a woman. Another reason why not is that pregnancy, childbirth, and breastfeeding limit a women's activities at least temporarily. If a man can subdue a woman, he can impregnate her; if he can impregnate her, he can slow her down.

Man could have "established his control at the outset by superior physical strength," as a judge wrote in 1908.[34] Did this happen? Could it have happened the other way around, as women, perceiving their inferior supply of brawn and/or wanting sex and/or children, found dependable men and submitted to them? The best guess is that all these things happened some of the time and that some of them happened all the time. Supreme Court Justice David Brewer preceded the sentence I quoted with a statement that "woman has always been dependent upon man."[35] Researchers with vastly more knowledge than he have had no greater success in determining the sequence of events. The first anthropologists to do field research found male dominance and female dependence coexisting.

Many studies of primitive cultures reveal complex courtship practices in which women were active. But researchers also found outright rape, as well as "bride kidnapping" or "marriage by capture." These customs have existed in many parts of the world throughout history and continue now.[36] They are the stuff of myth, as in the rape of the Sabine women, and folklore, as in the Hebrew Bible.[37] Capture marriage has returned to post-Soviet Central Asia, where communist rule had outlawed it, and is increasing there.[38] Male supremacy may have depended on conquest and kidnapping, as slavery did.

To the extent that male dominance was imposed by human beings on other human beings, a liberal defense of male dominance is impossible.[39] Power cannot substitute for reason.

Reproduction is necessary for species survival, but was male dominance necessary for reproduction? How long did it take for people to learn that all human beings die and that, therefore, children must be born for the group to survive? The supply of fertility has exceeded the demand. But was there a time when *Homo sapiens* was threatened with extinction? When infant mortality was high and life expectancy low, the species might have encountered a threat similar to that posed when Mao Zedong resolved to rid China of cats. The cats won because this species reproduces efficiently. Did we survive the same way? Would we have died out if only people who wanted children had them or if they had no more than they wanted? This last question is unanswerable, because the situation it describes has never existed. Human procreation still is not always voluntary. Many twenty-first-century women confront the situation Western women did in the eighteenth century: a woman was "unable to prevent conception reliably if she engaged in sexual intercourse" and facing "a strong possibility she would die as a result of pregnancy or childbirth."[40] However, some primitive and ancient societies had exceptions from the general rule of procreation. Infertility exists in every species. Alternatives to marriage and parenthood have existed.

> Such groups as monks, nuns, long-term spinsters and bachelors and permanent homosexuals are all, in a reproductive sense, aberrant. Society has bred them, but they have failed to return the compliment. Equally, however, it should be realized that an active homosexual is no more reproductively aberrant than monk.[41]

This writer was a zoologist. Human societies have recognized alternatives to majority lifestyles. The vestal virgins of ancient Rome were free to marry when their service ended at thirty, but they were not available for childbearing at the peak of their fertility. Buddhists and Roman Catholics have long had celibate religious orders. Entry into these may not always have been voluntary, but the celibate religious life has been an available alternative.[42] Homosexuality existed in many societies, with varying degrees of acceptance. The Native American Zuni *berdache* studied by Ruth Benedict "were men who at puberty or thereafter took the dress and occupation of women. Sometimes they married other men and lived with them."[43] Ancient Greeks accepted same-sex relationships.

Homosexual attraction did not necessarily preclude procreation any more than it does now. Aristophanes declared in Plato's *Symposium* that, while homosexual men "have no natural desire to marry and beget children," many "do so in deference to the usage of society."[44] Historian Carroll Smith-Rosenberg's study of American women's correspondence in the eighteenth and nineteenth centuries concluded that some pairs of friends "were lovers—emotionally if not physically." Many of these women married and had children.[45] But "Boston marriages" did exist. Classifying people as normal or aberrant according to their sexual identity or their desire to procreate is hard to justify in modern society, unless we want to make invidious distinctions.

Zoology and anthropology show that a useful concept of imperative theory must be more complex than what I started with. It must include wants as well as needs, power as well as necessity. Tasks do not get distributed without being assigned. Nature assigned childbearing and infant feeding to women. Societies assigned childrearing and homemaking to women. Men controlled public and private life in their own interests, but women often used the autonomy they retained to socialize the young into gender-role norms.

Technological advances have made motherhood voluntary, and less dangerous, for many women. Marriage is no longer an asymmetrical relationship. Intercourse is separate from reproduction—and vice versa. The cumulative effect of these developments has been to give people more choices. The cumulative effect of law, economics, and custom has been to channel these choices in socially acceptable directions. States and societies have regarded procreation as too important to be left to individual choice.

States and Procreation: The Politics of Fertility

The rest of this chapter shifts focus from societies, in general, to modern industrial societies, in particular. The norm is the nuclear family: a mother, a father, and their children. Fewer and fewer people choose this arrangement in the developed world, but it is still the model, as Americans relearn with every election and its accompanying rhetoric. This model is derived from ancient Greece and filtered through ancient Roman practices and Judeo-Christian traditions. People do not live in clans. Women do not live in camps with other women and children. Nuclear families do not routinely set up households near the wife's extended family. The Greek toleration of alternative patterns did not survive the contact with Abrahamic religions; homosexuals were long condemned and stigmatized. Christianity is the only world religion that insisted that procreation was the sole purpose of sex and denied women's capacity for sexual pleasure. The traditional family is one of the most patriarchal models in human history. The coexistence of this institution and liberal theory may have reinforced the common suspicion that liberalism and gender equality are incompatible. Changes in the Christian view of sex, prevailing attitudes toward homosexuals, and the balance of power between husband and wife have lessened sexism, but male dominance is "built into the house in which we live."[46]

Fertility rates fluctuate in predictable ways.[47] It is an old story for social science research: interviews and survey data generate individual explanations, while aggregate statistics reveal societal patterns. Fertility rates are relatively high in agrarian societies, where children are economic assets. Industrialization lowers fertility rates. Increased education for women, combined with development, lowers them further. Rates decline in hard times, but they do not necessarily increase as the economy improves. The fertility rate plummeted in the United States during the Great Depression, although barrier methods were the only available contraceptive techniques. Fertility declined again around the time of the 1970s "oil shock" and "since the onset of the recent recession in 2007."[48] The current fertility rate in the United States is 1.86, the lowest it has ever been.[49]

Governments have viewed both underpopulation and overpopulation as problems to be fixed. The medical advances that increased people's freedom have been used to curtail freedom. Authoritarian regimes use force, impose sanctions, and control access to family planning techniques. China is at one extreme. It reduced the population by imposing the "one-child policy" from 1978 to 2015. This policy was enforced by forced abortion and by punishments for those who disobeyed. The communist regimes in Europe had, or thought they had, the opposite problem. Their populations were declining or not growing fast enough—no surprise, given the hardships of life under communism.[50] Several countries imposed a tax on men and married women without children. The Ceausescu government in Romania banned abortion, then the commonest method of birth control. "Sudden shortages of condoms and birth control pills" have occurred in Cuba, where the "birthrate has been in free fall" for forty years.[51]

Popular sovereignty limits the power of countries like the United States to mandate family size. But representative democracies can regulate access to birth control. Discomfort with nonprocreative sex led many states to enact "little Comstock laws," patterned after the 1873 federal statute that banned the distribution of "obscene" materials through the mail. The last such law was invalidated by the Supreme Court in 1972.[52] The United States has practiced selective population control.[53] Some Americans are less sovereign than others: wards of the state, recipients of public aid, and, traditionally, women vis-à-vis men. Eugenics, popular in the United States and Europe in the nineteenth and twentieth centuries, encouraged forced sterilization and contraception.

These practices lasted long after eugenics had been discredited. The federal government allowed sterilization without informed consent until 1979.

Women subjected to mandatory sterilization were disproportionately poor and/or members of racial and ethnic minority groups. In the same years, the private sector limited middle-class women's access to voluntary sterilization. The American College of Obstetrics and Gynecology recommended that no woman be sterilized unless her age multiplied by the number of live children she had borne came to at least 120. Sterilization is available to any adult male on request.[54] Public and private power also cooperated in controlling access to contraception. Capitalist systems now distribute contraception and assisted reproductive technologies through the market. Some insurance carriers covered Viagra before they covered birth control pills.

Population trends in Europe and the English-speaking world, even where the economy is healthy, are raising warning bells. When times are bad, children are luxuries. When times are good, children have little or no economic utility. Residents of welfare states do not anticipate needing their children's care as they age any more than residents of industrial countries need their children's labor. Even countries with generous pronatalist policies like paid leave and parental subsidies experience population decline. Fertility rates of 2.1 or greater are necessary for a generation to reproduce itself; many developed countries are well below that.[55] Population decline need not result in extinction, but it reduces the size of the labor pool. As baby boomers retire, there are not enough workers to fill their jobs, including dependency work.[56] Economic growth stalls.

What can developed countries do? The radical solution of refusing to define underpopulation as a problem is not popular. But technological advances, twenty-first-century equivalents of gas, electricity, internal combustion machines, computers, and the internet, might reduce the demand for labor. Population decline might slow the pace of climate change and thus benefit the planet. Immigration could replenish the labor supply, but such policies are not popular in Europe or the United States in the aftermath of terrorist attacks. Shortening the working week might provide more jobs; the average full-time employee in Germany works four days a week.[57]

Would access to fertility treatments help? Sterility has only a small effect on population growth. Developed countries do not encourage treatment in any consistent way. Medically supervised artificial insemination is available in the United States only to women who can afford the required goods and services—or, if the reader prefers, to any woman who can afford it. Some states require some insurance plans to cover or offer coverage for infertility treatments. No state requires both insurance providers and employers to cover these treatments. Socialist governments may regulate access by law. Single women in Sweden got access to artificial insemination as recently as 2016.[58] Enough European countries permit artificial insemination to limit the effects of restrictions, because people can easily travel from country to country. The fact that artificial insemination does not require medical assistance limits restriction as well. The European Union has no uniform policy on using public funds for in vitro fertilization (IVF). Some countries do, and some do not. More consensus exists on defining the problem than on finding solutions to it.

One at a Time: Choice and Tradition

Adrienne Rich, in *Blood, Bread, and Poetry*, states:

> Women have married because it was necessary, in order to survive economically, in order to have children who would not suffer economic deprivation or social ostracism, in order to remain respectable, in order to do what was expected of women, . . . and because heterosexual romance has been represented as the great female adventure, duty, and fulfillment.[59]

Emma Woodhouse, the protagonist of Jane Austen's *Emma*, explains:

> I have none of the usual inducements to marry. Were I to fall in love, indeed, it would be a different thing; but I never have been in love; it is not my way, or my nature; and I do not think I ever shall. And, without love, I am sure I should be a fool to change such a situation as mine. Fortune I do not want; employment I do not want; consequence I do not want: I believe few married women are half as much mistress of their husband's house as I am of Hartfield; and never, never could I expect to be so truly beloved and important; so always first and always right in any man's house as I am in my father's.[60]

Adrienne Rich was an American poet and essayist who wrote in the twentieth and twenty-first centuries. Jane Austen's novel was published in 1816. Rich makes a generalization; Austen creates an exception. Reproductive functions controlled women's lives through most of human history. In parts of the world, they still do. They did when liberalism emerged as a philosophy in the seventeenth century. Marriage routinized sexual intercourse. Pregnancy and childbirth followed it. Infants had to be breastfed, usually by the mother. Alternatives did exist but not always, everywhere, and for everyone. These imperatives encouraged the development of the gender roles I have described. In developed countries, the roles survive the imperatives.

Rich's generalizations have been true more often than not. They were true for most of the women characters in Austen's novels. Although they were privileged by class and background, marriage was necessary for their economic security. Privileged men had reserved economic security for themselves and denied the opportunities for it even to the women in their lives. These women's alternatives were permanent dependency on family members or insecure, low-paying employment as paid companions, social secretaries, or tutors.

Emma has an immunity from need that most women of her time and place lack. She is not eager for motherhood. She has time and energy to spare for her efforts at matchmaking, with mixed results. As a spinster, she might be pitied, criticized, or gossiped about (her indifference to disapproval is another immunity), but she would not be poor. If heterosexual romance was "represented as the great female adventure, duty, and fulfillment" to her, she has remained unconvinced. An author could make Emma's immunity unravel—if not, there is no novel—in several ways, but Austen eliminates some possibilities. Emma has no rival for her widowed father's loyalty. He is disinclined to remarry. His property is not entailed, so no male relative can exile her from Hartfield after he dies. Austin has Emma fall in love with an older man who "loves to find fault with [her]" and marry him.[61]

Women like Emma have not been confined to fiction. The degree of comfort, privilege, and self-confidence necessary to provide immunity has been relative. A schoolteacher in the 1950s was more secure than a governess in the early nineteenth century. The teacher earned less than her brother, whether or not he went to college. He could buy a house, which she could not, even if a bank would approve a mortgage for a single woman. But she, with no children, had fewer expenses. The duty of caring for their aging parents usually fell on her, but the financial burden might be shared among siblings. Today, the male monopoly on education and financial security has been broken. Female immunity is more common in the developed world. Fewer women must marry to survive or to have children. Motherhood is more attractive now than in Austen's day, but marriage and motherhood are not interdependent. Babies can be bottle-fed. Medical science refined techniques of birth control, artificial insemination, and IVF in the twentieth century.

Custom and social expectation have been powerful influences in persuading people who have a choice to marry and have children. They do it because they want to. Society has worked hard to convince women to want marriage and motherhood. *The Angel in the House*, Coventry Patmore's ode to the Victorian wife and mother, was immensely popular in nineteenth-century England.[62] Barbara Welter's classic article "The Cult of True Womanhood," whose title is its description, showed that similar ideas were popular in the United States at the time.[63] These publications' intended audience included women who could choose whether to marry without facing poverty and who could resist social pressure. The American Birth Control League (ABCL) changed its name to the Planned Parenthood Federation of America in 1942. This name change not only distanced the ABCL from the eugenics of its founder, Margaret Sanger, but also implied that parenthood was the norm and childlessness the exception. The growth of the mass media made it easier for experts to circulate their ideas. The work of Sigmund Freud and his successors made it easy for experts to deny that people know what they really want. The psychological concepts of repression and denial have been at least as useful as the Marxist concept of false consciousness for discrediting what people say about themselves.

The propaganda machine really got going after World War II. Working women were urged to go home and concentrate on their families. Dr. Benjamin Spock's *Common Sense Book of Baby and Child Care* advised mothers, "The younger the child the more necessary it is for him to have a steady, loving person taking care of him. In most cases, the mother is the best one to give him this feeling of 'belonging.'" A mother who understands this need "may realize that the extra money she might earn, or the satisfaction she might receive from an outside job, is not so important after all."[64] Scholars echoed this opinion, although agreement was not unanimous. To Margaret Mead, "the specific biological situation of the continuing relationship of the child to its biological mother and its need for care by human beings are being hopelessly confused in the growing insistence that child and biological mother, or mother surrogate, must never be separated," although "anthropological evidence gives no support at present to the value of such an accentuation of the tie between mother and child." She labeled this "a new and subtle form of antifeminism in which men—under the guise of exalting the importance of maternity—are tying women more tightly to their children than has been thought necessary since the invention of bottle feeding and baby carriages."[65]

A woman who had no children did not need this advice. But twentieth-century "sex-directed educators" impressed on girls and women the idea that "Occupation: Housewife" was their destiny and that something was wrong with any woman who disagreed. The experts of the 1940s and 1950s ignored mothers who had to work outside the home. These women were not the intended audience. Neither were unmarried working women. But the books and magazines were available to all, with their implications that these readers were inadequate mothers or abnormal women.

Adults steered girls away from the professions and toward jobs that required less training and education. High schools and colleges had courses on marriage and the family that left a student "with the cheerful impression that if she chooses a career, she is choosing celibacy."[66] Women who remained single were considered abnormal. They were vulnerable to rumors that they were lesbians, rumors that could get them fired even when they were false. The combined message of expert opinion and popular social science was that women must have children when young (no modern equivalent of vestal virgins) and must stay home with them.

People in the developed world have much more freedom of choice now than they did in the 1960s. To the extent that sex is consensual, birth control reliable, and abortion available, parenthood is optional. People without children may be "child-free" instead of "childless." Nonparents may provoke envy or indifference rather than pity. They are less likely to be judged derelict in their duty than they were in the 1970s. The connection between marriage and parenthood has weakened. Parenthood without marriage does not entail the stigma it once did. Single adults adopt children, sometimes with financial aid from the government.

The relative importance of work and family in women's lives has also changed. "Occupation: Housewife" yielded to "work-life balance." This change was driven less by feminism than by economics. The disappearance of the family wage made full-time homemaking a luxury. Experts' opinions changed in response to this reality. Spock told *Working Mother* in 1987 that "women can go back as soon as they 'need to.'"[67] T. Berry Brazelton, an equally prominent expert, advocated a paid four-month maternity leave.[68]

But the twenty-first-century mommy manuals produced by Spock's and Brazelton's successors promote a "cult of true motherhood" that ignores gender asymmetry and economic realities.[69] The "attachment parenting" promoted by William and Martha Sears, for example, requires postpartum "babywearing" even at work.[70] The *What to Expect When You're Expecting* franchise emphasizes "prioritizing baby over cleanliness or baby over career." The authors advise mothers not to decide to return to work until after the baby is born, when they are dealing with hormonal changes.[71] Motherhood is still a full-time job. Once, mothers had to stay home; now, they must wear and, of course, breastfeed the baby. This overwhelming consensus that breastfeeding is mandatory, although the "science behind the consensus is deeply problematic," exemplifies what Joan Wolf calls "total motherhood":

> a moral code in which mothers are exhorted to optimize every aspect of children's lives, beginning with the womb. Its practice is frequently cast as a trade-off between what mothers might like and what babies and children must have, a choice that frames public discourse on breastfeeding. And when mothers have "wants"—such as a sense of bodily, emotional, and psychological autonomy—but children have

"needs"—such as an environment in which anything less than optimal is framed as perilous—good mothering is defined as behavior that reduces even infinitesimal or poorly understood risks to offspring, regardless of the potential cost to the mother. . . . Mothers are held responsible for matters well outside their control, and they are told in various ways that they must eliminate even minute, ultimately ineradicable, potential threats to their children's well-being.[72]

As imperatives die out, others are born. The headline of a news story in October 2015 read, "No Alcohol during Pregnancy—Ever—Plead U.S. Pediatricians."[73] The American Academy of Pediatrics, dismissing evidence "that a moderate amount of drinking during pregnancy is not linked to cognitive or behavioral issues," asserted that "the smartest choice for women who are pregnant is to just abstain from alcohol completely."[74] Is *plead* the right verb?

Not only is motherhood "total," but so, too, is parenthood. Responsibility for children is assigned to the parents, not—Hillary Rodham Clinton to the contrary—to the village.[75] In pregnancy and infancy, the responsible parent is the mother; no one else need optimize. Mothers must breastfeed their babies, but employers need not provide nursing breaks or lactation rooms; nor must a court exempt nursing mothers from jury duty or public places allow them to nurse on the premises.[76] Mothers work outside the home, but they must be hypervigilant or risk condemnation, shame, and guilt.[77] Women play at least as prominent a part in assigning this responsibility as men do. Nothing is new about women socializing women—some of the experts Mead and Friedan criticized were women—but contemporary activists often identify themselves as feminists.[78] The concrete results of these imperatives show how far we are from equality between the sexes.

Where Are We Now? Some Stories

To examine those results, I departed from conventional social science methods. I began not with facts or numbers but with stories. The time is the present. The setting is the workplace I know best, an academic department within a university.

Anita does not actually work for the department but for the buildings and grounds division. Some faculty members do not know her, because her shift begins at 2:00 A.M. and ends before noon. But she feels she knows them. She is sixty, earns minimum wage, and has always held additional part-time jobs in fast-food establishments. She helps care for her ailing mother and her grandchildren. She has type 2 diabetes and is often in pain from arthritis.

Susan, the receptionist, has just become a mother at twenty-five. Her pediatrician insists that she breastfeed. Her spouse, mother, mother-in-law, and best friend join the chorus. But Susan must return to work when her six weeks of paid maternity leave expire. She cannot afford to take any of the unpaid leave to which the law entitles her. The building where she works has no on-site child care and nowhere to nurse, pump, or store milk.

Joanne, the office manager, is in her late thirties. She and her second husband have been trying to conceive since their marriage three years ago. An infertility specialist has advised them to try IVF. This expensive procedure is not covered by their insurance and may succeed only after several tries, if ever. Joanne will have to miss work to undergo and recover from treatments. She does not have enough accumulated sick leave to cover IVF.

Every semester, the department hires adjuncts to teach undergraduate courses. This group of "freeway flyers" includes proportionately more women than any of the tenure-track ranks. Adjuncts include advanced graduate students, Ph.D. holders who do not work full time or whose spouses cannot move, and a local attorney teaching constitutional law. The adjunct faculty are worse off than the staff. They lack job security, insurance, and benefits. They are here because the teaching load for full-time faculty is two courses per semester and the demand for course sections exceeds this labor supply. Adjuncts are paid, below minimum wage, by the course, which can be canceled at the last minute. The academic job market is so bad that adjuncts have little chance of a permanent position even if they finish their degrees and publish their dissertations. The adjuncts have begun to organize, but the lawyer and the provost's spouse do not attend the meetings.

Rose and Violet are tenured professors in their sixties. They joined the department at the same time, right out of graduate school. Rose has modeled her behavior after that of her professors and senior colleagues. She has published extensively and is well known in her field. Violet has published much less than Rose but has won awards for teaching and service. When Rose is asked to undertake service obligations, her rule is "three nos for every yes." Violet feels guilty if she says no. She organizes the holiday party, the wedding and baby showers, and the retirement celebrations. These did not exist until she arrived. She may have created new expectations that will be imperatives by the time she retires.

Rose is one of the highest-paid faculty members. But she often feels she is failing a course she did not register for or has lost her place in a script. She is nowhere near as popular within the university community as Violet is. Susan, Joanne, and the other staff members do not like Rose; students complain about her; and her colleagues let her know that she falls short of their expectations. Violet senses her colleagues' disappointment, too. Successive department heads encouraged her to do more research but kept asking her to do more service. Colleagues have suggested that she volunteer for a 150 percent teaching load.[79]

Helen, a retired professor, joined the department twenty-five years ago. Her previous job was the presidency of a prestigious liberal arts college. None of her current coworkers knew why Helen had resigned her former position after two years until she published a memoir. She had been hounded out of her job after she exposed an academic fraud. The faculty had protested her decision to fire the perpetrator, a man with a family to support.

Helen is based on and named after Miss De Vine in Dorothy L. Sayers's mystery novel *Gaudy Night*. The other stories are fictional versions of common situations. These women fit the liberal and rational choice models of what it means to be a human being. Any of them might tell you that they have made free choices and accepted the consequences of these choices. They might also remind you that some women have it worse: few housecleaners earn even minimum wage, mothers have been fired for breastfeeding, and some workers have no paid maternity leave. Our subjects embody the mature, responsible adult that liberalism presupposes. Each has the power to change her situation. Anita could cut back on child care. Susan could bring a pump and a mini-fridge to work. Joanne and her husband could adopt a child or give up their plans for parenthood. Rose could conform more, and Violet less, to gendered norms of behavior. The ethic of individual responsibility encourages people to make their own arrangements and accept the consequences of their actions, even when others have the power to change those consequences. These women are rational actors and liberal subjects. The problem they share is that they confront conflicting expectations because they are women.

There are three obvious objections to this line of analysis. First, men also confront gendered expectations. Ask a bridegroom whose wife expects him to do home repairs or a father whose wife expects him to discipline the children. True, but most men are privileged with respect to similarly situated women,[80] and the expectations confronting men do not conflict as much. Second, class, status, and education privilege some women workers relative to others. Situations such as Rose's, Violet's, and Helen's are sometimes derided as "First World problems." They may seem trivial alongside Susan's, whose problems may pale alongside Anita's. Professors may be able to stop the tenure clock when they become parents and/or work out a deal to remain on full pay while reducing their teaching responsibilities. The adjuncts get no maternity leave. Full-time faculty and staff members have security and benefits that most American workers lack. And what about the Third World?[81] But I have committed this project to the premise that class is *a*, not *the*, crucial factor in social analysis. Despite the differences of degree, these women's situations are similar in kind. They all confront the classic gendered division of labor that assigns women to maintenance and nurturing functions and penalizes women who fail to fulfill these functions.

Third, I could be accused of what Angela Harris has called "gender essentialism—the notion that a unitary, 'essential' women's experience can be isolated and described."[82] By emphasizing similarities, have I trivialized differences in race, ethnicity, religion, sexuality, and so forth? I assigned my characters names without obvious ethnic origins. Susan might face less pressure to breastfeed if she were African American rather than Anglo or Hispanic.[83] But she might confront these difficulties no matter what her racial background or sexual preference. The factors that distinguish women in similar situations from one another make their realities different, and sometimes better or worse, but not different enough to preclude generalization. I am writing vignettes, not biographies. I do not deny the importance of race, ethnicity, religion, sexuality, and so on in these women's lives; I suggest that their situations affect them whatever those particulars are.

Why should anyone have to work to exhaustion like Anita?[84] Why should work conflict with motherhood for Susan now that a job is a necessity for most mothers? Why is professional work done by marginal employees? Why should some women be punished for conforming to gendered expectations and others punished for flouting them?

Anita's and Susan's difficulties reflect a tension between social and economic factors. Like many unskilled laborers, Anita cannot earn a living wage at a full-time job. She must moonlight, and these extra hours worsen common chronic conditions that may result, in part, from inadequate medical care. Even when she becomes eligible for Medicare and Social Security, she will have to work part time, and the demands from her family may increase. (She has seen it happen.) Susan may not earn a living wage, either; her family gets by because it has two full-time workers. But the demands that she breastfeed clash with the need to return to work so soon after birth that she and her baby may not have established a feeding schedule. Even in traditional women's jobs, the structure presumes an "ideal worker" for whom the job is the first priority.[85]

These workers' problems are capable of solution. Obamacare was a step in the right direction for Anita, especially if long-term elder care was available for her mother. On-site child care, parental subsidies, and paid family leave would help Susan. Many countries in Europe do it. Most of these governments are socialist, but why should capitalist businesses not compete for workers? To consider these possibilities in the American context is to realize how remote they are. Whether gender equality in the workplace is compatible with any capitalist system, it is incompatible with our entrenched political and economic system. The possibility that twenty-first-century pediatricians will follow Spock's and Brazelton's lead and moderate their expectations of mothers seems less remote. Waiting for markets to correct themselves and for experts to change their advice are passive strategies. Incremental changes, such as providing rooms for nursing and pumping, one workplace at a time, are happening in the public and private sector, with activist workers taking the lead.

Joanne may wish she had Susan's problems. She has a job and a husband and wants a baby. Should employers provide medical leave for IVF treatments? Should insurance plans cover it? This is likely to happen only if employers must compete for workers and carriers for clients, if then. Is it fair to have assisted reproductive technologies available only to people who can afford them? Are they luxuries or necessities? Is there a contradiction between classifying artificial reproductive technologies (ARTs) as luxuries and complaining about low fertility rates? A lack of access to ARTs might be a hidden benefit. A 2014 study showed that inadequately tested and misunderstood procedures have been aggressively marketed to women by those who are at least as eager to exploit women as to assist them; this result is no surprise to those familiar with the history of oral contraceptives, intrauterine devices, diethylstilbestrol, and hormone replacement therapy.[86] How, and by whom, should these decisions be made?

Economics has a greater effect than gender in creating the adjunct market. Both male and female adjuncts endure economic exploitation, but the "two-body problem" and "trailing spouse" status increase some academic women's vulnerability. Several factors contribute to the creation and maintenance of the adjunct market. First, the demand for courses exceeds the supply of teachers. Second, academia has set high standards for earning the terminal degrees in most fields. These degrees are awarded by R (for research) 1 programs. Ph.D. recipients who plan to teach do not get tenure-track jobs without a completed research project. Third, while teaching can and does complement research, one does not need to have done research to teach the introductory courses most adjuncts teach. Finally, more and more institutions of higher learning are run like businesses. While most do not maximize profit—those that do are not R1 institutions—they seek to increase input and reduce output. These needs and priorities encourage the growth of adjunct pools.[87] Any liberal will agree that people should be able to choose part-time and short-term employment. But what responsibilities do the employer and the state have to affect the consequence of the choice? Again, Europe has taken the lead.

Rose's, Violet's, and Helen's problems are easier to bear but no easier to solve. Business, law, medicine, and academia have often been described as two-class systems, structured like the feudal division of lords and serfs or the military division into commissioned and noncommissioned officers. Lawyers and paralegals, doctors and nurses, professors and adjuncts, and professional and clerical workers remain divided by gender and often by race. But describing the working world as a two-class system is no longer accurate. It has become a *three*-class system of professionals, aides, and maintenance workers. Men are disproportionately located in the upper tier, while women are disproportionately located in the lower two. The same is true for Anglo and Asian workers vis-à-vis African Americans and Hispanics.

The home, once called the "private" sphere, is the site of maintenance work traditionally assigned to women. The historical process that began with the Industrial Revolution and continued with the shrinkage of the domestic labor market sent tasks, and role expectations associated with them, into the workplace—the child-care center, the fast-food restaurant, the office, the university—although they still existed in the home. Patients, clients, students, and subordinates expect empathy and an "ethic of care."[88] So do colleagues and supervisors. Women who make it into the professions carry the lower-tier role expectations with them. If Rose and Violet have living parents, brothers, and no sisters, they will learn, if they have not already, that the burden of elder care is disproportionately theirs. The faculty Helen led turned against her because she dealt with fraud in a judgmental, rather than a nurturing, manner. Rose is disliked and snubbed because she is a "bad mother" to colleagues, staff members, and students. Violet is liked but not always respected.[89]

Would a woman now in Helen's situation meet the same fate? To forestall flippant responses to the effect that college presidents are too privileged to worry about faculty firings, I remind the reader that academic fraud is usually dealt with at a lower level. Department chairs are typical first responders. Many cases involve students, not faculty. The fact that the person Helen fired had a dependent family might not make much difference today. Vast disagreement exists within academia on how, under what circumstances, or even whether fraud should be punished. If faculty members and administrators are divided at this hypothetical institution, action or inaction by someone in authority might have no negative consequences other than a series of microaggressions of the type that Rose and Violet face.

These microaggressions are costly; they can sap the energy and lower the self-esteem of people subjected to them. The responsibility for change has rested with those who challenge them, the women who can absorb criticism and are immune from punishment. Violet could have looked for, and might have found, a job in an institution that rewards her talents. But why can her university not change? Why not reward people for conventional "womanly" behavior, the caring activities that improve the workplace? Would such a change make things worse or better for people who do not perform these tasks?

Conclusion

Imperative theory cannot stop with asking, "What must be done?" Malinowski's "secondary determinism" described how needs and wants become indistinguishable from wants.[90] Imperatives are assigned by both natural and human forces. Another question—"Who and what assign necessary tasks?"—is equally important. Sex differences in reproductive functions are givens; they are part of the reality with which civilization starts. But do sex differences in reproductive functions work as explanations for these different roles? No better than they do for male supremacy. Women bear children; then women breastfeed infants; then (not therefore) women care for children; then women care for others. Women bear children; then (not therefore) women do the necessary maintenance work; then women maintain the home for both children and adults; then women do the maintenance work outside the home. Once we realize that male power over women contributed to the development of gender roles, they lose much of their legitimacy.

Care and maintenance are time-consuming and under-rewarded. But both women and men expect women to do this work, whatever else any woman does. Susan and Joanne are less free than the male faculty and staff to carry out their reproductive functions compatibly with their jobs.[91] The three professors' childbearing years are behind them, but they still confront expectations their male counterparts do not.

Women will never be equal to men in more than a formal legalistic sense as long as they confront these situations. Feminists cannot accept the liberal subject model as adequate for women's interests. But the model also seems at variance with fundamental liberal principles of equality and of the primacy of reason over emotion. Where can we go from here?

That last sentence is only one of several questions I have posed: some rhetorical, some not. Constructing imperative theory raises more questions than it answers. Once we perceive that power is at least as important as nature in determining gender roles, we cannot accept male supremacy as natural or benign. Once we perceive that, even if reproductive functions are the source of gender roles, they do not justify them, we must challenge the role distributions we have now.

This project concentrates more on gender inequality than economic inequality. But my stories show how sex roles and economic inequality reinforce each other. The patterns of capitalism—the profit motive, supply and demand, the relationship between inflation and unemployment, and the like—are observed regularities, but they are not natural law principles any more than male supremacy is. Socialism is becoming respectable in twenty-first-century America—we have Bernie Sanders to thank for that development—and family-friendly policies once condemned as socialist may infiltrate, if not transform, a capitalist economy. Paid family leaves and parental subsidies need not lead to entitlements to several weeks at a health spa every few years at employers' expense. I wonder earlier in the chapter how women's lives would be affected if Greece became more like Germany. We know that American women's lives would improve if this country adopted policies familiar in Western Europe. A feminist post-liberalism must redistribute power from institutions to individuals and responsibility from individuals to institutions.

3

Liberalism and Feminism in the Courts

Between Lochner *and* Muller

Men are not in the U.S. Constitution. The use of the generic masculine was common in the Founding period, but the document refers to "person(s)" or "people."[1] The word *male* appears only once, in Section 2 of the Fourteenth Amendment, which imposed penalties on states that denied voting rights to adult male citizens. This clause was superseded by the Fifteenth Amendment's explicit prohibition of race discrimination in voting rights. So the qualifications for holding office, the rights and immunities, and the limitations on federal power applied to women as well as men. The victories of Ozzie Powell, Clarence Earl Gideon, Ernesto Miranda, and Clarence Brandenburg extended to women.[2] Linda Brown, Dollree Mapp, Madalyn Murray, and Mildred Loving won results that applied to all.[3]

The Constitution mentions sex discrimination only in the Nineteenth Amendment's elimination of sex as a legitimate qualification for voting rights. But women, like members of other disadvantaged groups, have used the equal protection and due process clauses of the Fifth and Fourteenth Amendments in making claims. Congress has prohibited or limited sex-based discrimination in employment and education.[4] Constitutional and statutory sex discrimination have brought gender issues to the courts.

In this chapter, I scrutinize three perfectly liberal Supreme Court opinions from the Rehnquist court: Harry Blackmun's majority opinion in *United Auto Workers v. Johnson Controls* (1991), Ruth Bader Ginsburg's majority opinion in *United States v. Virginia* (1996), and the plurality opinion in *Planned Parenthood of Southeastern Pennsylvania v. Casey* (1992). I argue that the theory generated by these cases has serious deficiencies from both feminist and liberal viewpoints. First, the court appears to be stuck between two obsolescent cases. *Lochner v. New York*, a split decision invalidating a maximum hour law for bakers, was reversed by the court itself.[5] *Muller v. Oregon*, a unanimous decision upholding a maximum-hour law for women laundry workers, was preempted by the Civil Rights Act of 1964.[6] The second error is the court's slowness to recognize a third type of case entailing the pronouncement on gendered issues without requiring courts to discuss them. The classic privacy rulings—those legitimizing birth control and homosexual activity, for example—are gender-neutral.[7] But the abortion decisions cannot be. Only women can get abortions. To discuss abortion is inevitably to discuss women's rights and equality between the sexes.

Why devote a chapter to appellate court opinions? Judges do not set out to write political theory. The authors of opinions are constrained by institutional norms. They are expected to, and usually do, resolve only the issues before them rather than seek an ideal conclusion. Restraints on judicial power, most of them self-imposed, limit the scope of appellate court decisions. The idea that decisions are at least as much the product of politics as of ideologies has long been conventional wisdom. But not all decisions have political salience. *Craig v. Boren*, for example, is an important case because it established the equal protection doctrine for gender discrimination, not because the public cared whether young men could buy 3.2 percent beer or whether venders could sell it to them.[8] The ruling is obsolescent now, since the legal drinking age is twenty-one, but the decision continues to have an impact. My justifications for using court opinions as examples of political theory are, first, that many opinions can stand on their own merits as theory; second, that court decisions are influenced by the judges' ideologies; and, third, that liberalism and legal doctrine have a close relationship.

A minimalist view of the judicial role is as old as judicial review itself. *Marbury v. Madison* declared that the courts' function was to "apply the rule to particular cases."[9] Owen Roberts, writing for the majority in *U.S. v. Butler*, used similar language: the judicial role was "to lay the article of the Constitution which is invoked beside the statute which is challenged and decide whether the latter squares with the former."[10] But readers of these opinions know it was not that simple; both accompanied blatant judicial activism. The most frequent sources of admonitions against writing theory into law are dissenting opinions and scholarly critiques that accuse court majorities of doing just that. Oliver Wendell Holmes insisted that *Lochner* was "decided on the basis of an economic theory which a large part of the population does not entertain."[11] Hugo Black criticized his colleagues for enacting a "natural law due process philosophy . . . which I cannot accept."[12] William Rehnquist characterized the idea of a "living Constitution" as "a formula for an end run around popular government."[13]

These judges were propounding, momentarily at least, the "legal model" of judicial decision making. Black and Rehnquist may have thought they practiced judicial restraint, but neither is remembered that way. Holmes suspected that judges normally decided cases on the basis of personal opinions, if not economic theories. Later realists, notably Jerome Frank, had no doubt that both judges and juries decided this way. Frank accused critics of legal realism of reducing the law to "gastronomical jurisprudence": the idea that judges decide cases on the basis of their digestion. But the term was Frank's, not his critics'. He did not dismiss the idea outright.[14]

Current theories are more sophisticated and better supported by evidence. The "attitudinal model" holds that rules and precedents are less important factors in Supreme Court decision making than political philosophy. As Jeffrey Segal and Harold Spaeth explain, "Simply put, Rehnquist votes the way he does because he is extremely conservative; [Thurgood] Marshall voted the way he did because he is extremely liberal."[15] Like the legal model, this hypothesis oversimplifies. It is circular, at best, and tautological, at worst. The attitudinal model purports to explain votes, not opinions. It does not explain all votes because some decisions are unanimous and not all cases have political salience to all judges. Different philosophies can lead to the same conclusion, and vice versa; what explains justices' votes may not explain the opinions they write or join. But the Supreme Court databases contain more evidence in support of the attitudinal model than any other model.[16] Applying rules to cases has generated quite a bit of political theory. *Lochner* and *Muller* read quaintly in the twenty-first century: the former, a throwback to laissez-faire; the latter, an exercise in "romantic paternalism."[17] Yet *Lochner* and *Muller* were liberal decisions for their time, and their brand of liberalism continues to shape judicial thinking about gender and law.

In *Lochner*, the theory "the Fourteenth Amendment does not enact" was social Darwinism, which Holmes identified with "Mr. Herbert Spencer's *Social Statics*."[18] Lawyers and judges in the early twentieth century might not have read Spencer, but they were familiar with social Darwinism in a legal context. The writings of Justice Thomas Cooley of the Michigan Supreme Court and Dean Christopher Tiedeman of the University of Buffalo Law School were widely read within the legal profession. These jurists defended laissez-faire as a means of natural selection.[19]

Lochner survived as precedent for only thirty-two years. The court repudiated it, not once but twice.[20] But it remains a potent symbol of what courts should not do. Cass Sunstein, writing in 1987, characterized *Lochner* as "the most important of all defining cases" since it was decided.[21] Another constitutionalist wrote that "avoiding 'Lochner's error' remains the central obsession, the (oftentimes articulate) major premise, of contemporary constitutional law."[22] To "Lochner" is to ground a decision in personal preferences rather than legal doctrine. Dissenters from the conservative majority in a 5–4 decision limiting Congress's commerce power accused their fellow justices of returning to *Lochner*'s "expansive conception of Fourteenth Amendment substantive due process."[23] The conservative scholar Robert P. George describes twenty-first-century court decisions extending rights to homosexuals as "*Lochner*izing on a massive scale."[24]

Many critics of this sort disagree with the philosophy enacted, the result reached, or both. But Holmes himself was "sympathetic" to Spencer's *Social Statics* "as a matter of personal predilection."[25] The first author to use "Lochner" as a verb was John Hart Ely, who affirmed his support for legalized abortion even as he called *Roe v. Wade*[26] "a very bad decision . . . because it is bad constitutional law, or rather because it is *not* constitutional law and gives no sense of an obligation to try to be."[27] Arguing with Ely's assessment is difficult, but is *Roe* really the *worst* example of judicial usurpation? The commonest example of judicial activism on steroids is not a commerce clause case, *Citizens United v. Federal Election Commission*, or even *Bush v. Gore*.[28] It is the case that legalized abortion. A 7–2 decision endorsing a women's right to reproductive choice is a worse exercise of judicial power than any of these 5–2 decisions denying Congress the power to keep firearms away from schools, gutting the Violence against Women Act, negating efforts to control campaign financing, and determining the result of a presidential election. To protect exclusively female rights is unacceptable.

Lochner: The "Old Constitutionalism"?

Lochner, to which *Roe* is so often compared, has enjoyed some rehabilitation since the 1990s.[29] This change did not come from defenders of *Roe*. A few scholars have defended *Lochner*'s result, although not necessarily its dependence on the due process clause.[30] One article suggested that *Lochner*'s "unprincipled judicial activism" led to better public policy.[31] A centrist critique does not defend the result but the *Lochner* majority against Holmes's accusation that they wrote social Darwinism into the Constitution. Holmes may have heard these principles invoked in conference, conversation, or correspondence, but no records survive.

Recent studies have insisted that the ruling was based on established constitutional principles. Howard Gillman wrote that *Lochner* and similar rulings "represented a serious, principled effort to maintain one of the central distinctions of nineteenth-century constitutional law—the distinction between valid economic regulation, on the one hand, and invalid 'class legisla-tion,' on the other—during a period of unprecedented class conflict."[32] The term *class legislation* was at least as old as the congressional debates over the Fourteenth Amendment in 1866. There, it referred to discrimination against members of racial minorities.[33] But appellate court judges in the early twenti-eth century were not in the habit of citing original constitutional sources. For them, *class legislation* meant laws singling out any group for special treatment without sound reason. Justice Rufus Peckham wrote that "there can be no fair doubt that the trade of a baker, in and of itself, is not an unhealthy one to that degree which would authorize the legislature to interfere with the right to labor, and with the right of free contract on the part of the individual, either as employer or employee."[34]

Owen Fiss stressed the majority's reliance on freedom of contract: "Peck-ham did not—to put to rest another misinterpretation of *Lochner* also tied to Holmes's dissent—'find' liberty of contract of the interstices of the Fourteenth Amendment. He instead was trying to preserve the then fairly well recognized limits on the police power."[35] Peckham condemned the state law as a regulation of "the hours in which grown and intelligent men may earn their living" and waxed eloquent about "the rights of individuals . . . to make contracts regarding labor upon such terms as they may think best."[36] This is established law, as the cited precedents show. Although contrary precedents, upholding regulations while recognizing that they "legitimately promoted the general welfare," were available,[37] the majority did not need to resort to Spencer, Cooley, or Tiedeman to support its decision. No other justice joined Holmes's opinion. Justice John Marshall Harlan's dissent, joined by three colleagues, argued that baking was, in fact, a dangerous occupation calling for the exercise of police power.

If the rehabilitators are correct that the majority followed settled legal doctrine, *Lochner* was a liberal decision for its time and place. (One switched vote would have turned it into a progressive decision.) So what was "*Lochner's* error"? A suspicious feature of the ruling is that the court did not decide the controversy presented to it. Joseph Lochner was not a worker asserting a right to work longer hours; he was an employer asserting a right to make his em-ployees work longer hours. *U.S. v. Lopez* and *U.S. v. Morrison* made a similar mistake: they found that Congress had usurped the powers of the state where no state was a party.[38] But this sort of lapse need not vitiate a ruling. *Griswold v. Connecticut*, the doctrinal ancestor of *Roe*, involved a birth control clinic, not "the sacred precincts of marital bedrooms."[39] *Roe* refused to choose be-tween "a woman's decision whether or not to terminate her pregnancy" and "the pregnant woman's attending physician" (always "he").[40]

The crucial defect of *Lochner* was the court's failure to recognize that lib-eral premises of equality between contracting parties did not apply. Couched in neutral language, the proscription of class legislation and the endorsement of freedom of contract favored employers at the expense of workers, the ruling class over the working class. Most American workers had lost any freedom to contract with their employers they had ever had. Labor was a buyers' market. In the absence of collective bargaining or government intervention, employers set hours and conditions of labor. History had answered Alexander Hamilton's rhetorical question in *Federalist* 35—"Will not the merchant understand and be disposed to cultivate, as far as may be proper, the interests of the mechanic and manufacturing arts to which his commerce is so nearly allied?"—in the negative.[41] If the justices in the majority recognized that the decision would help employers and hurt workers, they did, indeed, write laissez-faire and social Darwinism into the Constitution. The majority was either ignorant or devious.

A familiar radical feminist critique of privacy doctrine holds that these cases had an effect on gender relations that was similar to *Lochner*'s effect on class relations. Whereas *Lochner* increased the power of employers over workers with respect to labor, *Griswold* and *Roe* left undisturbed the power of men over women with respect to sex and reproduction. Catharine MacKinnon wrote, "To the extent that abortion exists to control the reproductive consequences of intercourse, hence to facilitate male sexual access to women, access to abortion will be controlled by a man or The Man."[42] But these critics do not argue that the privacy cases were a pretext for reinforcing male supremacy or that they were wrongly decided. The rulings did not increase male power while pretending to increase women's freedom; they increased women's freedom without ending male supremacy.

The court also cannot fairly be accused of substituting liberalism for laissez-faire or Mill's *On Liberty* for Spencer's *Social Statics*. *Griswold* and *Roe* recognized privacy rights that had been read into the Constitution over time and accepted, at least tacitly, in American culture. The specific result of *Roe* remains unacceptable to many. The opinion was far from persuasive. The justices may have overestimated their own power. Those who prioritize collective democracy over individual autonomy, or process over result, may argue that judges usurped the power of the people. But, compared with recent examples of judicial activism, *Roe* does not warrant a comparison to *Lochner*.

Muller: The "New Realism"?

"How," asks Fiss, "could the justices who condemned the maximum hours statute in *Lochner* have embraced one in *Muller*?"[43] The fact that an experienced legal scholar could pose that question in 1993 indicates the extent to which his contemporaries "tend to view the constitutional community as embracing all adults."[44] No one asked that question in 1908 or even in 1974, when I wrote my dissertation on protective labor legislation. Fiss answered his own question: for the 1908 court, "women and men stand in a different relationship to the community that constitutes the state—women are not full members, men are."[45] This liberal position was acceptable, although contested, at the time. Twelve years later, the Nineteenth Amendment's grant of voting rights to women negated it. *Adkins v. Children's Hospital* cited this amendment in striking down a minimum wage for women, thereby extending *Lochner*-style membership to women workers.[46]

Gender equality had gotten off on the wrong foot in Fourteenth Amendment litigation. *Minor v. Happersett* rebuffed a claim that voting was among the privileges and immunities granted by Section 1.[47] *Bradwell v. Illinois* upheld a state bar association's refusal to admit a woman to practice. *Bradwell* became notorious for a concurring opinion by Justice Joseph Bradley. "The lawyers in the courtroom laughed aloud"[48] as Bradley declared, "The paramount destiny and mission of woman are to fulfill the noble and benign offices of wife and mother."[49] Bradley was thinking exactly as Rousseau had. No one laughed at David Brewer's opinion in *Muller*. He answered Fiss's question as Bradley might have: women were different from men. They were physically weaker, and they bore children. Woman "has been looked upon by the courts as needing especial care that her rights be preserved. . . . She is not upon an equality" with man.[50] Once again, bearing rights is incompatible with bearing children.

Brewer's anthropology was less simple than his jurisprudence and, with a century's hindsight, more interesting. Man "established his control at the outset by superior physical strength, and this control . . . has continued to the present."[51] Therefore, woman "still looks to her brother for protection . . . from the greed, as well as the passion, of man."[52] Men gain power over women, so men must protect women from this power. The predators guard the prey. *Muller* allowed the substitution of the power of the state for the power of the market. Paternalism, maybe, but hardly romantic.

A second possible answer to Fiss's question stems from "the brief filed by Mr. Louis D. Brandeis for the defendant in error" with its "very copious collection of all these matters."[53] *Lochner* had no equivalent brief. The four *Lochner* dissenters remained on the court three years later, but so did four members of the majority. To urge a reversal of *Lochner* would have been a risky strategy. Oregon did not use it. While the Brandeis brief contained abundant evidence that working long hours was dangerous for women, it would not pass muster in an undergraduate methods course today. The brief did not compare women who worked outside the home to women who stayed home; nor did it compare working women to working men. The latter comparison would have been futile, since working men and women had different occupations, and most women's hours were (even) longer and conditions (even) worse than most men's.[54] Physiological differences between men and women were safer and easier grounds on which to rest the decision.

The progressives' hope that *Muller* would encourage judicial rethinking of general-hour legislation was realized within ten years.[55] But the long-run effects of *Muller* were disastrous for women's rights, in general, and their work opportunities, in particular. The decision's impact extended far beyond labor law. It was cited in cases "upholding the exclusion of women from juries, differential treatment in licensing various occupations and the exclusion of women from state supported colleges."[56] The phrase "Sex is a valid basis for classification" came to express the constitutional doctrine laid out in *Muller*. When special labor laws for women morphed into a tool for labor unions to reserve good jobs for men, courts took no notice. The International Union of Hotel and Restaurant Employees had opened the bartending trade to women during World War II, but the organization lobbied the Michigan legislature for a law prohibiting most women from this work that was enacted in 1945 and took effect in 1947. The court upheld this law, treating it as a classic example of protective legislation. Three justices dissented on the grounds that the statute did not provide equal protection to women owners of bars, who, unlike their male counterparts, could not employ their daughters as bartenders.[57]

Lochner did not survive progressivism. *Adkins* did not survive the New Deal.[58] Hours limitations and minimum wage laws are gender-neutral. *Muller* is obsolescent because the Civil Rights Act of 1964 preempted it. The original draft of Title VII, forbidding employment discrimination on the basis of race, religion, or national origin, contained no mention of sex. That provision was inserted by opponents as a "joke" and interpreted by the agency charged with enforcing it as a "fluke."[59] When the Equal Employment Opportunity Commission (EEOC) vacillated, the courts followed the rule of federal preemption. The Ninth Circuit ruled in 1971 that women-only labor laws illegally discriminate based on sex. These laws did not make sex a "bona fide occupational qualification" for any job.[60] But what Congress can do, it can undo. If Title VII were repealed, no national barrier would exist between women and special labor laws.

Lochner is a dead letter, but *Muller* only looks dead. The impact of contemporary feminism has erased the judicial blank check for sex discrimination. The Supreme Court of the 1970s progressed from a realization that sex discrimination might not be reasonable to a near acceptance of strict scrutiny to the declaration that "classifications by gender must serve important governmental objectives and must be substantially related to the achievement of these objectives."[61] Could *Muller* survive this intermediate scrutiny?

Lochnerian Equality: Can Liberalism Be Enough?

Johnson Controls and *U.S. v. Virginia* illustrate the problematic relationship between feminism and liberalism. Neither case was an intellectual challenge. Precedent supported a ruling in favor of women's rights as strongly as text did. The vote in *Johnson Controls* was unanimous; only one justice dissented in *Virginia*. Neither case would have reached the Supreme Court at all were it not for the emotions connected with it.[62] *Casey*, by contrast, *was* a challenge. By enacting several restrictions on a woman's right to abortion, Pennsylvania all but dared the court to overrule *Roe*. The court did not, but the opinion showed how weak a foundation liberalism is for gender equality. I discuss these three cases in ascending order of complexity.

"In the field of public education, the doctrine of 'separate but equal' has no place. Separate educational facilities are inherently unequal."[63] So the Supreme Court proclaimed in *Brown v. Board of Education* with respect to segregation by race. Men and women excluded from public colleges and universities were quick to ask state and federal courts to apply this bold principle to sex segregation. The only successful litigants were four women who sought admission to the University of Virginia in the late 1960s.[64] Not until 1982, when the Supreme Court ordered a woman-only nursing program to admit men (in Sandra Day O'Connor's first majority opinion), did feminist constitutional doctrine cancel single-sex education.[65] No decision has ruled that all sex discrimination in higher education is unconstitutional. But the Virginia Military Institute (VMI) case came close.

Descriptions of campus life at VMI and at its South Carolina counterpart, the Citadel, create an impression of West Point on steroids. VMI's "adversative" military training, modeled on Marine Corps boot camp, featured a lack of privacy, rigorous physical training, frequent punishment, hazing, and the like. The goal of this treatment was to produce "educated and reliable men" who were "advocates of the American democracy and free enterprise system, and ready as citizen-soldiers to defend their country."[66] This training appealed to few young men and even fewer young women. Nevertheless, admission to VMI has been and continues to be a commodity of which the demand exceeds the supply. More men and women apply each year than the college can accept.[67]

VMI and the Citadel have long been supported, in the financial, emotional, and political senses of the word, by enthusiastic alumni. Many VMI graduates throughout the Southeast are prominent in public service, business, and community affairs. When a young woman instigated a complaint against VMI in 1990, the school and its alumni, almost to a man, rose up in indignation. Unintimidated, the U.S. Justice Department under President George H. W. Bush sued the school on the woman's behalf. The district court agreed with VMI that "key elements of the adversative VMI system, with its focus on barracks life, would be altered, and the distinctive ends of the system would be thwarted, if VMI were forced to admit females."[68] The circuit court sympathized with VMI's position but did not let the state off the hook. The panel gave Virginia three possibilities: turn VMI into a private institution, admit women to VMI, or create a comparable single-sex public college for women.[69] The Virginia Women's Institute for Leadership (VWIL) was the state's response to the Fourth Circuit. Located at Mary Baldwin College, an otherwise private institution, VWIL substituted "a more psychologically nurturant leadership training program" for VMI's adversative approach.[70] The Justice Department appealed to the Supreme Court.

Justice Ginsburg had no trouble disposing of VWIL by comparing it to *Sweatt v. Painter*, a 1950 decision rejecting Texas's similar effort to pass off the Texas Law School for Negroes as providing separate but equal education. Ginsburg's use of a race discrimination case as an authority for a ruling on gender discrimination suggested that the court might be on the verge of declaring gender a suspect classification, as Bill Clinton's Justice Department had urged it to do. *Virginia* did not go that far, but it reaffirmed O'Connor's statement in the 1982 case that the party seeking to uphold a statute that classifies individuals on the basis of their gender must show an "exceedingly persuasive justification" for the classification:[71]

> "Inherent differences" between men and women, we have come to appreciate, remain cause for celebration, but not for denigration of the members of either sex or for constraints on an individual's opportunity.... However "liberally" this plan serves the Commonwealth's sons, it makes no provision whatever for her daughters. This is not *equal* protection.[72]

U.S. v. Virginia is a clear victory for liberal feminism and a less clear, but significant, victory for feminist liberalism. Ginsburg's opinion is a stellar piece of liberal rhetoric, on a par with Robert Jackson's majority opinion in *West Virginia State Board of Education v. Barnette*.[73] The VMI opinion was premised on constitutional principles associated with *Lochner*. These principles were all the court needed. Women who desire this kind of education are no longer denied the right to compete for admission to VMI. The ruling privileged individual freedom and gender equality and rebuffed an influential, tightly knit community that defined itself by the exclusion of women and was united in its desire to keep women out. To be more precise, the community excluded women as peers. The VMI and Citadel websites list many women employees in support services.[74] What, then, is so bad about individualism? Here, it was all the court needed. A feminist victory in this case demanded a decision for the individual against the community.

Two decades after the first women cadets entered VMI, the institute's experiences are similar to those in the service academies.[75] Gender-specific standards of physical fitness have been developed for women, while female cadets have graduated with honors, been expelled for infractions, faced sexual harassment, filed complaints, and gone on to military service (or not). There is no reason to worry that women are being forced (by whom? their parents?) to attend VMI or that the choice of VMI is coercively structured. Nor has the inclusion of women driven men away from VMI and made military training less attractive to them.[76]

Liberals accept the possibility that people will disagree about what they want. Feminists may find this possibility harder to accept. The American feminist movement is rooted in pacifism as well as in abolitionism. Pacifists were active supporters of women's rights years before the Seneca Falls convention in 1848 and have made their presence felt ever since, from the Women's International League for Peace and Freedom in World War I to contemporary scholars who promote "a politics of peace." Some feminist pacifists make a connection between their rejection of war and their gender identity, positing an innate female desire for peace that may or may not emerge from their experience as mothers.[77] Nothing about maternalist antiwar rhetoric is feminist. The Women's Strike for Peace, founded in 1960, based its antinuclear activism on traditional notions of sex roles.[78]

Might feminists such as these oppose a ruling that makes training in warfare accessible to women? Maybe, but to adopt that position would be to misunderstand the character and purpose of the hyper-military academies. Their students do not necessarily aspire to become warriors. At least one Citadel graduate went there to play basketball.[79] A young woman might also pick one of these institutions for the athletics, or to test her capacity to withstand harsh training and rigorous conditions. The value to society of self-discipline, endurance, and toughness is independent of war. Nothing about the VMI decision is antifeminist.

Johnson Controls: The End of Exclusion

Calling exclusionary policies fetal protection policies renders women invisible—mere vessels that may contain a fetus. Once women are

mere vessels, we can conceive of the woman as separate from the fetus
. . . rather than seeing the fetus as part of the woman. Fetal protection
policies seek to protect potential fetuses rather than women. The term
protective suggests a benign and laudable policy, yet one that is also
paternalistic. Potential fetuses cannot protect themselves, so employers must intervene on their behalf.[80]

United Auto Workers v. Johnson Controls, decided in 1991, was an exercise
in statutory construction rather than constitutional interpretation. By then,
courts had less leeway under antidiscrimination law than they did under the
equal protection clause. Some strictures were self-imposed; they came from
cases decided twenty years earlier. *Rosenfeld v. Southern Pacific Co.* struck
down women-only labor laws under Title VII.[81] *Phillips v. Martin-Marietta*
held the line against "sex plus" policies by remanding a case involving an
employer's refusal to hire women with preschool children.[82] But the decisions
of the EEOC and the courts applied only to laws that existed at the time.
These rulings were not prospective. Any deterrent effects that they might
have on employers were limited by the fact that antidiscrimination laws are
not self-enforcing.

Congress went further than the courts, amending Title VII by the Pregnancy Discrimination Act of 1978. But exclusionary policies and sex-plus
discrimination returned the same year under the label "fetal protection."
American Cyanamid made headlines when it forced women workers exposed to toxic substances to undergo sterilization or transfer to safer jobs.[83]
Again in 1978, the Olin Corporation refused to hire women of "childbearing age"—between five and sixty-three—for high-exposure jobs. Johnson
Controls barred fertile women from jobs that exposed workers to blood lead
levels unacceptable for pregnant women in 1982.[84] The circuit court issued a
summary judgment for Johnson Controls.[85]

Lead, gases, and asbestos are only a few of the toxic substances that per-
vade the environment, the home, and the workplace. Many workers are exposed to radiation. These substances, at high enough levels, injure anything
and anyone exposed to them: women, men, sperm, ova, and fetuses. By the
1970s, infertility, impotence, miscarriages, and cancer had been observed in
exposed workers; except for a few widely publicized instances, these consequences did not raise alarm. Most actual studies of workplace hazards concentrated only on women workers.[86] As infertility, miscarriages, and birth
defects increased, fetal damage was perceived as a greater danger than damage to workers. After all, more research had been done, and funded, about
the effects of toxic substances on fetuses than on workers.

Occupations that expose workers to toxic substances include skilled blue-collar jobs of the sort that Title VII had opened to women. "Rigorous implementation of fetal protection policies," wrote a dissenter in the lower court, "could close more than 20 million jobs to women."[87] Those familiar with labor history might wonder if concern with reproductive hazards was a pretext for reserving these jobs for men. Not for the union; it sided with the women in *Johnson Controls*. This choice was part of a radical change in organized labor's attitude toward women workers that deserves mention, even as the power of organized labor continues to decline. Perhaps expecting the unions and the employers to cooperate on a strategy was too much. But, if the employers' concerns were protective, why were their solutions so draconian? Instead of allowing workers who were pregnant or trying to conceive to transfer temporarily to less risky positions, why prohibit all women, or at least any fertile woman, from taking jobs that entailed exposure? Why offer the choice to get sterilized or get out? Sally Kenney's insight was apt: employers were treating women as vessels.[88]

Blackmun's opinion put a stop to that. "With the Pregnancy Discrimination Act," he wrote, "Congress made clear that the decision to become pregnant or to work while being either pregnant or capable of becoming pregnant was reserved for each individual woman to make for herself. . . . Decisions about the welfare of future children must be left to the parents who conceive, bear, support, and raise them, rather than to the employers who hire those parents."[89]

Johnson Controls and *Virginia* were significant victories for liberalism. Both decisions reflected liberal priorities: reason over emotion, law over fiat, autonomy over paternalism. That *Johnson Controls* provoked an op-ed piece titled "What Feminist Victory in the Court?" illustrates the gulf between liberalism and feminism.[90] Feminist theorists have argued that the listed liberal priorities are masculine; that some pairs of opposing terms are not, in fact, contradictory; and, for that matter, that reasoning by dichotomy is problematic.[91] Telling workers in the era of two-income families that they are free to work or not during pregnancy is roughly equivalent to telling bakers in 1905 that they were free to negotiate their working hours with their employers. Blackmun's rhetoric evokes the majority opinion in *Lochner*. Fortunately, that liberal rhetoric was enough to reach the correct result in *Johnson Controls*, but it did not solve the problem of exposure to toxic substances in the workplace. The feminist and liberal theory that would justify such a result is not within the courts' present constitutional repertoire.

Johnson Controls was essentially a choice (or a ratification of Congress's choice) of *Lochner* principles over those of *Muller*. Which ruling is the rock, and which the hard place? Even if the choice between endangering your un-born child and reducing your earnings were free, this situation falls far short of any feminist ideal. Liberalism turns on itself. The principles that limit employers' power over workers also limit employers' obligations to reduce dangers in the workplace.

Privacy Meets Equality: From *Roe* to *Casey*

Roe v. Wade proved easy to criticize and hard to defend. The majority opinion and separate concurrences suggest that at least some justices found the step from birth control to abortion easy.[92] In 1973, seven male jurists presuming that the right of men and women to make decisions about conception en-tailed the right of women to make decisions about pregnancy was encourag-ing, but a nuanced, comprehensive discussion of why the similarities between birth control and abortion were more important than the differences would have made the ruling less vulnerable. Instead, the core of Justice Blackmun's majority opinion consisted of a list, a proclamation, and a non sequitur. "This right of privacy," Blackmun announced, "is broad enough to include a wom-an's decision whether or not to terminate her pregnancy."[93] Why? Because unwanted pregnancy harms pregnant women and their families. But the law can force people to do or not do many things that can cause harm. No one in the majority could summon anything more eloquent than "detriment" (Blackmun), "interests" (Potter Stewart), and "preferred lifestyle" (William O. Douglas), making it easy for Byron White to counter by speaking of "the convenience, whim, or caprice of the putative mother."[94]

The Supreme Court did strike down Missouri's spousal and parental consent requirements in 1976.[95] But a series of decisions between 1977 and 1980 sustained prohibitions on the use of public funds for abortion.[96] These decisions were made with only one new justice since *Roe* while Democrats controlled the presidency and Congress; the judicial retreat started before the Republican victories happened. Ronald Reagan, George H. W. Bush, and George W. Bush sought out antichoice judicial appointees. They succeeded often enough to ensure that the trend was consistently pro-restriction. Parental consent requirements morphed into parental notification requirements, which have been upheld.[97] We do not yet know what Donald Trump's justices will do.

Would it have made any difference if the *Roe* opinions had been bet-ter reasoned? Certainly not to the antichoice lobby. Probably not to Justice White, who trivialized the pregnant woman's interests.[98] Some critics of *Roe* should have known better.

But there were judges like William Rehnquist, whose dissent in *Roe* em-phasized not (preferred) result but (due) process.[99] And scholars like Ely, who welcomed the result in *Roe*.[100] Judges read legal scholarship, professors teach future judges and become judges themselves, and they all meet at conferences. Suppose solid arguments for privacy rights had influenced the bench, bar, and academy in the generation since *Roe*. Would the pool of antichoice candidates now available for judgeships exist? Would those members of the attentive public who oppose legalized abortion but who consider other issues more important have put abortion on the back burner?

Planned Parenthood v. Casey, my third model of liberal rhetoric, presented the Court with an opportunity to overturn *Roe*. Pennsylvania, that haven for antichoice Democrats, had enacted a law placing several restrictions on access to abortion. By 1989, the Abortion Control Act required counseling designed to dissuade the woman seeking an abortion; informed, written consent; a twenty-four-hour waiting period between the consent and the abortion; parental notification with a judicial bypass for minors; and spousal notification for married women. Although state funds could not be used for abortions, facilities that performed abortions and received public funds for other services were required to submit data on abortions. The ruling was neither the disaster that pro-choice Americans had feared nor an "I told you so" moment for populists. At the same time *Casey* removed limitations on the states' powers to regulate and discourage abortion, it reaffirmed a woman's right to choose abortion. The plurality opinion issued by Sandra Day O'Connor, Anthony Kennedy, and David Souter—all selected by anti-*Roe* presidents—is eloquent:

> At the heart of liberty is the right to define one's own concept of existence, of meaning, of the universe, and of the mystery of human life. Beliefs about these matters could not define the attributes of personhood were they formed under compulsion of the State.
>
> . . . Abortion is . . . fraught with consequences for others: for the woman who must live with the implications of her decision; for the persons who perform and assist in the procedure; for the spouse, family, and society which must confront the knowledge that these procedures exist, procedures some deem nothing short of an act of violence against innocent human life; and, depending on one's beliefs, for the life or potential life that is aborted. Though abortion is conduct, it does not follow that the State is entitled to proscribe it in all instances. That is because the liberty of the woman is at stake in a sense unique to the human condition, and so, unique to the law. The mother who carries a child to full term is subject to anxieties, to physical constraints, to pain that only she must bear. That these sacrifices have from the beginning of the human race been endured by woman with a pride that ennobles her in the eyes of others and gives to the

infant a bond of love cannot alone be grounds for the State to insist she make the sacrifice. Her suffering is too intimate and personal for the State to insist, without more, upon its own vision of the woman's role, however dominant that vision has been in the course of our history and our culture. The destiny of the woman must be shaped to a large extent on her own conception of her spiritual imperatives and her place in society.[101]

Would the reaction to *Roe* have been calmer if similar language had been used? The *Casey* plurality makes explicit what *Roe* fudged: women share liberty equally with men; having babies is no barrier to having rights. The opinion is a categorical statement that women are liberal subjects. This legalistic commitment to universal equality, however slowly and reluctantly it was arrived at, may help explain why the *Roe* majority did not indulge in stirring rhetoric: Why belabor the obvious? But while the general principle is obvious, the specific conclusion is not.

Justice Ginsburg, who successfully argued several significant women's rights cases before the court, is "troubled that the focus on *Roe* was on a right to privacy, rather than women's rights."[102] But in 1973, a decision based on the equal protection clause would have been a dramatic departure from precedent. Feminism was alive and well in the 1970s, but feminist equal protection doctrine was in its early stages. The court decided *Roe* a year and a month after it rejected the old rule that sex was a valid basis for classification, in a case where Ginsburg coauthored the brief.[103] She wrote the ACLU's amicus brief in *Frontiero v. Richardson*, decided a few months after *Roe*, in which the court came within one vote of declaring sex a suspect classification, like race.[104] But three years later, the court, apparently reluctant to render the proposed Equal Rights Amendment (ERA) superfluous, compromised in *Craig v. Boren*.[105] This "intermediate scrutiny" has been the standard for equal protection cases involving gender since then, long after the ERA was defeated. The court has not moved from this position for more than forty years. Despite Ginsburg's efforts in the VMI case, there is little or no indication that the court will demand strict scrutiny in gender-based equal protection.[106]

Casey is symmetrical to *Craig*. The 1992 case does to abortion what *Craig* does to gender-based classifications. Both types of claims are relegated to a status somewhere between an ordinary interest and a first-tier right or immunity. Compelling justification is no longer required for restricting access to abortion, any more than it is for sex discrimination. For all its brave talk about women's freedom, the *Casey* plurality opinion invites legislatures to limit legal abortion. And they did. In June 2015, the Fifth Circuit sustained a Texas requirement that abortion clinics meet the same building, staffing, and equipment standards as hospitals. If affirmed, this ruling would have forced all but seven clinics in the state to close. There were forty-one in 2013, the year the law was enacted.[107]

On June 29, the court struck down the law by a 5–3 vote. Justice Stephen Breyer's majority opinion reaffirmed *Casey*, ruling that the law placed an undue burden on the exercise of the right to terminate a pregnancy.[108]

Could an argument for legal abortions be based on women's rights without declaring gender a suspect classification? A future Supreme Court majority could begin with the recognition that this particular privacy claim is unique in the sense that it belongs only to women. An opinion could go on to argue that equality between the sexes entails the right to abortion. This hope is not realistic at present, but this scenario is plausible in the long run. *Casey* proclaims what *Roe* implied: women do not have equal autonomy and rights with men unless they can choose to end unwanted pregnancies.

Two common objections to *Roe* and *Casey* invoke liberal values as important as the ones already mentioned: a belief in individual responsibility and a commitment to the democratic process. Should a pregnant woman, like any liberal subject, not accept the consequences of her behavior? This question has lost much of its rhetorical clout under an onslaught by scholars who have deconstructed the presumption that sex is consensual and by the twentieth century's separation of sex from pregnancy. Even if all or most sexual activity fit the rational decision-making model, if couples had intercourse primarily to conceive, or if birth control methods were 100 percent reliable, the fact that two people who perform the same act face drastically different consequences conflicts with the principle of gender equality.

The second question pertains not to the conclusion but to its source. Should the abortion question not be resolved by the democratic process? Justice Ginsburg has expressed this view repeatedly. "My criticism of *Roe*," she said in 2013, "is that it seems to have stopped momentum on the side of change." She would have preferred "that abortion rights be secured more gradually, in a process that included state legislatures."[109] Laurence Tribe has argued that few, if any, states were poised to follow New York's and Hawaii's lead in legalizing abortion before *Roe*; no momentum existed.[110] Moreover, the "democratic process" is an abstraction; weighed against the concrete reality of reluctant pregnancy, it must yield. I agree with Tribe that *Roe* effectively assigned the abortion decision to pregnant women themselves. This action fits within David Easton's definition of politics as the authoritative allocation of values for society as a whole. We know that courts make political decisions, even if they avoid political questions. *Roe v. Wade* may have been bad politics, but it is not wrong. Liberal constitutionalism and rights theory recognize limitations on majority rule.

The result of *Casey* negated the rhetoric. The majority upheld all provisions except the husband notification requirement. The decision demoted abortion from the status of a fundamental right and substituted the "undue burden" text for strict scrutiny. The court conceded to the government the power to discourage abortion as an end in itself, inviting legislators to make this liberty harder to exercise. *Casey* gets women no closer than *Roe* did to full reproductive and sexual freedom. Feminists on both sides of the abortion debate have pointed out that permission to get an abortion does not help, and may harm, women coerced into having abortions by partners or families.[111] It makes it no easier, and may make it harder, for women to refuse sex, and it does not affect women's freedom to initiate sex.[112] Liberalism often fails women when it presumes that adult behavior is voluntary and consensual.

Liberal principles cannot get us all the way to substantive equality between the sexes. *Casey*, *Virginia*, and *Johnson Controls* reinforce the lessons feminists have already learned about "the poverty of liberalism."[113] Liberal principles are not sufficient foundations for gender equality. But the three opinions convincingly establish that, in a legal context, these principles are necessary to achieve it.

These three cases show that, in the context of actual public decision making, gender equality requires an adherence to liberal principles in preference to other principles that are actually available for guidance. Together, the rulings reveal the importance of liberalism's emphasis on reason, of a liberal conception of what it means to be an adult human being, and of a liberal prioritization of the individual. Without these principles, we are left with custom, emotion, paternalism, and exclusion.

Motherhood and the Court: *Muller* Revived

Justice O'Connor retired in 2006. George W. Bush replaced her with Samuel Alito, the appeals court judge who voted to uphold the spousal notification requirement in *Casey*. A 2007 decision illustrates just how dangerous a departure from liberal jurisprudence can be and how much feminist jurisprudence has lost in the Roberts court. *Gonzales v. Carhart* upheld the most recent in a series of congressional attempts to prohibit some techniques of late-term abortion, or what antichoice activists call "partial-birth abortion." Justice Kennedy's opinion for the court indicated that his views had changed since he joined O'Connor and Souter in *Casey*:

> Respect for human life finds an ultimate expression in the bond of love the mother has for her child. Whether to have an abortion requires a difficult and painful moral decision. While we find no reli-

able data to measure the phenomenon, it seems unexceptionable to conclude some women come to regret their choice to abort the infant life they once created and sustained. Severe depression and loss of esteem can follow. . . . It is self-evident that a mother who comes to regret her choice to abort must struggle with grief more anguished and sorrow more profound when she learns, only after the event, what she once did not know: that she allowed a doctor to pierce the skull and vacuum the fast-developing brain of her unborn child, a child assuming the human form.[114]

No longer is the woman a liberal subject making adult decisions; now she must be protected from a decision she might regret. Kennedy's opinion in *Carhart* echoes the principles of *Muller* as powerfully as Blackmun's opinion in *Johnson Controls* recalls *Lochner*. If a woman no longer "looks to her brother and depends upon him for protection," she must now look to the state for protection against her own decisions.[115]

What Kennedy does *not* do here is important to note. He does not reject abstract rights in favor of democratic decision making. Nor does he argue for the separation of powers and judicial self-restraint. Instead, he does what the court did in *Muller*: he defends the law on its merits. The 1908 court had little choice. If it wanted to uphold the Oregon law without reversing its own recent precedent, it had to distinguish the case from *Lochner*.[116] But no such imperative confronted the justices in *Carhart*. The ruling replaces liberalism with paternalism. It implies what *Muller* announced and *Casey* denied: a tension between women's childbearing capacity and their status as liberal subjects.

The best news about *Carhart* is that it remains the low point for gender-equality jurisprudence. It did not signal a downhill progression. The courts have deferred to Congress in construing antidiscrimination law once Congress spelled out its intentions.[117] In the unlikely event that Congress passed laws facilitating access to abortion, the courts might go along. But in constitutional cases, the Supreme Court takes the lead. Since the 1970s, several decisions suggest that *Carhart* is not an abrupt departure from precedent.

The court ruled that laws based on "old notions" of gender roles, "stereotyped distinctions between the sexes," or traditional notions of marriage did not bear substantial relationships to important purposes.[118] Neither did laws using sex as a proxy for need or for drinking and driving.[119] But some laws survived intermediate scrutiny, usually by close votes. *Fiallo v. Bell* and *Rostker v. Goldberg* emphasized deference to Congress.[120] *Fiallo* upheld a provision of the Immigration and Naturalization Act that allowed unwed mothers, but not unwed fathers, to obtain preferred immigrant status for their minor children born outside the United States. The decision in *Goldberg*, upholding a draft registration for men only—a law still in effect—relied on the policy of excluding women from combat positions. The Defense Department dropped this ban in 2013. We can predict that a young man will challenge the draft registration law or that Congress will change it. *Fiallo*, on the other hand, might have survived judicial scrutiny if Congress had not amended the law.

The remaining rulings upholding the constitutionality of gender discrimination under intermediate scrutiny relate it to women's childbearing capacity. All have been superseded by legislative action. None of these rulings deprived women of any rights. They upheld discriminations against men. Two cases involve accusations of, and one of these a conviction for, sexual assault. *Michael M. v. Superior Court of Sonoma County* upheld California's "statutory rape" law, which made it a crime for a male to have intercourse with a female under eighteen but not vice versa. The state had already replaced this law with a gender-neutral prohibition of "unlawful sexual intercourse," but seventeen-year-old Michael had been convicted under the old law for having sex with sixteen-year-old Sharon. Six justices concluded that this law was substantially related to the important objective of discouraging teenage pregnancy:

> We need not be medical doctors to discern that young men and young women are not similarly situated with respect to the problems and risks of sexual intercourse. Only women may become pregnant and they suffer disproportionately the profound physical, emotional, and psychological consequences of sexual activity. The statute at issue here protects women from sexual intercourse at an age when these consequences are particularly severe.[121]

"Would a rational parent making rules for the conduct of twin children," a dissent retorted, "simultaneously forbid the son and authorize the daughter to engage in conduct that is especially harmful to the daughter?"[122] But physiological differences between the sexes trumped common sense. In 1998 and 2001, two rulings reaffirmed the result in *Fiallo* by upholding similar distinctions between the unwed mothers and fathers of children born outside the United States.[123] *Miller v. Albright* upheld a provision barring these children from citizenship unless the father declared paternity while they were minors: "There is no doubt that ensuring reliable proof of a biological relationship between the potential citizen and its citizen parent is an important governmental objective. Nor can it be denied that the male and female parents are differently situated in this respect."[124] *Tuan Anh Nguyen v. INS* produced a similar ruling, even though this child had been brought up by his father, Joseph Boulais, in the United States. Did the fact that Nguyen was fighting a deportation order following his conviction for sexual assault on a child affect the justices' votes? The majority opinion indicated no such influence:

> The first governmental interest to be served is the importance of assuring that a biological parent-child relationship exists. In the case of the mother, the relation is verifiable from the birth itself. The mother's status is documented in most instances by the birth certificate or hospital records and the witnesses who attest to her having given birth. In the case of the father, the uncontestable fact is that he need not be present at the birth. If he is present, furthermore, that circumstance is not incontrovertible proof of fatherhood.[125]

DNA testing had proved that Boulais was Nguyen's father, but sexual differences preempted science in the judicial mind.[126] The court went on to recognize Congress's concern "that the child and the citizen parent have some demonstrated opportunity or potential to develop a relationship that . . . consists of the real, everyday ties that provide a connection between child and citizen parent and, in turn, the United States."[127] The opinion continued:

> In the case of a citizen mother and a child born overseas, the opportunity for a meaningful relationship between citizen parent and child inheres in the very event of birth, an event so often critical to our constitutional and statutory understandings of citizenship. The mother knows that the child is in being and is hers and has an initial point of contact with him. There is at least an opportunity for mother and child to develop a real, meaningful relationship. The same opportunity does not result from the event of birth, as a matter of biological inevitability, in the case of the unwed father. Given the 9-month interval between conception and birth, it is not always certain that a father will know that a child was conceived, nor is it always clear that even the mother will be sure of the father's identity. This fact takes on particular significance in the case of a child born overseas and out of wedlock.[128]

The majority's discussion of gender differences in parent-child relations was hardly profound or original. It ignores the facts of the case. The court seemed stuck on the issue of reproductive physiology. *Muller*-style thinking lingers, although only in *Carhart* does this thinking restrict women's rights. Legislatures and state courts have been ahead of federal courts on this issue.

Sessions v. Morales-Santana may or may not indicate a change in the court's thinking about sex-based discrimination.[129] A unanimous holding rejected yet another gender-based congressional distinction in the Immigration and Naturalization Act, this one concerning children born outside the United States who had one citizen parent. When Luis Ramon Morales-Santana was born in the Dominican Republic in 1962, children of a married citizen parent or an unmarried citizen father were eligible for U.S. citizenship if the parent had lived in the United States for ten years, at least five of them after age fourteen. The children of an unmarried citizen mother, however, were eligible if she had lived in the United States for at least one year.[130]

Luis's father was an unmarried U.S. citizen who had moved to the Dominican Republic only days before his nineteenth birthday. Luis and his parents, who eventually married, lived together in the Dominican Republic until he was thirteen, when they moved to the United States; he had lived there ever since. By 2000, Luis had been convicted of several crimes, including robbery and attempted murder. An immigration judge ordered him deported for crimes of moral turpitude (see Chapter 4). He appealed and won in federal appellate court. The Supreme Court invalidated the discrimination but did not affirm his citizenship. Congress must treat unwed mothers and fathers equally, but it could choose to treat fathers more leniently or to treat mothers more severely. Whatever Congress did, the change would not affect Morales-Santana unless the law applied retroactively.

Justice Ginsburg's opinion for the court repeatedly used words such as *overbroad generalizations* and *stereotype* to describe the rationale for the law:[131]

> Under the once entrenched principle of male dominance, the husband controlled both wife and child. . . . For unwed parents, the father-control principle never held sway. Instead, the mother was regarded as the child's natural and sole guardian. . . . Hardly gender-neutral, that assumption conforms to the long-held view that unwed fathers care little about, indeed are strangers to, their children. Lump characterization of that kind, however, no longer passes equal protection inspection.[132]

Morales-Santana is an important precedent because, for the first time, the court critically scrutinized generalizations derived from reproductive function and rejected them as bases for sex discrimination. The opinion refused to reason from the fact that women bear children to the conclusion that children's relationship with their mother differs qualitatively from that with their father when the two are not married. Reproductive roles may justify some sex-based discrimination, but generalizations based on these roles did not. This is a step toward gender equality. But constitutional law has yet to recognize that policies based on reproductive function are inseparable from stereotypes and old notions.

Conclusion

The task of reconciling feminism with American law fell to the Supreme Courts led by Warren Burger, William Rehnquist, and John Roberts, in ascending order of conservatism. The justices' output from 1971 to the present has shown that conservative judicial philosophy is no barrier to liberal feminist decisions. Feminist post-liberalism, however, has come from sources outside the federal judiciary. Official jurisprudence has not gotten further than *Lochner* or much further than *Muller*. This liberalism serves gender equality well in cases such as *Johnson Controls* and *U.S. v. Virginia*. That federal courts have gone no further may be an artifact of the limits of their powers. Donald Trump's addition of conservatives Neal Gorsuch and Brett Kavanaugh to the Supreme Court makes the reversal of *Roe* more likely. The task of reconciling bearing children with bearing rights is too important to be left to judges.

Gentlemen's Rights and Gender Equality

What We Think about When We Think about Crime

The Bill of Rights was written by the privileged for the privileged. The framers gave priority to freedom of expression and property rights.[1] The provisions reflected the experience of an elite that had been suppressed. "The right of the people to keep and bear arms" and to be secure "from unreasonable searches and seizures," the prohibition of forced self-incrimination and double jeopardy, the ban on cruel and unusual punishments, and other provisions were designed to protect the authors and people like them.[2] Gentlemen created rights for gentlemen. The Federalists' efforts to stifle Republican opposition by the Alien and Sedition Acts of 1798 provided early evidence that gentlemen needed protection.

Privilege does not confer immunity from accusation. Officeholders are accused of malfeasance, executives of corrupt practices, and celebrities of white-collar and violent crimes. Sometimes they are punished. Justice Felix Frankfurter's admonition, "It is a fair summary of history to say that the safeguards of liberty have frequently been forged in controversies involving not very nice people," referred to Elmer Rabinowitz, a seller of forged stamps.[3] In the 1960s, the Supreme Court reversed the convictions of offenders who were far less nice than Rabinowitz.[4] Crime became an issue of "us versus them." The Bill of Rights protected them against us. The "war on crime" of the late twentieth century was partly a reaction to these Supreme Court decisions. Notorious cases involving members of minority groups made the defendants more vulnerable to marginalization. It became easy for privileged white Americans to associate crime with violent offenders who escaped punishment. But if you were not white or privileged or American, you risked joining "them."

Federal and state governments sought to staff their courts with judges more friendly to law enforcement, with limited success. Later decisions weakened, but did not reverse, due process cases.[5] Fighting crime did not stop with prioritizing law and order. Crime became an excuse for creating what scholars have called a "carceral state," "prison America," "mass incarceration," and "the new Jim Crow." Members of a permanent underclass risk arrests, prosecutions, imprisonment, and punishments that preclude their full participation in society. Constitutional rights rarely matter, because most sentences result from guilty pleas. These rights do not always apply to noncitizens, even to those who are in this country legally. President Donald Trump has committed himself to the deportation of undocumented aliens accused even of misdemeanors.[6] The federal government has created "extraconstitutional" categories for people, such as the "enemy combatants" at Guantanamo.[7] A movement for dismantling the carceral state is growing in the United States. If this movement succeeds, it will end criminal justice as we know it.[8] But Trump's victory in the 2016 election brought one more "tough on crime" politician to the White House.

Liberals helped create mass incarceration. It took them a long time to realize that their efforts vitiated their principles and took power away from potential allies. Liberals, along with moderates, progressives, and even some conservatives, are working to dismantle the carceral state. Yet this issue is problematic for feminists. Women become victims of the criminal justice system. They are subject to mass incarceration. But many crimes that go unpunished or are treated leniently are crimes against women, such as sexual assault and domestic violence. People who commit them, privileged or otherwise, escape punishment more often than not. Gender is the oldest us-versus-them dichotomy.

This chapter addresses several important questions. First, how did we get from gentlemen's rights to mass incarceration? Second, what kind of argument is the carceral state thesis; how is it similar to, and how different from, other arguments? Third, can we dismantle the carceral state without further endangering women? Finally, are the procedural rights that liberals value compatible with feminist principles?

The War on Crime: Civil Liberties Meets Law and Order

The original Bill of Rights limited only the national government. It had no effect on the powers of the states. So the Supreme Court ruled in 1833, in a civil case involving the takings clause of the Fifth Amendment.[9] That ruling did not stop abolitionists from arguing that slavery violated the Bill of Rights.[10] The ratification of the Fourteenth Amendment in 1868 was widely regarded as the inclusion of abolitionist principles in the Constitution. It encouraged new claims that guarantees also bound the states. In 1937, Justice Benjamin Cardozo tried to distinguish between provisions that should be "incorporated" onto the states through the due process clause and those that should not. Rights that are "of the very essence of a scheme of ordered liberty" according to "principles of justice so rooted in the traditions and conscience of our people as to be ranked as fundamental" were in. Freedom of expression, "the matrix, the indispensable condition, of nearly every other form of freedom," was in. The right to counsel and immunity from torture were in. The right against self-incrimination and to immunity from double jeopardy were out because they "might be lost, and justice still be done."[11]

Cardozo did not clarify what he meant by "justice," reaching the correct result, perhaps: illegal searches and seizures uncover valid evidence of crimes, whereas those wrongly suspected may confess if they are tortured or be convicted if they lack a lawyer. Equating justice with result accords with Cardozo's criticism of the exclusionary rule when he was on the New York Court of Appeals: "The criminal is to go free because the constable has blundered."[12] But this reading does not quite work. Defendants who confess under torture or who must defend themselves may have done what they are suspected of doing. Perhaps Cardozo's concept of justice included both reaching the right result and prohibiting official abuse of power, even when those goals conflicted. The prohibition of torture and the right to counsel might have expressed an idea that there are things decent governments must not do. Cardozo's distinction between essential and nonessential rights guided the court through the 1940s. *Betts v. Brady* limited the Sixth Amendment right to counsel to capital cases. *Wolf v. Colorado* refused to impose the exclusionary rule on the states.[13]

Earl Warren's tenure as chief justice (1953–1969) brought a radical rethinking of the relationship between the federal government and the states, of which the unanimous decision in *Brown v. Board of Education I* was the primary manifestation.[14] The change also affected due process doctrine. The court incorporated the right to counsel and the exclusionary rule, making them binding on the states through the Fourteenth Amendment.[15] Justice was no longer conflated with result. Tom Clark's majority opinion in the exclusionary rule case confronted Cardozo's objection squarely: "The criminal goes free, if he must, but it is the law that sets him free."[16] *Miranda v. Arizona* and its companion cases applied the same Fifth and Sixth Amendment requirements to both the federal government and the states.[17] Federalism disappeared as an issue. Today, those who oppose the exclusionary rule oppose it for both jurisdictions.

A venerable maxim holds that it is better for ten guilty men to go free than for one innocent man to be punished. Few will dispute this, at least aloud, but liberals have owned it. Long committed to procedural rights, and tolerant of the risks they pose, liberals welcomed these decisions. When a crime is not punished, an injustice is done; an offender does not get what he or she deserves. When someone is wrongfully convicted, the injustice is official and collective. Government abuses the power it gets from the people.

Mapp v. Ohio, the exclusionary rule case, is a good example of this abuse. In 1957, Dollree Mapp, an African American resident of dubious reputation, was lied to by the Cleveland police, had her home illegally searched, and was convicted of possessing obscene material. The procedure that led to her arrest and the law she was convicted of violating were invalid.[18] Decisions such as *Mapp* have not ended abuses of power. The conviction of the "Central Park Five" for the 1989 rape and beating of Trisha Meili exemplified us-versus-them thinking run riot. It pitted African American and Hispanic youth against a zealous white prosecutor and a sympathetic white victim. These suspects confessed under vigorous questioning, but their stories contradicted one another. They went to prison, although the DNA found in Meili's body did not match theirs. Another man confessed and was convicted in 2002, after the original defendants had served their time.[19]

Whether or not Mapp was a nice person—accounts vary—she had committed no crime.[20] But the Supreme Court also reversed the convictions of rapists, such as Andrew Mallory and Ernesto Miranda, and murderers, such as Danny Escobedo, Robert Williams, and Patrice Seibert.[21] Williams and Seibert murdered children; Seibert may have caused the death of her own son.

These rulings invoked provisions of the Bill of Rights to nullify convictions for crimes the defendants had obviously committed. Miranda and Williams were reconvicted of the same offense.[22] Mallory and Escobedo served sentences for crimes committed after they left prison—the worst-case scenario envisioned by critics of the Warren court. Miranda and Escobedo were Hispanic; Mallory, Williams, and Seibert were black. They were "them." When society is divided between us and them, the privileged lose their ability to identify with the accused. False convictions and mass incarceration have both resulted, in part, from this marginalization. But false convictions are dramatic. Mass incarceration is normal.

Most criminal proceedings are not worst-case scenarios. They typically involve less severe and less violent crimes. We can question whether violent crime does more damage than white-collar crime—or, indeed, whether any crime does as much damage as legal business practices do[23]—but correctional facilities are full of people charged with trivial offenses, people whose punishment continues long after their sentences end.

Error in all directions is inevitable. Procedural safeguards are not the only reasons criminals escape punishment. People get away with crimes because police, prosecutors, judges, and juries blunder. Actors in the criminal justice system make mistakes that have nothing to do with rights. Some crimes go unsolved. Weapons are not found. Juries nullify. So, too, do flawed investigations and prosecutions result in guilty verdicts. Defendants get what they had coming to them, but the government gets a result it has not earned. Defendants are at a disadvantage because an informal assumption of guilt undergirds formal presumption of innocence. Juries convict on flimsy evidence. Defendants who plead guilty do not get trials. People are punished for crimes they did not commit even when everyone involved follows the rules and acts in good faith.[24] The stakes are so high and errors so common that punishment must be finite, proportional, and equitable. No punishment should be irreversible: no amputation, no mutilation, and no death penalty.

The Carceral State Thesis

A 2014 National Research Council report found, first, that "the U.S. penal population of 2.2 million is the largest in the world" and the U.S. rate of incarceration, 707 per 100,000 in 2012, is "by far the highest in the world." Second, "after decades of stability from the 1920s to the early 1970s, the rate of incarceration in the United States more than quadrupled in the past four decades." Finally, "the growth in incarceration had disproportionately large effects on African Americans and Latinos" to the extent that "serving time in prison has become a normal life event among recent birth cohorts of African American men who have not completed high school."[25]

Five studies published since 2010 confirm these assertions. *The New Jim Crow*, whose title is its thesis, was written by Michelle Alexander, a law professor. Two books by three political scientists appeared in 2015. "Prison America" comes from the subtitle of Naomi Murakawa's *The First Civil Right*.[26] *Arresting Citizenship* presents Amy Lerman's and Vesla Weaver's analysis of the impact of crime control on American democracy. Marie Gottschalk's *Caught* describes "a tenacious carceral state" that "has sprouted in the shadows of mass imprisonment and has been extending its reach far beyond the prison gate."[27] Historian Elizabeth Hinton explores the roots of the incarceration boom in *From the War on Poverty to the War on Crime*.[28]

Perspectives in Politics published a "critical trialogue" in which Gottschalk, Murakawa, Lerman, and Weaver review one another's books.[29] They found, and my reading confirms, more difference in emphasis than in opinion. Alexander's and Hinton's books fit this pattern. All six scholars agree that too many people are arrested, that too many go to prison, that punishment does not end when sentences do, and that "vast racial and ethnic disparities" exist "between those who serve time and those who do not."[30] They reaffirm Alexander's account of "the magnitude of the crisis faced by communities of color as a result of mass incarceration."[31] Their interpretations do differ. Murakawa maintains that "liberals built Prison America." Gottschalk and Hinton make a convincing case that liberals have not acted alone.[32]

All five books agree that mass incarceration and custodial citizenship undermines democracy and reinforces racial, ethnic, and class inequality.[33] I call this the carceral state thesis. The National Research Council (NRC) report contains ample data to support it. The books stress different aspects of the problem, together providing a comprehensive overview. Hinton studies the history of the criminal justice system from the 1960s to the Reagan era. Gottschalk is particularly good on how the "prison industrial complex" has become such a big business that it may resist change as forcefully as the tobacco industry did.[34] Alexander introduces five generations of disenfranchised African American men, the first a slave, his great-great-grandson a felon on parole.[35] Lerman and Weaver begin their study with arrests, necessary conditions for transforming people into "custodial citizens." An arrested suspect may resist, thereby committing a misdemeanor that can result in a jail sentence. The results can be far worse. In July 2016, two unarmed African American men, Alton Sterling in Baton Rouge, Louisiana, and Philando Castile near St. Paul, Minnesota, were shot and killed by police officers after routine stops. These were not the last such deaths that year.

Criminal justice policies have "increased the number of citizens who are represented in the custodial population but have never been convicted of a crime" and produced "a growing disconnect between those who engage in criminal behavior and those who encounter criminal justice."[36] The authors' interviews with custodial citizens reveal heightened police surveillance, the loss of the right to vote, ineligibility for government benefits, and difficulties in finding legal employment. These consequences often follow criminal convictions, usually arrived at not through jury trials but through plea agreements, thus circumventing constitutional guarantees. Forfeiture of property is a common punishment that can be imposed on people who have not even been charged with any crime.[37]

Incarceration does not turn inmates into independent, responsible, law-abiding adults. Some prisoners manage to make this transition, but the process militates against it. Inmates share skills that make them more successful criminals.[38] As cheap labor in the prison industrial complex, inmates may learn more respectable skills, but these skills are not marketable for unemployable ex-convicts. Rehabilitation is no longer taken seriously as a goal of punishment. The 2014 NRC report reveals arbitrary discipline and harsh punishments, including solitary confinement; limited access to medical care, counseling, and psychotherapy; inadequate education and training; "material deprivations; restricted movement and liberty; a lack of meaningful activity; a nearly total absence of personal privacy; and high levels of interpersonal uncertainty, danger, and fear."[39]

Most convicts remain custodial citizens after they serve their sentences, even if they never went to prison.[40] Probation and parole enmesh the convict in restrictions that are difficult to follow and easy to violate.[41] "In the United States today, 5.85 million Americans—about one in every forty voting-age adults—are disenfranchised due to a criminal conviction," Hinton writes. "One out of every thirteen African Americans will not vote in the 2016 election due to a prior conviction."[42] The racial disproportion in these statistics indicates that "many of the immediate gains of the [1965] Voting Rights Act have been dismantled."[43]

The authors of the books I discuss are women. This may or may not be coincidence. None identifies herself as either a feminist or an antifeminist; only Gottschalk critically engages with feminist positions.[44] Mass incarceration is a women's issue. Although women compose less than 5 percent of the inmates in the United States, they suffer at least as much as their male counterparts do. Minority women are disproportionately represented among carceral citizens. The incarceration boom of the 1970s began at a time when minority women and welfare recipients were being sterilized without informed consent.[45] Coincidence? Imprisoned women are more likely than imprisoned men to be custodial parents. They lose the company and may lose the custody of their children. They become single parents when their children's fathers go to prison. The carceral state creates the father absence so deplored by conservatives and liberals alike. The same Daniel Patrick Moynihan who found a "tangle of pathology" in African American families in Lyndon Johnson's Labor Department recommended "benign neglect" of the race issue as Richard Nixon's assistant for domestic policy.[46] But that administration's approach was neither benign nor neglectful.

The fate of Sandra Bland illustrates the dangers women face in the criminal justice system. Bland, a twenty-eight-year-old African American woman, was a graduate of Prairie View Texas A&M University, near Houston. She struggled to find work during a recession. She was arrested for failure to pay traffic tickets and for marijuana possession in an area where "proportionately three times as many blacks as whites were being arrested and subjected to some of the harshest punishments in the country." Because she could not pay the tickets, she did jail time. Her record made job hunting even more difficult. In July 2015, "she was pulled over, brutalized, and arrested" by a state trooper. Four days later, she was found dead in her cell. The coroner ruled her death a suicide.[47]

Women, men, and children also enter the criminal justice system as victims. Some common crimes, such as sexual assault and domestic violence, tend to have male perpetrators and female victims. Here, the authors fail the feminist reader. Lerman and Weaver trivialize family crimes by sympathizing with a carceral citizen who was "arrested and locked up briefly on a domestic violence charge and served twelve months for failing to pay child support."[48] (Couldn't the authors find examples that involved arrests for, say, nonpayment of traffic fines?) Murakawa endorses Gottschalk's call to "relinquish . . . mainstream feminist investments in mandatory imprisonment for domestic violence."[49] Gottschalk herself devotes a chapter to "the war on sex offenders."[50] She presumes the accusations are false. In 2006, she wrote, "The contemporary women's movement in the United States helped facilitate the carceral state."[51] Feminist scholars and activists who have worked hard to draw attention to these crimes and to reform the laws must pay careful attention to these arguments.

The Growth of the Carceral State

Mass incarceration has a thousand parents. The federal government funded it, the states executed it, and the public and private sectors of the economy intensified it. The process began at least ten years before rates of incarceration began to soar. Hinton traces it to John F. Kennedy's antidelinquency programs, which were designed to provide aid to poor, high-crime areas. The expected decrease in crime did not materialize either in Kennedy's term or in that of his successor.[52] Lyndon Johnson gave priority to social welfare, education programs, and his war on poverty, but that war included efforts to reduce crime by paying for more police in the same areas the government wanted to help. Police who can help can also arrest. The Crime Control and Safe Streets Act of 1968 was the Democrats' futile election-year response to the Republicans' emphasis on the increasing crime rates in the 1960s.[53] Under Richard Nixon, the Law Enforcement Assistance Administration grew exponentially, while the Office of Economic Opportunity was abolished in 1974.[54]

A pattern in federal crime policy was established that persisted until the Obama administration: the Republicans became the sun, and the Democrats, the moon. Republicans accused Democrats of being soft on crime while Democrats tried to prove that they, too, were tough. Liberals collectively froze in reaction to conservative accusations. The Democratic Leadership Council and other "neoliberal" forces retreated, endorsing the death penalty and removing civil liberties from the Democrats' agenda. The Republicans became more conservative, and the Democrats became less liberal. Rehabilitation gave way to retribution and deterrence as the goals of punishment (see the discussion in the next section).

The Violent Crime Control and Enforcement Act of 1994 was no more effective in preventing a Republican takeover of Congress than the 1968 law had been in retaining the White House. The Personal Responsibility and Work Opportunity Reconciliation Act (PRWORA) of 1996 ratified the conservative agenda by replacing Aid to Families with Dependent Children with Temporary Assistance to Needy Families.[55] The welfare state, paltry as it had been, became a bully state. Since Nixon, Republicans have won elections by promising to be tough on crime. Republicans fought crime while Democrats, until Barack Obama's presidency, conformed. Crime is easy to oppose. The tough-on-crime lobby joined the media in teaching Americans to think of crime in terms of violent offenders.

The federal government could not institute mass incarceration alone. About 181,000 prisoners are in federal custody.[56] The other two million or so are in state facilities. Most arrests, adjudications, and sentences involve violations of state laws. The states also control, with limitations, the right to vote.[57] The federal government has funded programs that enabled the states to build and staff correctional facilities, hire police, maintain supervision in probation and parole, and the like. Voices within the executive and legislative branches have encouraged the states to punish more severely. President George H. W. Bush's support for the death penalty in the 1988 presidential campaign is one example. Before he became a candidate, Donald Trump advocated the death penalty for the Central Park Five.[58] The Supreme Court, whose criminal procedure rulings were often blamed for the rise in crime, has adopted a permissive stance since the 1970s. *Richardson v. Ramirez* upheld states' power to deny convicts the right to vote.[59] *McCleskey v. Kemp* upheld the death penalty despite evidence of racial disparity in sentencing.[60]

States took the hint—and the money. They concentrated police strength in African American and Hispanic neighborhoods. This is one reason why "blacks are ten times as likely" as whites "to spend time in prison for drug offenses," although they are less likely than whites to use illegal drugs except for crack cocaine.[61] Mandatory minimum sentencing, the war on drugs, and "three strikes and you're out" were popular policies in the late twentieth century.[62] One career criminal found that by 1992, during his last prison term, "more than half the guys, they were in for drugs, for possession, I mean for *nothing*."[63] Probation and parole became more rigorous. State and local governments joined the federal government in refusing to hire convicts. So did the private sector. Ironically, social welfare agencies became punitive. Andrew Solomon writes of a rape survivor whose attacker "brought charges against her for stalking, so she was fired from Head Start, where employees cannot be the subject of a criminal investigation."[64] Head Start is a children's education program, part of the war on poverty, which, unlike most of that initiative, has survived to the present. The bully state prevailed. And now we have a bully as president.

The carceral state thesis is subject to verification or refutation. Evidence that "big punishment" has succeeded in making people safer might provide a basis for defending these policies.[65] "Violent crime rates have been declining steadily over the past two decades, which suggests a crime prevention effect of rising incarceration rates."[66] But association does not imply causation; making this inference risks committing the logical fallacy of post hoc ergo propter hoc. Evidence for and against this judgment is mixed. The NRC report concludes that "lengthy prison sentences are ineffective as a crime control measure."[67] We do know that other factors, such as the strength of the economy, the proportion of young men in the population, and the weather, affect the crime rate. The studies I analyze here argue convincingly that big punishment, however effective, has proved too high a price for a reduction in crime.

Punishment: Its Purposes and Consequences

All societies identify actions to require and to forbid. These are not the same actions everywhere, but every society punishes people who flout criminal laws. The official purposes of punishment are well known to both experts and the public. The distinction between retributive and utilitarian theories of punishment that Joel Feinberg makes in his article "The Classic Debate" is a staple of jurisprudence. Utilitarians hold "that punishment of the guilty is at best a necessary evil justified only as a means to the prevention of evils even greater than itself."[68] Retribution is not a legitimate utilitarian goal, but rehabilitation and deterrence are. Retributivists argue that punishment for wrongdoing is a good in itself, regardless of its utility.[69]

Utilitarian and retributive theories are mutually contradictory, but the American criminal justice system has never chosen between them. Retribution—injuring someone who has caused harm, however *harm* is defined—is accepted as a legitimate goal. Words such as *reformatory* and *penitentiary* convey the importance once given to rehabilitation. The law recognizes two kinds of deterrence. General deterrence presumes that the threat of punishment is a disincentive to the commission of the crime. Specific deterrence, or incapacitation, seeks to prevent inmates from committing crimes.[70]

These are the official purposes and consequences of punishment. Whether or not these consequences serve these purposes, and how well, is subject to dispute. The six authors I discuss do not reject any of these purposes as they apply to violent crimes, although Gottschalk is uneasy about retribution.[71] None of these books recommends the abolition of imprisonment for violent crimes.[72] The books show that punishment attaches to crimes that do not cause serious harm, that the consequences of punishment are severe and permanent, and that these consequences further disempower marginalized groups. The carceral state thesis holds that punishment has consequences beyond the official ones. This kind of argument is common in political discourse. Consider, for example, China's one-child policy. Imposed to reduce the population, it led to the abandonment of infant girls.

For American liberals, the consequences of punishment were unintended and ironic. Democrats have disenfranchised people who might have voted Democratic, most recently in 2016. To what extent are Democrats responsible for their defeats? Republicans intended these consequences at least some of the time. Dan Baum reports a 1994 conversation with John Ehrlichman, a top Nixon aide:

> "You want to know what this was all about?" he asked with the bluntness of a man who, after public disgrace and a stint in federal prison, had little left to protect. "The Nixon campaign in 1968, and the Nixon White House after that, had two enemies: the antiwar left and black people. You understand what I'm saying? We knew we couldn't make it illegal to be either against the war or black, but by getting the public to associate the hippies with marijuana and the blacks with heroin, and then criminalizing both, we could disrupt those communities. . . . Did we know we were lying about the drugs? Of course we did."[73]

There is irony in "the contradiction between Richard Nixon's pursuit of law and order and the lawlessness and criminal behavior rampant in his own administration."[74] The Watergate scandal exposed Ehrlichman as a liar, so anything he said invites skepticism. But the way the Republicans "turned America from blue to red" by gerrymandering districts in state legislatures and the House of Representatives provides more evidence of a deliberate intent to weaken the opposition. There is no irony in this result.[75]

The idea that punishment has secondary consequences, in addition to the primary ones, has been around for a while.[76] The carceral state thesis is the latest in a series of arguments that the work of the criminal justice system accomplishes goals and has consequences separate from and in addition to the recognized goals of punishment. Some of these arguments suggest that the official purposes of punishment are not the real reasons we punish: some ulterior motive or process is the primary explanation. Chapter 2 shows that Marxists and Freudians like this kind of argument and often dismiss opposition as "false consciousness" or "denial." Less radical critiques accept the official reasons but insist that something else is also going on.

Émile Durkheim thought crime and punishment had positive effects in addition to the negative ones. They increased social solidarity:

> Crime therefore draws honest consciousnesses together, concentrating them. We have only to observe what happens . . . when some scandal involving morality has just taken place. People stop each other on the street, call upon one another, meet in their customary places to talk about what has happened. A common indignation is expressed. From all the similar impressions exchanged and all the different expressions of wrath there rises up a single fount of anger . . . which is that of everybody without being that of anybody in particular. It is public anger.[77]

Thus, "to classify crime among the phenomena of normal sociology is . . . to assert that it is a factor in public health, an integrative element in any healthy society."[78] Is what Voltaire said about God true of crime: If we didn't have it, we'd have to invent it? We do invent it—at least, whoever "we" are, crime is invented. But is crime necessary for social cohesion, or is cohesion a by-product, a collateral benefit, of crime? Reactions to the assassination of President Kennedy in 1963 and the terrorist attacks of September 11, 2001, provide examples of what Durkheim was talking about. But noncriminal events, such as the coronation of Elizabeth II in 1953, the explosion of the space shuttle *Challenger* in 1986, and natural disasters like hurricanes and earthquakes, also increase social cohesion.[79]

The title of *The Crime of Punishment*, published in 1968 by the American psychiatrist Karl Menninger, is its thesis. Society imposes punishment—"the deliberate infliction of pain . . . , the penalty out of all proportion to the offense"—because "we need criminals to identify ourselves with, to secretly envy, and to stoutly punish. Criminals represent our alter egos—our 'bad' selves—rejected and projected. They do for us the forbidden, illegal things we *wish* to do."[80] Menninger's idea has something in common with the then popular idea that the most homophobic people are the ones repressing their own same-sex attractions—an opinion that seems quaint in the twenty-first century. When we punish the criminal, we punish our own conscious and subconscious desires to commit crimes. What we think of as retributive justice is a smokescreen for projection. Menninger's position does not exactly refute Durkheim's. But violent crimes have victims, who get lost in Menninger's argument.

Like other ideas derived from Freudian theory, Menninger's can neither be proved nor disproved. Menninger's conclusions do not follow from his premises. Might judges and juries tend to impose light sentences if they identify with the accused? Anecdotal evidence supports this counterhypothesis (see the discussion later in the chapter). Menninger reasoned from his belief that criminal punishment was the result of unacknowledged hostile motives to the conclusion that rehabilitation was punishment's only legitimate goal. But by the time he wrote, rehabilitation had been left behind in the face of evidence that incarceration and rehabilitation were incompatible.

As Menninger channeled Freud, Michel Foucault channeled Marx. Foucault argued that the state extended its control beyond prison bars into society to create a kind of permanent *lumpenproletariat*.[81] This theory is compatible with the carceral state thesis. The geographer Ruth Wilson Gilmore's argument in her study of California's mass incarceration makes use of both Foucault and Marx: "Prisons are partial geographical solutions to political economic crises, organized by the state, which is itself in crisis."[82] These crises include surpluses of capital, labor, land, and state capacity that provided places to build prisons, money to fund them, and more workers than the economy could absorb. Like Menninger, Foucault and Gilmore have an us-versus-them explanation of the role of the criminal justice system.

The Carceral State and Feminist Post-liberalism

Carceral state explanations hold that the system creates and reinforces a dichotomy between law-abiding people (us) and criminals (them). But gender has also been understood as a dichotomy. As Simone de Beauvoir wrote, "He is the Subject, the Absolute—she is the Other."[83] Men's crimes against women threaten women's freedom and safety as much as mass incarceration threatens minority men and women. Perpetrators get away with sexual assault and domestic violence. These crimes are among the least likely to be reported to the police. The carceral state thesis is not part of the solution. It is part of the problem.

These authors' primary concern is with the victims of the criminal justice system. They have little to say about victims of crime. But a full understanding of criminal justice entails a recognition that some crimes inflict serious harm. These crimes do not justify the permanent stigmatization and disempowerment that attach to punishment. There are no good reasons to deny even violent criminals the right to vote after they have served their sentences or to make it impossible for them to earn a living by legal means. But women are disadvantaged in comparison to men. One gendered disadvantage is vulnerability to violent crime.

Marie Gottschalk devotes a chapter of *Caught* to "the new untouchables." Few of them are batterers or rapists. People become sex offenders as a result of "tough sanctions and restrictions on . . . everything from making obscene phone calls to urinating in public to consensual sex between teenagers to the rape and murder of a child." She acknowledges that "these measures have disproportionately swept up older white men, not young men and women of color."[84] One common punishment is the requirement to register as a sex offender, often for life. "Possession of child pornography has been conflated with actual sexual abuse, despite weak or inconsistent evidence about the likelihood that people who possess child pornography also sexually abuse children."[85] These regulations, along with residency restrictions and "Megan's laws" requiring convicted sex offenders to register, create "ritual exile," which "misleads society into thinking that the primary threat to public safety comes from strangers" rather than the "friends, acquaintances, and family members" who commit 90 percent of the abuse.[86] The original Megan's Law, enacted in New Jersey, does not apply to offenders who commit incest.[87] Sexual abuse and domestic violence are instances of what Shatema Threadcraft calls "intimate injustice."[88] But does that fact preclude punishing aggressive strangers?[89]

Prosecutions of unlawful sexual intercourse—what used to be called statutory rape, now gender-neutral—against people whose partners are below the legal age of consent have been brought and won in what Gottschalk calls "Romeo and Juliet" cases.[90] This term has infiltrated the media. A 2016 article in the *New Yorker* defines these offenses as "involving consensual sex between teens."[91] Why use the most idealistic, romantic term possible for ordinary teenage sex?[92]

Gottschalk presumes that sex is consensual. A generation of radical feminist discourse has not proved the opposite, but this wealth of material has led many readers to question, and some to discard, the premise of mutual consent.[93] *Michael M. v. Superior Court of Sonoma County* was not a Romeo and Juliet case. Michael, seventeen, and Sharon, sixteen, had sex only after he repeatedly hit her. The Supreme Court upheld Michael's conviction for what California law then called statutory rape, later revised to unlawful sexual intercourse. Justice Harry Blackmun's concurring opinion noted that Sharon "appears not to have been an unwilling participant in at least the initial stages of the intimacies" and included the section of the trial transcript in which she reported having been assaulted.[94] Gottschalk's preference for the consensual version omits too much.

Gottschalk's 2006 book, *The Prison and the Gallows*, has chapters on sexual assault and domestic violence. Her accusation that feminists contributed to the development of the carceral state has some merit. She shows that the feminist "antirape movement" of the 1970s went along with the transition to the bully state by downplaying prevention and women's empowerment in favor of offenders' punishment.[95] (In fact, feminists were quite critical of the "prevention" that was available at the time: the ubiquitous advice telling women how to avoid becoming victims, which implied that women were responsible for male violence.)

Gottschalk notes, "The U.S. women's movement was more vulnerable to being co-opted by crime-control proponents than were feminists in other Western countries." Among American feminists, "the equal rights approach" won out over demands for "a wholesale restructuring of societal values and the reorganization of institutions to end the subjugation of women."[96] Gottschalk does not explain why this choice was necessary or how effective restructuring and reorganization would be in preventing sexual assault in the short run.

James Forman, Jr., made a parallel argument ten years later with respect to black activists and the war on crime in the 1960s and 1970s. *Locking Up Our Own*[97] shows how many black police, judges, politicians, and community leaders in Washington, D.C., "embraced the Nixonian law-and-order mood of the nation, passing increasingly tougher laws and adopting aggressive policing practices into the 1990s."[98] Although feminists did not turn on members of their own group, they displayed a similar insensitivity to class issues.

The battered women's movement

> turned out to be even more vulnerable to being co-opted by the state and conservative penal forces than the anti-rape movement that emerged before it. . . . The mobilization against domestic violence in the United States converged with the state in ways not seen in other countries. It increasingly reflected rather than challenged the growing state interest in taking a hard line against crime and criminals. In Britain, Sweden, Germany, and elsewhere, the issue of domestic violence did not propel a conservative law-and-order movement premised on the needs and rights of victims.[99]

Socialist countries have welfare states. The only tool the United States has is a hammer, so all its problems look like nails. Liberals and conservatives disagree about whether the government should help, but everyone agrees that the government may punish. Victims have rights but only to the punishment of those who harm them.

No feminist consensus exists about how to treat crime, in general, or crimes against women, in particular. Contrary to what Murakawa implies, feminists are not united in favor of mandatory imprisonment for domestic violence.[100] Some feminists have supported mandatory *arrest*, but no consensus exists even on this issue. Feminist activism does not explain why or how "presumptive arrest and mandatory arrest policies became the central pillars of criminal justice remedies for domestic violence."[101] Feminists contributed to this development, but they did not cause it and could not have prevented it. Gottschalk correctly implies that feminists failed to perceive a connection between male supremacy and the bully state and the incompatibility of the bully state and gender equality. But those missed opportunities do not explain or excuse the trivialization of violence against women.

Privilege and the Limits of Leniency

Keeping rapists and batterers out of prison would have little effect on mass incarceration. Too few are convicted to make a dent in the statistics. Only 8 percent of all black men in state prisons were incarcerated for rape/sexual assault in 2013.[102] U.S. Department of Justice survey data and aggregate statistics show that punishment for sexual assault is the exception, not the rule. The Bureau of Justice Statistics' National Crime Victimization Survey reported 28.4 rapes per 1,000 persons over the age of twelve in 2014, which averages out to more than 7 million rapes nationwide. But the National Incident-Based Reporting System of the Federal Bureau of Investigation (FBI) estimated about 84,000 rapes "reported to law enforcement" in that year.[103] "Out of every 1,000 sexual assaults, 995 perpetrators will walk free."[104] Only 230 rapes, less than one-quarter of the total, are reported to police. Only about 5 of these cases result in imprisonment.[105] General deterrence may prevent some assaults, but it does not prevent enough of them.

No bright line exists between cooperation and coercion. Rape cases rarely "come down to he said, she said." Instead, "the most current thinking on sexual-assault investigations is that there is always corroborating evidence."[106] Society has so internalized male viewpoints about sex that only radical feminist resistance can overcome male bias in rape cases. One aspect of this internalization familiar in fiction, drama, and journalism is the idealization of the criminal as rebel and hero—not only Robin Hood types, such as Pretty Boy Floyd, but also "the myth of the heroic rapist."[107] A twenty-first-century example comes from Adrian Nicole LeBlanc's book *Random Family*, an exploration of "class injustice" in a Bronx ghetto. LeBlanc devotes much attention to Boy George, a local drug dealer. He had several girlfriends whom he often beat up and locked in their apartments. LeBlanc calls him "a remarkable young man."[108]

Society's ambivalence about violence against women becomes clearer when the offender resembles a gentleman. Cases involving celebrities become controversial. Another episode is always on the way. Accusations against student athletes generate one case after another. Three 2016 cases involved people who became notorious by being accused. Yong Chen, a finance professor at Texas A&M University, gained local notice when he was charged with trying to strangle his wife, a felony. She had called the police before, but no charges had been filed. Chen was convicted of a Class A misdemeanor, the prosecution having failed to convince the jury that the attempted strangulation had occurred. District Judge Steve Smith sentenced him to thirty days in jail, twenty months' probation, and an eighteen-week course on preventing domestic violence. Smith said he "did not want Chen's students at the Mays Business School to be punished." The university took away Chen's endowed professorship but did not revoke his tenure.[109]

Brock Allen Turner, a twenty-year-old Stanford University student and champion swimmer, raped an unconscious twenty-three-year-old woman. Bystanders caught him in the act. Since an unconscious victim is incapable of giving consent, the discovery of his DNA in her body inculpated him. He was convicted, but Santa Clara County Superior Court judge Aaron Persky sentenced him to only six months in prison. He must register as a sexual offender for the rest of his life. Persky, a Stanford graduate and varsity athlete, declared, "A prison sentence would have a severe impact on him. I think he will not be a danger to others."[110] Persky's indifference to the victim's impact statement—"I wanted to take off my body like a jacket and leave it at the hospital with everything else" and "Having too much to drink was an amateur mistake that I admit to, but it is not criminal" are representative excerpts—matched Smith's indifference to Chen's abused wife.[111] Persky was recalled in June 2018.[112]

Turner's victim's statement went viral, as did a letter from Turner's father pleading for mercy for his son. "He will never be his happy go lucky self. . . . His every waking minute is consumed with worry, anxiety, fear, and depression."[113] Disinterested observers might hope that anyone who committed such a crime would experience worry, anxiety, fear, and depression at the expense of his happy-go-lucky self. Readers of the letter might also wonder where this young man learned his attitudes about women.

The final case involves Martin Blake, a Glasgow, Montana, man who repeatedly raped his twelve-year-old daughter. State law requires a minimum sentence of twenty-five years in prison for anyone convicted of rape, incest, or sexual abuse of a child twelve or younger, but the judge may reduce punishment on the recommendation of a court-appointed evaluator. Judge John McKeon sentenced Blake to sixty days. He pointed out that the man had a job and no criminal record. The girl's mother pleaded for clemency, insisting that her husband "needs help" and "has two sons that still love him and need their father in their lives. . . . [She] would like to see [her] children have an opportunity to heal the relationship with their father."[114] Blake is required to register as a sex offender but may return to the home where all three children live. Protestors called for McKeon's removal from office, but he retired on full pension shortly thereafter.[115] Rehabilitation lived. Psychobabble replaced judgment. Even the child's mother identifies her other children's interests with those of the attacker. Family overrode gender. Patriarchy overrode children's safety.

In all three cases, a male view of the world prevailed. That fact alone does not condemn the punishments. The sentences might or might not work as specific deterrence. The publicity might shame Chen, and jail might scare him, into stopping the violence. Jail time separates abuser and abused at least temporarily. His wife has relatives in the United States with whom she had taken refuge in the past. Probation entails continued supervision. The mandatory class provides an opportunity for rehabilitation, obsolescent as that goal of punishment may be. Without a conviction for attempted murder, a light sentence was predictable. Brock Turner's penalty might, as Persky implied, keep him from reoffending. So might Martin Blake's. The registration requirements, which apply everywhere in the United States, impose ritual exile (unless they choose real exile and become fugitives).

Specific deterrence is a utilitarian goal, but it does not satisfy utilitarian demands. What happened to general deterrence? None of these three judges sought to make an example of the offender. A commentator proposed that Turner be required to fund a campus tour after his prison term "to talk about how a privileged life can be destroyed by 20 minutes of irresponsible, selfish, and hurtful actions."[116] The longer Turner spent in prison, the more deterrent force that message would have had.[117]

Society has not rejected retribution as a goal of punishment, but retribution played no part in these cases. These offenders are not "them." Chen is neither white nor American, but he is a middle-class professional. The judges may have identified, consciously or unconsciously, with the offenders they sentenced. But any projection had the opposite result than what Karl Menninger expected. When the offender looks like one of us, rehabilitation reappears and retribution disappears, along with the victim. Readers of a certain age may hear an echo of Gerald Ford's statement that "Richard Nixon and his loved ones have suffered enough and will continue to suffer."[118]

Turner and Chen faced civil penalties that might act as general deterrents for people in similar circumstances. Turner received some. Stanford not only expelled him but banned him from campus for life.[119] USA Swimming permanently excluded him from competition.[120] Chen escaped similar sanctions. He is a Chinese citizen with a permanent residence visa. He risked deportation because domestic violence is a "crime of moral turpitude" under immigration law. No such efforts were underway in 2017. Is exile an acceptable penalty? Did the privileged status that triggered the publicity prevent deportation?

Chen is not typical of convicted batterers. His jail term did not cost him his job. Is it fair to sentence a batterer without stable employment or community roots to a more severe sentence? Both cases present the classic dilemma of justice: the tension between giving each what he or she deserves and ensuring that similar crimes bring similar penalties. But these privileged criminals were treated as individuals, not as people involved in and responsible to society. Gentlemen got gentlemen's rights.

The Turner case was not the last occasion in 2016 that *Stanford* and *rape* appeared together in the headlines. On December 29, the *New York Times* ran a story about a varsity football player who escaped punishment for an alleged rape because an ad hoc disciplinary board voted 3–2 against him. A 4–1 majority is required for punishment. This bar is unusually high for judgments; among comparable schools, only Duke, which has had its own problems with rape allegations, has a similar rule. The accused played in the Sun Bowl game the following day.[121]

Stanford's willingness to impose more punishment on a student convicted in criminal court was not matched by similar severity on its own campus. This ruling sets a precedent for the majority of Stanford students who are not varsity athletes. The Obama administration treated college sexual assault as sexual harassment under Title IX of the Education Amendments of 1972 and applied the preponderance of evidence standard to these cases. Betsy De Vos, Donald Trump's secretary of education, removed this requirement.[122] But neither the presumption of innocence nor the reasonable doubt standard applies in other civil cases. Internal disciplinary proceedings—for plagiarism, cheating, fraud, misuse of funds, and the like—are commonplace in academia. Most cases are decided by simple majorities under the "preponderance of the evidence" standard. The danger of false accusations is no greater in sexual assault cases than in any others. Why treat them differently?

A liberal case can be made that preponderance of the evidence is too weak a burden for accusers. Does my questioning Head Start's firing an accused worker contradict with my dismissal of presumption of innocence? No; that employee was presumed guilty and received no process whatsoever. Right or wrong, fair or unfair, none of these practices resembles judgment under preponderance of evidence. Here process exists, and presumptions are neutral.

But should preponderance of evidence be the academic standard of proof? Unlike juries, the members of the ad hoc committees and honor boards who make the decisions are insiders with a stake in the system. Power imbalances favor accusers over the accused. Why not impose a more stringent burden? Clear and convincing evidence, perhaps, which the state of Texas must show to deprive parents of custody of their children.

Cases of academic dishonesty often meet that standard. There is corroborating evidence; in its absence, the charge is suspect. Plagiarism of a published source is easier to catch than a paper written by someone other than the student. But in campus sexual assault cases, corroboration is rare. No DNA or other concrete evidence that a sexual encounter took place is required. Some cases could become criminal matters. The imbalance of power that favors accusers is reversed. The accused have the advantage because society has long presumed that unsubstantiated accusations of sexual assault are false.[123] Boomers raised in liberal homes grew up hearing about Scottsboro, Emmett Till, and *To Kill a Mockingbird*.[124] Understanding that false accusations might not be limited to members of minority groups was easy. Liberals may no longer find rape heroic, but they are not immune from the attitude that male sexual aggression is healthy.

Modern liberalism has long been committed to ending race and class injustice. But gender injustice gets lost. Feminist post-liberalism must rank women's rights to protection from crime and freedom from fear equally with their immunity from carceral citizenship. Freedom from intimate injustice is no less important than freedom from mass incarceration.

Dismantling the Carceral State

Does serious punishment for serious crime sustain the carceral state? Must we close all the prisons to stop mass incarceration? Some experts argue that we must. Ruth Wilson Gilmore, Angela Davis, and Maya Schenwar are prominent advocates of prison abolition.[125] They agree with the conclusions that Alexander, Gottschalk, Murakawa, Hinton, Lerman, and Weaver reach: prisons are crowded with people who should not be there; custodial citizenship is permanent, disabling, and disempowering; the economy depends on prison labor; and the carceral state reinforces racial and class injustice. The abolitionists go a step further, concluding that these factors are so entrenched in the criminal justice system that mass incarceration "generates profits as it devours social wealth, and thus it tends to reproduce the very conditions that lead people to prison."[126] The carceral state is self-perpetuating. It will persist unless incarceration is abolished.

Gilmore and Davis helped found Critical Resistance, a grassroots organization that seeks to "end the Prison Industrial Complex by challenging the belief that caging and controlling people makes us safe" and convincing people "that basic necessities such as food, shelter, and freedom are what really make our communities secure."[127] Davis ponders "why . . . prisons tend to make people think that their own rights and liberties are more secure than they would be if prisons did not exist."[128] Mass incarceration "relieves us of the responsibility of seriously engaging with the problems of our society, especially those produced by racism and, increasingly, global capitalism."[129] But these abolitionists have done little more than replace one myth—"prisons make us safe"—with another—"we would be safe if only [fill in the blank]."

For more than twenty years, the national trend has been in the opposite direction from providing basic necessities. "The era of big government is over," Bill Clinton proclaimed in his 1996 State of the Union address.[130] The welfare state, if the United States had ever had one, was dead. A bully state replaced it. The two major political parties have combined to create a permanent class of carceral citizens. The new challenge is dismantling Prison America while protecting Americans from violent crime. Providing necessities would, no doubt, reduce property crime motivated by need, but how would it reduce property crime motivated by greed? Does anyone believe that mitigating racism and controlling global capitalism will stop sexual assault and domestic violence?

Schenwar is a journalist, not an academic. Unlike Davis and Gilmore, she does not base her arguments on Marxist theory. Her "restorative justice," seeks "to guide people who have hurt others toward addressing the ways *they* have been hurt—the root causes of their harm-doing—so they can be fully accountable for what they've done."[131] Techniques include "peace circles" that bring together offenders, victims, survivors, and community members "with the goal of working toward understanding, healing, and, in many cases, reconciliation and reparations."[132] Whether or not the reader accepts Schenwar's premise about the causes of crime, these programs have had some success in avoiding or reducing prison sentences. But restorative justice cannot deter crime. It works only after a crime has occurred.

Schenwar acknowledges that "when it comes to sexual and domestic violence, the prospect of community 'restoration' may well ring discordantly. . . . For survivors of gender violence, the key factor in whether a restorative justice process can be effective is whether a community unites with the victim in holding the perpetrator accountable. Often, communities end up siding with the perpetrator."[133] The reader will search other abolitionist and reformist literature in vain for such an admission.

Abolitionists fail to make a tenable feminist post-liberal argument that their remedies are realistic alternatives to incarceration. But their recommendations might go a long way toward creating substitutes for custody. Their implications that incarceration is inseparable from race and class injustice may apply to gender violence as well as to any other crimes. Abolitionist positions are part of a larger argument about whether incremental change can solve problems or radical change is necessary. This argument has been going on since the nineteenth century and shows no signs of abating. The abolitionists have not proved their case, but neither has anyone disproved their assertions. They may be right.

Could requiring rapists to register as sex offenders be enough to inflict damage that would act as both a general and specific deterrent? Could probation and mandatory classes do the same for battering? We will not know unless we try; the first possibility may be more likely than the second. Should we abandon retribution as a goal of punishment and/or reemphasize rehabilitation? If not, how can we end mass incarceration without abolition?

The Supreme Court has insisted that a facially neutral policy that, in effect, discriminates on the basis of race, class, or gender does not violate the Constitution unless the effect was intentional.[134] That principle is entrenched in American constitutional law. But those decisions are permissive, not restrictive; the government has the power to reject such policies and make them illegal. But most carceral citizenship is imposed by states and their subdivisions. One way to reduce arrests is to decriminalize certain behaviors. Legalizing drug use would remove a frequent cause of arrests. The government could regulate the manufacture, sale, distribution, and use of drugs as it does with alcohol. Calls for legalizing drugs emphasize how this step would reduce the size of the custodial population.[135] Legalizing sex work, but not forced prostitution, would have a similar impact.[136] Legislatures have the power to prohibit imprisonment for unpaid fines and to prevent civil forfeiture.

Relaxing the employment disqualifications imposed on felons would make it easier for them to legally earn a living. Any necessary prohibitions should be tailored to specific situations. *Richardson v. Ramirez* allowed the states to disenfranchise felons, but states can repeal these laws. Terry McAuliffe, Virginia's Democratic governor, has restored voting rights to all felons after they serve their sentences. The Maryland legislature overrode the Republican governor's veto of a similar measure.[137] There is no good reason to deprive convicts of voting rights after they have "paid their debt to society." Even without racial bias, economic bias would continue; the poor would be disproportionately affected. A case can be made for allowing inmates and those on probation or parole to vote. By keeping people out of custody and ameliorating the consequences of punishment, reforms such as these would weaken the carceral state.

These reforms will not change the prison system itself. Prison, a total institution, demoralizes and dehumanizes its inmates. Its structure militates against rehabilitation. Can this situation be changed? State legislatures can institute, and local criminal courts implement, restorative justice programs. The government can create or subsidize education and training programs. Sentences can be shortened. Why not institute terms of mandatory public service after release? Military service could be an option. States could create suitable civilian jobs.[138] To equalize penalties, convicts with secure employment might have to take on extra burdens. We could explore alternatives to prison, like resident-run halfway houses.

That reforms have occurred in states with Democratic majorities is no accident. Republicans control most state governments as they do the national government. There is no cause for optimism that states *will* do anything they *can* do. But there is no reason to give up either. Republican control may not be permanent. Senate seats and governorships are immune from gerrymandering. States that enact reforms can act as sociological laboratories, teaching other states that the outcomes of drug legalization or convict enfranchisement are more positive than negative.

Conclusion

The U.S. Constitution was written by gentlemen for gentlemen. Its authors were no strangers to us-versus-them thinking. The fact that "we the people of the United States" excluded more residents than it included is familiar. The framers thought about people like themselves when they thought about crime. Recent history had exposed them and their contemporaries to the threat of arrest, trial, imprisonment, and even execution. By the mid-twentieth century, the demographics of crime had changed. Landmark due process decisions upheld the rights of people who committed serious crimes and sometimes got away with them. Such people were easy to identify as "them," especially if they were members of "outsider" groups. The incarceration boom that began in the 1970s reinforced the us-versus-them dichotomy. But some criminals do not fit this model.

The word *gentleman* has fallen out of vogue in twenty-first-century American English. Using it can raise eyebrows because it presumes the class division many Americans refuse to recognize. The word also does not mean quite what it meant in the 1770s. It now describes an educated, middle- or upper-class adult male. By this definition, Yong Chen, the batterer, and Brock Allen Turner, the rapist, are gentlemen. That status worked in their favor. Not only did they get the procedural rights that become irrelevant for the majority of offenders who plead guilty, but they also got the privilege of empathy. Retribution gave way to rehabilitation. Sentencing judges ignored victims while considering third parties, such as Chen's students and Turner's father.

Empathy disappears in the carceral state. Arrests lead to fines that lead to imprisonment. Plea agreements replace trials and may entail imprisonment. Incarceration leads to unemployability and disfranchisement. Former inmates may have no legal way to support themselves and no power to participate in change. These developments gave advantages to one major political party while depriving the other of part of its base. Once mass incarceration was polarized, activists began opposing it. But in their opposition, many seemed to forget a distinction older than the Constitution itself. Women are vulnerable to violent crime in ways that most men are not. The criminal justice system has failed to protect women from violence. We must avoid reforms that make life more dangerous for women. Feminists must sensitize critics of the carceral state to these dangers. Mass incarceration has not made women safer; efforts to end it must avoid making them less safe.

5

Gender Equality and the Family

Compatible or Contradictory?

"The family is the natural and fundamental group unit of society." Thus reads the Universal Declaration of Human Rights (UDHR).[1] In this context, *family* denotes what Martha Fineman calls the sexual family, "the traditional or nuclear family, a unit with a heterosexual, formally celebrated union at its core."[2] "Upon [marriage] society may be said to be built," wrote the U.S. Supreme Court in *Reynolds v. U.S.*, rejecting the claim that Mormon polygamy was protected by the free exercise clause of the First Amendment.[3] The Defense of Marriage Act of 1996 proclaimed that "the word 'marriage' means only a legal union between one man and one woman." This was the law of the land until 2013, when the court struck it down.[4]

The sexual family is not now, was not when UDHR was promulgated in 1948, and has never been a universal arrangement. "The modern Stone Age family" existed only in the television show *The Flintstones*. People lived in clans then. In some parts of the world, they still do.[5] The nuclear family is neither natural nor fundamental. But the idea that "the family is the basis of civil society" is popular in modern Western society, even among some feminists and liberals.

What do people mean by this cliché? Sometimes they mean that society as we know it would not exist without the family as we know it, a hypothesis incapable of proof or disproof. Karl Marx and Friedrich Engels held that the family was an essential bulwark of capitalism.[6] No one need embrace Marxism to agree that the two institutions are compatible. The statement can also be an outlook, a viewpoint, an "as if": we have agreed to presume that it is true and to regard the family as "entitled to protection by society and the state."[7] The nuclear family, two parents and their children, is the norm; everything else is an exception.

Some political practices accommodate arrangements outside the family. The Census Bureau, charged with collecting data without causing offense, abandoned the old "Head of Household; Wife of Head" format in 1980. Residents of a dwelling may be listed in any order. But immigration law gives priority to applicants for permanent residence visas with family members who are legal U.S. residents. Prospective immigrants without American relatives are at a disadvantage. The fact that this chain migration is now in jeopardy shows that family concerns do not get priority over all other issues all the time.[8] The Trump administration's separation of immigrant children from their families, even after a federal court invalidated the practice, is another indication that border security supersedes family values.[9] But special rules for families are common. This chapter reveals instances of families granted exceptions to general rules.

Every election cycle brings rhetoric about "our children and grandchildren." That a twenty-first-century author would label nonparents "aberrant," as Desmond Morris did, is unlikely, but mainstream rhetoric ignores them.[10] True, this discourse marginalizes fewer people than it once did. Unwed motherhood is not universally stigmatized; no children are termed "illegitimate"; the Supreme Court legalized same-sex marriage.[11] But the discourse excludes Americans who live alone, 27 percent—about eighty million—in 2013.[12]

My own experience informs my analysis. Never married and child-free, I count as an outsider. I am expected to defer to the opinions of parents and grandparents. Oppose censorship? You do not have kids. Question Megan's Law? You do not have kids. Object to obstreperous children in airplanes or indoor swimming pools? If you had kids, you would understand. Never mind that parents and nonparents line up on all sides of these issues or that the defensive parent does not know whether the complainer has children. Woe betide the nonparent whose detachment allows insight. Queries such as "If you're worried about her weight, why do you make her drink milk three times a day?" or "Would the boys get along better if you stop comparing them to each other?" can end friendships.

No one attempts to persuade me that reversing climate change or reducing the federal deficit serves my interests. No one talks about younger friends and neighbors, students, or even nieces and nephews, let alone about groups or institutions. Natural resources, animal species, plant life, land, water, and clean air are not recognized as interests. The implication that only parents have a stake in what happens after they die insults people like me. But does the implication that parents are concerned only about their own families not insult them? The word *our* is inclusive when opposed to *my* but exclusive when opposed to *your* and *their.*

My own "minority" status enables me even as it isolates me. Chapter 2 discusses the immunities that some women have from some gendered expectations some of the time.[13] I have been criticized for acting like a "bad mother." Lack of experience does not provide an acceptable excuse. But nonparticipation in marriage and parenthood frees me from the constraints of these roles and—more important for scholarship—the need to justify my own behavior. The more I stand away from these institutions, the more clearly to see them. I do not presume that parents do the best they can. I do not consider the family a "haven in a heartless world"[14] or agree a priori that "truly rotten families are, thank God, few and far between. Most commonly we have good enough families or almost good enough ones."[15] The uninvolved have contributions to make to the discourse. Of course, hands-on experience is necessary for knowledge. But so is perspective. The two are complementary, not contradictory. My skepticism about the conventional family informs my approach to the questions I ask here.

Is a feminist post-liberal family possible? The conventional Western family is derived from patriarchy, which presumes male superiority. Liberalism no longer does. But does liberalism entail patriarchy? The patriarchal family is, in many respects, what we have now, when push comes to shove. Can we reconstruct the institution of the family to make it more egalitarian and more inclusive?

How Liberal Is the Family?

Merriam-Webster defines *familism* as "a social pattern in which the family assumes a position of ascendance over individual interests."[16] It is thus incompatible with the presumptions of equality and autonomy that underlie liberalism. Liberal rights include the right to form counter-liberal associations. The family is an involuntary association, in two senses. First, even the majority of Americans who choose their own spouses do not choose their ancestors, their in-laws, their biological children, or their siblings. Depending on law and custom, we may have obligations to, and/or claims on, some of our kin.

Second, by founding a family, we create a relationship whose structure and content are predetermined. Reciprocal rights and duties of family members have changed over time, in ways that improved women's status. Unions are no longer limited to heterosexual couples or denied to interracial couples. Parenting is no more connected to sex for same-sex couples than it is for adoptive parents. But no one can form a family of parents and adult children;

of siblings and one's own children; with the parent of a dead spouse; with that in-law, a future spouse, and future children; or of people unrelated by kinship or marriage, or any "caretaking family" except for a single parent and one or more children.

Third, the structure of families consisting of parents and minor children is hierarchical. Anglo-American law presumes, subject to rebuttal, that the parent speaks for the child.[17] Parents have power over their children. This power, like all power, is subject to misuse and abuse. Misusing parental power without abusing children is possible—in fact, it may be unavoidable. But abuse can happen when some family members have resources, such as size, strength, and income, that others lack. This possibility cuts both ways; children who have greater resources than parents can abuse them. But minor children have an obligation to obey their parents. This chapter shows how the institution becomes the excuse for condoning and even rewarding violence.

Yet tangible, extrinsic benefits do not attach to family status in the United States: no child allowance, no subsidized child care, no visiting nurses or counselors. The only benefits conventional families get are immunity from criticism and encouragement to think of themselves as normal and of others as deviant. Otherwise, families are on their own.

Chapter 2 shows that human beings could imitate and obey before they could form opinions and write them down. Power and structure precede analysis. The sexual family was in place in the West before political theory appeared and was entrenched by the time liberal theory developed. Thinkers could praise it, accept it, tolerate it, criticize it, reject it, or ignore it, but it forms part of "the house in which we live."[18]

Patriarchy and Male Supremacy

Liberals were not the first thinkers to connect male supremacy and the family. Liberals, like their intellectual predecessors, wrote after the fact; patriarchy was already in place.[19] These thinkers produced rationalizations, not explanations. Plato, who acknowledged that "many women are better than many men in many things," has Socrates ask, "Do you know of anything that is practiced by human beings in which the class of men doesn't excel that of women?"[20] Book I of Aristotle's *Politics* declares, "The relation of male to female is naturally that of the inferior to the superior." Any deviation from this pattern was a "departure from nature."[21] But the two philosophers took their belief in male superiority in different directions.

Plato's observation seems to be based on casual empiricism, "what everybody knows" (and, as such, is vulnerable to criticism). The generalization has little relevance to the abilities of individuals. Book 5 of *The Republic* admits able women into the class of guardians and defends coeducation so that women will be able to raise future guardians. Conventional families would not exist among the guardians, but male dominance would. In the ideal state

> you, their lawgiver, just as you selected the men, will hand over the women to them, having selected them . . . with natures that are as similar as possible. And all of them will be together, since they have common houses and mess, with no one privately possessing anything of the kind. And . . . they'll be led by inner natural necessity to sexual mixing with one another.[22]

Free sex would replace monogamy among the elite. Without private property, the traditional rationale for female monogamy disappears. Men need not know which children are theirs when there is nothing to hand down. "But how," asks Glaucon, "will they distinguish one another's fathers and daughters?" Socrates keeps the incest taboo by reinventing it: a married man will call all children born at specific times of the year sons and daughters, "and they will call him father."[23] Was Plato on to something when he perceived a contradiction between justice and the conventional family? He never got to put his arrangement into practice. History shouted him down.

One translator called book 5 "preposterous."[24] That was also Aristotle's view. "The scheme of Plato means that each citizen will have a thousand sons," and "any and every son will be equally the son of any and every father; and the result will be that every son will be equally neglected by every father."[25] Aristotle won the argument. The idea of alternative family arrangements was no more palatable late in the twentieth century, when Martha Fineman called for "the abolition of the legal supports for the sexual family and the construction of protections for the nurturing unit of caretaker and dependent exemplified by the Mother/Child dyad."[26]

Aristotle rooted male superiority, as he did just slavery, in nature. Free men, free women, slaves, and children fulfilled the roles for which nature fitted them. "The soul rules the body with the sort of authority of a master." Therefore, "all men who differ from others as much as the body from the soul . . . are by nature slaves, and it is better for them . . . to be ruled by a master."[27] Unlike the slave, the woman possessed "the faculty of reason" but "in a form which remains inconclusive." Her "moral goodness" showed itself in "serving" rather than "ruling."[28] Aristotle recommended that men marry at thirty-seven and women at eighteen;[29] most Greek men in his time married closer to thirty and women closer to fourteen.[30] Marriage was the only possibility available to all but a few women in ancient Greece.

The belief in male superiority may, therefore, have been affected by the intervening variable of age. But if that were true, it would contrast with Aristotle's defense of slavery. Ancient Greek slavery was usually the result of war or piracy. Some slaves were black Africans, but not all slaves looked different from free Greeks.[31] Far from being forbidden to learn to read and write, like plantation slaves in the American South, some Greek slaves were scribes, managers, or physicians. They worked in a variety of occupations such as domestic servants, miners, farmers, and craftspeople. So where did Aristotle get his notion of the natural slave? His beliefs, that distinction and hierarchy characterized highly developed societies and that "there must necessarily be a union between the naturally ruling element with the element which is naturally ruled," may have predisposed him to create these categories for human beings to fill.[32] A twentieth-century translator suggested that slavery and male dominance could also "afford the citizen leisure for the high purposes of the state."[33]

The twenty-first-century family departs from its ancient and early modern ancestors. The Greek and Roman versions of what Aristotle called the household included slaves and often combined home and livelihood. *Domus*, the equivalent Latin word, carried the same meaning. *Familia* was what language teachers call a "false friend." It included household staff, slave or free. Opposition to slavery antedated the growth of liberalism. Household slavery was rare by the seventeenth century.[34] By the eighteenth century, liberals had concluded that "just slavery" was an oxymoron.

Multigenerational families were more common then than they are now. The workplace was less often separate from the dwelling, both physically and socially. The availability of land on the American frontier allowed nuclear families to establish farms. The Industrial Revolution encouraged the separation between public and private spheres. These changes had ramifications that went far beyond economic development. The division between public and private brought a separate spheres ideology that relegated women to the home.[35] The demarcation of a private sphere led to a privacy doctrine that had contradictory results for women, enhancing their marital and reproductive freedom while reinforcing the power of husbands and fathers over them.[36] "Privacy doctrine is most at home at home," where "women have no privacy to lose or guarantee."[37]

Male supremacy was a constant. The fact that "Sophia, a woman of quality," titled her 1739 essay "Woman Not Inferior to Man" indicates that the opinion she rejected was alive and well.[38] Challenges to male supremacy may have had some relationship to the steady decline in the age gap between husbands and wives since ancient Greece. By the 1700s, the typical age of marriage in rural England was twenty-five or twenty-six for women and thirty for men. In the New World, where more land was available for young adults to live on, women usually married at about twenty-two and men at twenty-six.[39] But belief in gender equality remained a minority viewpoint even among liberals.

Jean-Jacques Rousseau based his defense of female subordination on his theory of the family. Women bore children; therefore, children's health depended on women; therefore, women must be educated to please men. This argument not only ranks women below men but also wipes out any notion of women's separate interests.[40] Aristotle thought male supremacy served the interests of both men and women. Nor did he link women's subordination to their reproductive function. Liberal male supremacy was thus nastier and more selfish than classical male supremacy. Male dominance may or may not have *caused* the development of the conventional Western family or even have been a necessary condition for it. But the history of that family is inexorably intertwined with the history of male dominance. Some critics have argued that liberalism is inseparable from patriarchy.[41]

Saying that women were inferior to men gradually became unfashionable. Some nineteenth-century writers even made the opposite claim while endorsing traditional gender roles; the angel in the house must remain there. Twentieth-century scholars such as Desmond Morris and Lionel Tiger related male dominance to differences in reproductive function rather than female inferiority.[42] But one defense of male superiority persisted long after women had won formal legal equality. The textbook for the introductory sociology course I took in 1964 at a women's college was Robert Bierstedt's *The Social Order*. Bierstedt took the "Why are there no great women X?" line: "In the entire history of music there is no woman composer of the rank of Beethoven or Brahms or Wagner. . . . Where is the woman whom one can place with a Rembrandt, a Michelangelo, a Titian, a Leonardo?"[43] Whether or not most men were superior to most women, all the luminaries were men.

Twentieth-century feminists criticized this reasoning by rhetorical question. They pointed to factors such as a lack of opportunity and revealed that work done by women was often attributed to men.[44] But why did anyone ask such questions at all? Bierstedt mentioned seven people who lived over four centuries. Considering the population of Europe in those years, how significant is it that all these geniuses were male? The argument is bad science; what was it doing in a discipline that claimed to be scientific? Was it about science at all? It helped keep women in their place. The "no great women X" approach provided a rationale for discouraging women's ambitions.[45] My cohort was the last to be fed this sort of argument and the first to dismiss it. Bierstedt's ideas are no more current than those of Paul Goodman, Erich

Fromm, or Daniel Patrick Moynihan.[46] Twentieth-century feminism accomplished at least that much.

The arguments for male superiority do not survive scrutiny. The rationalizations of male supremacy were made obsolescent by industrialization and fertility control. Sexist premises morphed into neutral premises. Moynihan's female-headed family became a single-parent family. Women became different from men rather than inferior to them. It became easier not to notice the discrepancies in freedom, power, resources, burdens, and responsibilities. But patriarchy, like most social arrangements, persists without justifications or causal connections. It reinforces itself. Getting rid of it is one of the many goals feminism has not yet achieved.

Second-wave feminists lost no time in subjecting the conventional family to criticism. Asking whether justice prevailed in the family, and often answering no, they challenged liberal acceptance of the institution as a given.[47] But once again, liberals were ahead of whoever was in second place. Conservatives tend to idealize the conventional family. They regard bad families as exceptions to a general rule of benevolence. Radicals, for their part, tend to regard the family as of secondary importance to class oppression and imperialism.

The Family in Political Discourse

On the right, familism gets in the way of change. Two books targeted to a conservative Christian audience provide examples from American inner cities. The lead author of *When Helping Hurts*, an economics professor at a Christian college, writes, "Well-intentioned welfare programs penalized work, undermined families, and created dependence."[48] A community organizer declares in *Toxic Charity* that "when we do for those in need what they have the capacity to do for themselves, we disempower them."[49] It is not either author's fault that, late in 2017, these statements called to mind Donald Trump's throwing packages of paper towels to Puerto Ricans after Hurricane Maria. Traditional Christian economics in the United States defends capitalism as strongly as traditional Christian theology defends patriarchy. Yet Christian theologians are not united in equating interdependence with dependence.

Both books note occasions when men were absent from holiday giveaways. *Toxic Charity* urges donors to "give the gift of dignity to the dads" by bringing their donations to a thrift store.[50] *When Helping Hurts* declares, "The last thing these fathers needed was a group of middle-to-upper-class Caucasians providing Christmas presents for their children . . . that they themselves could not afford to buy."[51]

The threshold questions are how the authors knew, first, that the households in question included a man and, second, if they did know, that the man was the father of any children in the household. Assumptions preempt facts in both accounts. These books superimpose a model of a two-parent family on households that may not fit that model. They presume the existence of a man whose pride is hurt, who is deprived of his rightful place in the family. Altruism must accommodate the male ego. Daniel Patrick Moynihan, whose ideas permeate these books, although he goes unmentioned, was right; male leadership is essential.

But is it? Suppose the child of a single mother gets a bicycle for Christmas. With her increased mobility, the child can now run errands for the family. She can earn money by doing the same for neighbors. A teenager might even get a paper route, if children still deliver newspapers anywhere. Altruism need neither frustrate independence nor undermine the family.

Voices on the left scorn efforts to bring about incremental change in the Third World. Several years ago, *New York Times* columnist Nicholas Kristof, commonly regarded as liberal/progressive, publicized child prostitution in Asia, bought and released two young prostitutes who were sold by their families, and encouraged his readers to do the same. His columns revealed occasions when family members sabotaged a former prostitute's efforts to conduct a business. The reforms Kristof sponsors are instances of "microfinance." This practice provides loans to low-income clients who set themselves up in business. The word *micro* describes both the loans and the businesses. Women are the preferred recipients, because entire families benefit from their earnings. A generation of micro-financiers could help to break entrenched cycles of poverty, malnutrition, and helplessness.[52] Succeeding generations might include activists who call for "macro" change.

But some leftists find the source of intrafamily cruelty in exogenous factors, such as economic oppression. Alexander Cockburn takes this position in a 2006 article in the *Nation*. He criticizes Kristof for ignoring what Cockburn identified as the root of the problem: neoliberal "reforms" by the World Trade Organization that have destroyed Third World industries. Cockburn invites Kristof to "take his video camera to the World Bank and confront its current president, Paul Wolfowitz."[53] Criticizing Western practices is easier for radicals than is scrutinizing Eastern ones.

The *New York Times* is read at the World Bank, whereas the *Nation* may not be. Is it so clear that the World Bank was the "prime promoter of prostitution"?[54] We can concede the truth of Cockburn's implication that prevention is better than cure. Without exonerating neoliberal trade policies, however, the child prostitution that Kristof publicized could not have occurred unless parents had the power to sell their children and governments allowed or ignored this practice. Cockburn assumes that only a desperate parent would sell a child; there would be no child prostitution if families had better economic options. Presumably, less childhood prostitution would exist if Third World industries were healthier. Cockburn may have identified a cause; Kristof may have found a cure.

We know too much about intrafamily abuse to believe in miracle cures. Western parents hire out their children for pornographic films—and, more often, as actors or models. Poverty may explain some of these actions, but abusive practices exist that have nothing to do with money. Female genital mutilation (FGM) and honor killings are standard practices in some parts of the world. Families subject girls to FGM in the United States, although it is illegal here.[55] These families have emigrated from countries where FGM is practiced. But other abusive practices occur in native-born American families. Kristof wrote an op-ed column about an eleven-year-old Florida girl raped and impregnated by an adult who attended the same church as her family did. She was forced to marry him. Florida is one of twenty-seven states that have no minimum age for marriage.[56]

Familism, Law, and Bureaucracy

When the state gets involved with a family, something bad has happened. The government does not get involved in all cases in which bad things have happened. The vast majority of offenses go unreported. This next section, therefore, deals only with the tip of the iceberg. A critic might complain that my treatment is one-sided. Why do I not discuss battered men or the abuse of parents by adolescent and adult children? If I found similar patterns in such cases, my argument that family tyranny is tolerated would be strengthened even as my argument that family patriarchy persists would be weakened. But, with one partial exception, comparable cases do not exist. The victims are women and children.

Much official discourse reflects a commitment to the conventional family and to accommodating specific families in the face of overwhelming contrary evidence. As with crime in Chapter 4, there is always another example. Reconsider the case of Martin Blake, the father-rapist who was set free and allowed to return to his family. His wife insisted that their sons needed their father. But what did the boys need their father for? So he can influence them as Dan Turner may have influenced his son Brock? Apparently, the boys' needs overrode those of their sister.[57] The mother also said that the children needed "an opportunity to heal the relationship" with their father. Did she think it was *their* responsibility?

In September 2017, former U.S. Representative Anthony Weiner was convicted of sexting a fifteen-year-old. Judge Denise L. Cote sentenced him to twenty-one months in prison. Seeing this weeping, self-ruined man in court may have inspired pity and the belief that he had suffered enough and should serve no prison time. Weiner's estranged wife, Huma Abedin, herself a victim of collateral damage, wrote Judge Cote asking for leniency in the interests of their young son.[58] No one asked if contact with this particular father would benefit the boy.

A notorious case a month later went against the father but revealed a little-known fact: in seven states, rapists who impregnate their victims retain parental rights. Christopher Mirosolo was convicted in Michigan in 2008, on the basis of DNA evidence, of raping a twelve-year-old, who bore a son in 2009. She kept him, at what personal cost only she knows. Mirosolo was later convicted of another rape and served four years in prison. He applied for public assistance in 2016. Without his knowledge, or that of the mother, the state filed an application to award him joint custody of their seven-year-old son. A judge granted it, although no one—mother, father, or advocate for the child—wanted it. The judge had not known that the child resulted from a rape and reversed himself the next day after the news hit the media,[59] but one scholar called rapists' retention of parental rights a "second rape" of the victim.[60]

Family loyalty has led some parents to welcome the Trump administration's rejection of the preponderance of evidence standard in campus sexual assault cases. Several mothers whose sons had been punished met with Secretary of Education Betsy De Vos in July 2017. De Vos rescinded the Obama administration's rule in September.[61]

These women did not evince shame for their children's behavior, any more than Dan Turner did. The son of one mother interviewed by the *New York Times* had intercourse with a woman too drunk to resist. "In my generation," said the mother, "what these girls are going through was never considered sexual assault. It was considered, 'I was stupid and I got embarrassed.'"[62] In the good old days, we blamed the girls, and the girls blamed themselves. Rape was a rite of passage, a learning experience, a part of growing up. Victims were responsible, not aggressors. Before second-wave feminism, this view was popular among baby boomers across the political spectrum. This one lesson from older generations went unquestioned even by rebels. "Stop rape: say yes" was a popular 1960s slogan. The picture emerges of a state of nature, a Hobbesian war of all against all. Predators aggress. Prey yield, or protect themselves. This version of heterosexual relations in the 1960s, the present, or any time in recorded history is, of course, incomplete. Now, family loyalty becomes an excuse for returning to the old days.

That parents defend their accused children is depressing but predictable. That officials responsible for enforcing laws side with them without seeking input from other actors is inexcusable. That a baby boomer (De Vos was born in 1958) would act this way indicates that the fight against sexual assault, the progress from the state of nature to civil society, will be long and difficult. But at least it has begun.

So judges defend bad fathers, and parents defend bad sons. My last case involves a woman who committed family violence and was punished for it. Michelle Jones spent twenty years in prison for the murder of her son. While incarcerated, she got a college degree, published articles, won awards, and wrote plays and dance compositions. Having paid her debt to society, she was admitted to graduate school at Harvard. But the university's president, provost, and graduate deans took the extraordinary step of reversing a departmental decision and revoking the offer of a fellowship "out of concern that her background would cause a backlash among rejected applicants, conservative news outlets or parents of students."[63]

Harvard is the richest university in the world and the oldest in North America, more than 150 years older than the United States itself. A less vulnerable institution is difficult to imagine. But even Harvard yielded to *anticipated* threats. The knowledge and perspective this forty-five-year-old African American female ex-convict could have brought to and shared in the graduate program counted for nothing. Ironically, the law prevents institutions receiving federal funds from discriminating on the basis of gender, race, or age.

The conventional family remains a site of violence. Bullying takes place within the family as it does within the state. We have seen how defenders of the family insist that benevolence is the rule and violence, the exception: at least, a phenomenon of less than 50 percent. This argument seems to reassure many who hear it. We do not really know how many or what proportion of families are pathological. Numbers do not matter much, because the cases that the government must deal with are already pathological. Everybody knows that the government cannot stop family violence, but the law and the bureaucracy condone it too often. Bad fathers are let off the hook, while bad mothers are condemned in perpetuity. Parents devote more energy to excusing their sons' aggression than to preventing their daughters' victimization. The twenty-first century has not untangled the family from patriarchy.

What Is to Be Done?

So what do we do about this? A necessary step is to publicize as many episodes like these as we can. The autumn of 2017 brought new media attention to sexual harassment and misconduct in both the public and private sectors. The same must be done with family violence and legal leniency. The important difference between these two sets of victims is that the former are legally competent adults and can decide for themselves whether to face the publicity.

Children, such as the Montana incest victim or the Michigan girl who bore her rapist's child, are more vulnerable. The residents of Glasgow, Montana, probably know who Martin Blake's daughter is. But some adult and child victims do remain anonymous. Once child victims grow up, they can decide whether to tell their stories. Those who do will benefit society.

Institutions can also publicize intimate injustice. Professional athletic teams have started to discipline players for domestic violence. The Department of Education no longer requires colleges and universities to decide sexual assault cases on the preponderance of the evidence, but it has not forbidden them to do so. The more resistance the Trump administration gets from institutions, the less damage it can do.

Some families should not exist. No victim should have to marry her rapist or co-parent with him. The state should not use its power to return an incestuous father to his family, making the victim responsible for reconciliation. Yes, people can heal from terrible experiences and reconcile with those who abuse them. But this girl is not on equal footing with her parents. Her father abused his daughter, and her mother abused her power over her daughter. The parents are in the position of strength, and the children are in the position of weakness. The victim is surrounded by people who, at worst, rank her father's needs above hers and, at best, identify her needs with his. This is familism run riot.

Anthony Weiner presents a more complex case. There is no family, just two ex-spouses and their son. Is having this man for a father better than having no father at all? An affirmative answer to this question does not settle the question of what punishment Weiner should receive. Should we use minor children as a mitigating factor in sentencing their parents? If we find that public embarrassment and registration requirements for sex offenders are strong enough general deterrents to lower the incidence of sex crimes, we can revisit this issue. But for now, prison may be the best place for sex offenders.

What can government do besides punish? Suppose Blake's wife had been offered a choice between separating from her husband and losing custody of her children. That solution is not only a choice but also a threat. It might appeal in a bully state, but where would the children go if the threat must be carried out? Into foster care, or an institution? Might this wife and mother (whose name goes unmentioned) have feared the loss of her husband's income? Most husbands earn more than their wives, and many families need two incomes. Blake could be required to pay child support, but these payments are notoriously hard to collect. His wife might have suspected that mouthing psychobabble would be more effective than pleading economic necessity.

Suppose, instead, that the state provided parental subsidies and affordable child care. Socialist governments do this, but the era of conflating socialism with communism is over. The Democratic Socialists of America have been gaining influence since the 2016 election.[64] Emulating the governments of Western Europe would not automatically transfer control of the means of production from the private to the public sector. Parents who do not need a subsidy, such as Huma Abedin, would qualify, too, but why not find a way to compensate people who forgo the entitlement? Would subsidies reward lazy custodial parents as well as deserving ones? Yes, but why deprive children because of parental shortcomings? Would subsidies encourage teenage parenthood? Why not discourage it by providing access to birth control? The government could also provide job training and counseling. Therapy might help the Davis children heal themselves. Both parents are good candidates for mandatory counseling. But even in a welfare state, prison might be the only way to keep Blake away from his children.

How would we pay for family subsidies? Through tax increases, unless the private sector starts paying workers a living wage. Residents of welfare states pay much higher taxes than Americans do. So far, bully-state solutions to family violence are much more popular than welfare-state solutions. Public shame and registration requirements extended to perpetrators of incest might eventually work as general deterrents to sex crimes and family violence. But we are not there yet.

Might family subsidies have other advantages? The U.S. fertility rate has declined since the 2007 recession and reached a record low in 2016. It has been below the replacement level for several years.[65] Might subsidies encourage people to have or adopt children? Countries with generous pronatalist policies have also experienced population decline. Several have fallen below the 2.1 births per woman required for a generation to reproduce itself.[66] The United States may have to rely on technology and immigration like the rest of the developed world. But a welfare state might be worth a try.

No one expects these changes to happen anytime soon. Family subsidies and parental benefits are long-run solutions. Public shaming and extending sex offender registration requirements to perpetrators of incest may eventually work as general deterrents to sex crimes and family violence, but waiting for attitudes to change is reactive. What, if anything, can we do in the short run?

Reconstructing the Family

We can redefine the family to include arrangements not based on sexual union. Martha Fineman to the contrary notwithstanding, we need not replace the nuclear family with the mother-child bond. Society teaches people to want monogamy and parenthood; the (revised) sexual family survives as both ideal and reality. But the connections among sex, reproduction, and parenthood are broken. Even before same-sex marriage was legalized, people—heterosexual couples, gay couples, and single adults—were allowed and even encouraged to adopt children. Birth control and abortion have separated sex from reproduction; assisted reproductive technology (ART) has separated reproduction from sex. There is no magic about the number two. Reproduction requires ovum and sperm, but parenting does not. Conception requires one female and one male progenitor, but childrearing does not require two and only two parents. These generalizations cover both single-parent families and multiparent families. "We now live in an era where a child may have as many as five different 'parents.' These include a sperm donor, an egg donor, a surrogate or gestational host, and two nonbiological relatives who want to raise the child."[67]

This scenario gibes with Andrew Solomon's account in the autobiographical final chapter of *Far from the Tree.* He is the biological and legal father of Blaine and George. Blaine's biological mother, also named Blaine, is her legal mother, who later married Richard. Andrew and his husband, John, are George's legal parents. Laura, George's volunteer surrogate mother, is also the biological and legal mother of John's two children. Laura's legal co-parent is her partner, Tammy. John renounced parental rights to these two children; Laura and Tammy relieved him of parental obligations. Laura has neither with respect to George. But Laura is involved in George's life, as Richard is in Blaine's.[68]

Andrew and John are middle-class professionals. Laura was John's co-worker. Blaine senior went to college with Andrew. So at least one partner in each dyad is a typical ART parent. ART is available only to those who can afford it or find volunteer donors. Ova are less expensive than surrogates, and semen less expensive than ova. Prices may decline with time as the prices of many big-ticket items have declined. But for now, ART is a luxury. My justification for starting with ART arrangements is their ability to suggest alternative parenting arrangements that are more widely available.

Why could Richard not be a third parent to young Blaine? Why could Laura not be a third parent to George? Surrogacy might be less worrisome if the biological mother and intended parents shared rights and duties. What would have happened if Mary Beth Whitehead Gould, William Stern, and Elizabeth Stern had all been recognized as parents of Baby M, if the adults' relationships had been cooperative instead of adversarial? Would the adult Melissa Stern have severed all ties with her biological mother?[69] No one should be forced into these arrangements, but what if all the adults wanted them? Should the law not allow them?

The implications of multiple parenting go far beyond ART. Why should a single mother not form a family with her parent(s) or sibling(s)? If she begins a romantic relationship later, her partner or spouse might become a co-parent—or not, if they prefer. Must someone who marries a parent become a co-parent or even a stepparent? Why should I not form a family with an aging parent or one or more siblings? Why should I not be able to include them on my health insurance by paying the family rates? Why not multigenerational families? Why should friends not build families, with or without children? These relationships would be subject to dissolution, as marriage is now. Co-parents might be relieved of rights and duties by mutual consent. The ability to add parents might alleviate the problem of the "deadbeat ex." Caregiving families might supplement, but need not replace, the conventional family.

Courts in nine states have allowed third-party adoptions, known as "tri-parenting." The third party is usually a grandparent, a stepparent, or the spouse of a biological parent.[70] The judges who decide these cases confront what Benjamin Cardozo called "the serious business of judging," which begins "when the colors do not match, when the references in the index fail, when there is no decisive precedent."[71] No state legislature has yet acted on this matter, nor has the federal government. But two Canadian provinces, British Columbia in 2013 and Ontario in 2017, have legalized multiple parenting by statute. In both countries, lesbian, gay, bisexual, transgender, and queer (LGBTQ) activists have been leading advocates of these reforms.[72]

Redefining the family leads inexorably to the question of polygamy. Western polygamy has its roots in Mormonism, a belief system as sexist and patriarchal as any that shaped our culture. The Supreme Court's opinion in *Reynolds* combined prejudice with xenophobia: "Polygamy has always been odious among the northern and western nations of Europe, and, until the establishment of the Mormon Church, was almost exclusively a feature of the life of Asiatic and of African people."[73] The Church of Jesus Christ of Latter-Day Saints (LDS) gave up polygamy in 1890 as a condition of Congress's admitting Utah to the union. But a breakaway sect, the Fundamentalist LDS (FLDS), continued to practice polygamy. Driven underground, members lived inconspicuously to avoid prosecution but were not always successful. The next time the court heard a case involving polygamy, it quoted the previous quotation verbatim, upholding the conviction of an FLDS member for interstate travel with his wives. Eight justices agreed that polygamy was an "immoral purpose" under the Mann Act.

Justice Frank Murphy's dissent in this case, *Cleveland v. U.S.*, described polygyny (a marriage of one husband and more than one wife) as one of the basic forms of marriage. Historically, its use has far exceeded that of any other form. It was quite common among ancient civilizations, and was referred to many times by the writers of the Old Testament; even today, it is to be found frequently among certain pagan and non-Christian peoples of the world. We must recognize, then, that polygyny, like other forms of marriage, is basically a cultural institution rooted deeply in the religious beliefs and social mores of those societies in which it appears.[74]

These opinions fail as guides for twenty-first-century jurisprudence. *Reynolds* predated the development of equal protection and individual rights doctrine. No opinion in *Cleveland* reveals any hint of feminist consciousness. To the cynic, polygyny may look like a device for freeing men from the constraints of fidelity while providing them with multiple helpmates and sexual partners. The worst-case scenario is represented by the FLDS president, Warren Jeffs, who is serving a prison sentence of life plus twenty years for child sexual abuse. A 2008 raid of the sect's YFZ Ranch in Texas found households in which men lived with several much younger wives. Girls and women were forced to marry husbands chosen for them, while boys and young men were forced to leave. If this were all we knew about polygamy, rejecting it would be easy. Did polygamy cause the violence? Did the sect's near invisibility make it easier for the perpetrators to get away with it? Two popular, long-running television shows have presented FLDS in a positive light. *Big Love*, an HBO drama series, premiered in 2006, the year of Jeffs's first arrest. *Sister Wives*, a TLC reality show, ran from 2010 to 2016. Some episodes suggested that the wives' shared duties lightened the burdens on all of them.

Some polygamists seem to have progressed from male supremacy toward equality. The Confederate Nations of Israel, another Mormon sect, was organized in 1977 by Alex Joseph and survived his death in 1998. Members of this sect do not fear prosecution, because each husband is legally married to only one wife and extramarital cohabitation is no longer a criminal offense. One of Joseph's wives, Elizabeth, who is not a Mormon, wrote a column in the *New York Times* in 1991 and gave the keynote address at the 1997 conference of the Utah National Organization for Women. She described polygamy as "the ultimate feminist lifestyle." Polygamy "enables women, who live in a society full of obstacles, to fully meet their career, mothering, and marriage obligations. . . . I believe American women would have invented it if it didn't already exist."[75] A critic argued that "modern polygamy takes trappings of the feminist movement but still hangs them about a world where partnerships are still defined by traditional roles."[76]

I share this author's belief that the eradication of conventional gender roles is necessary for gender equality. I have described asymmetrical responsibility as "the problem that won't go away."[77] A quarter century after I wrote those words, progress toward equality remains slow. These roles are so deeply entrenched that they resist change. But, to paraphrase *Federalist* 10, controlling their effects may be possible when removing their causes is not.[78] Elizabeth Joseph's claim to is no more suspect than that of a monogamist feminist who hires another woman to share her household duties or a mother who assigns to her daughters and sons the tasks their father shirks. Mothers like this may be generating progress. As the Jeffs case shows, abuse does occur within polygamist families, as it can occur within the alternative families I describe. But, since these arrangements are not proclaimed natural and fundamental, abusers within them are unlikely to be granted exceptions to the rules.

Conclusion

The conventional family originated in patriarchy. Wives obeyed husbands, and children obeyed parents. Children grew up and assumed adult status, but beliefs about women's inferiority to men rationalized permanent male supremacy. These beliefs have fallen out of fashion but not into desuetude. The vision of the male family herd gets in the way of efforts to end poverty. Traditional views of the family reinforce themselves in situations involving criminal behavior. Mothers defend rapist sons. Violent fathers get lenient treatment, while violent mothers get double punishment. People can, of course, form families that reject patriarchal norms. But women's economic and social dependence must end for this to happen. One way to encourage independence and interdependence is to establish a welfare state. The other way is to encourage people to form alternative family arrangements. This chapter shows that liberalism without feminism has not, cannot, and will not protect women and children from violence.

6

Freedom from Guilt?

Possibilities of Feminist Post-liberalism

"A Brief History of Liberal Demonization," a cartoon by Jen Sorensen, appeared in the *Nation* in June 2017. The first three panels show Rush Limbaugh, Fox News, and Ann Coulter hurling insults like "feminazi," "arrogant," "slut," "elites," "slanderous," and "demonic." In the final panel, "liberals demonize themselves." A dark-skinned woman and a light-skinned man are drinking coffee in what appears to be a staff break room. She reads an op-ed column headlined "Liberals, We Must Stop with the Elitist Condescension." Both recall nasty things they said about their adversaries. He groans, "Trump is our fault!"

"The Dumb Politics of Elite Condescension" appeared on the *New York Times* op-ed page a few days earlier. Legal scholar Joan Williams criticized liberals for slighting the interests of white working-class people and using derogatory terms to describe them: "Something is seriously off when privileged whites dismiss the economic pain of less privileged whites on grounds that those other whites have white privilege."[1] Williams was not blaming the left for Trump's victory; she was suggesting strategies to avoid repeating it. I found it impossible to disagree with her. But Sorensen predicted that the column would move liberals to self-criticism. This result seemed all too likely.

The "elite condescension" argument was already old by the time of Williams's article and Sorensen's cartoon. In the weeks after the election, I heard myself and others like me described as inhabitants of a "bubble" impervious to the concerns of the less privileged. Self-criticism was easy. But my guilt did not survive my scrutiny. Had I alienated students by talking about "invidious" and "innocuous" classifications instead of "harmful" and "safe" ones? Latinate words are no problem for those who grew up speaking Spanish. What about the intellectual bullying I did in school, when "smart" and "stupid" was a popular binary and I did not know it could be a proxy for class? Most of my victims still live near where we grew up, in a state that went for Clinton. For that matter, how many white working-class people read the *Times*? I cut down on the professor-speak, but the causal connection between action and result is tenuous at best. In questioning this connection, I was reasoning like a liberal, but I was not reacting as many liberals and many women do. Liberal guilt is a familiar phenomenon. Women's susceptibility to guilt feelings is old news to feminists, who seek to understand and eradicate women's guilt. Yet guilt feelings thrive in these groups. Not all feminists are women, not all women are feminists, and not all feminists are liberals, but the three groups overlap.

Whatever its basis in fact, the self-criticism after the 2016 election was relatively benign. It held people to account for things they had actually said and done. But liberals and women are vulnerable to guilt feelings that have nothing to do with their behavior. The idea of guilt separate from action combines uneasily with the liberal emphasis on individual freedom and responsibility. Liberal feminists prioritize the individual as much as any liberals do. But beliefs that appear contradictory coexist in practice. I have suggested elsewhere, and argue here, that liberals feel guilty because they recognize their privilege and women because they presume their responsibility.[2]

Guilt and Power

Authoritarian governments find guilt feelings useful. Alma Guillermoprieto's memoir, *Dancing with Cuba*, recounts a conversation with Galo, a fellow dancer. He was middle class before the revolution; now he is poor. His homosexuality was tolerated by his society and accepted in his milieu; now he risks imprisonment for it. Almost every consumer good is scarce. Galo cannot afford to buy much anyway, because the job market in the performing arts is all but nonexistent. Even if dance companies were hiring, the government has imposed forced labor for the sugar cane harvest. Many Cubans like Galo have left the country. Why, then, does he support the regime?

> "Do you know what it is," he inquired, "to wake up in the morning and know that what you're eating for breakfast hasn't been stolen from anybody else's mouth? That if your son or your nephew

graduates from medical school, you don't have to feel guilty, because the son of the guy who cleans your building can be a doctor if he wants to? It's all because of Fidel and Fidel alone."[3]

Did Fidel Castro invent a new freedom to replace every guarantee of the Bill of Rights plus Franklin Roosevelt's four? Freedom from guilt is so precious to Galo that it compensates for the freedom from want and fear that he has lost. There is only so much any regime, however brutal, can do to keep order. Some voluntary compliance is necessary. Religions have facilitated obedience by conflating God and country. Atheistic regimes needed a substitute. Cuba followed the USSR and the People's Republic of China in substituting self-criticism for confession and in proclaiming that "suffering will make you a better Communist" instead of "unearned suffering is redemptive."[4]

Theology and law emphasize guilt for what people have actually done or left undone. Communist indoctrination, Cuban style, extended the notion of guilt to include the effects of accidental circumstances. Postrevolutionary propaganda proved effective in the short run. Taking away privileges and convincing people to embrace the deprivation by rescuing them from an emotion they had not previously felt are feats worthy of Aldous Huxley's *Brave New World*. Without genetic engineering, soma, or sleep-learning, the new Cuba instilled a morale fit for a communist state.

The psychological effects of communist indoctrination were not permanent. Stalin, Mao, and Castro may have hoped that subsequent generations would accept austerity as a given, but those hopes were not fulfilled. The Soviet Union collapsed, China turned entrepreneurial, and Cubans continued to leave, as Galo eventually did. North Korea's response to a food shortage caused by the regime's economic mismanagement was to tell people to eat less. The failure to cooperate with international aid agencies resulted in a famine that killed an estimated 10 percent of the population.[5]

Capitalist systems may not encourage guilt feelings, but guilt and its close relative, shame, can thrive in that environment, too. The economic collapse of 2008–2009 led to renouncements that suggest the power of both emotions. Rather than being imposed from above, these feelings appear self-generated. Two pieces from the *New York Times* in 2009 report sacrifices that range from the trivial to the remarkable. Susan Dominus's account of a Corcoran Group executive who decided to give up her leased Rolls-Royce, at huge cost and bother to herself and no benefit to anyone else, because she came "to feel deeply uncomfortable riding around in the Rolls, spacious and well-appointed though it may be" provided some comic relief.[6]

But when schoolteachers making "on average $67,000 a year" voted to give up their 5 percent pay raise "so programs and teachers would not have to be terminated," columnist Thomas L. Friedman found this sacrifice heroic.[7] Maybe it was. Teachers are better off than many American workers. They are eligible for tenure in a nation of at-will employees, they enjoy benefits many workers lack, and they are often unionized. Teachers' unions have been consistently maligned for doing their job: advancing the interests of the workers they represent. Did this hostility influence the teachers who gave up their raise? Had they internalized the guilt attributed to them? Guilt feelings are useful in democracies as well as in dictatorships. These feelings keep people quiet and undemanding. Whatever the teachers' motives, their sacrifice may have done some good.

But from a feminist post-liberal viewpoint, this episode is deeply disturbing. The renunciation came from members of a profession that, however privileged, is notoriously overworked and under-rewarded—a group that, in comparison to the general population, is disproportionately Democratic, disproportionately liberal, and disproportionately female. Were the teachers being heroic or being good girls? Is feminist post-liberalism about women making sacrifices?

Guilt: Fact? Feeling? Symptom?

Dictionaries define *guilt*, first, as wrongdoing and responsibility and, second, as a sense of culpability or inadequacy. Dictionary.com recognizes a third usage that it labels "informal": a transitive verb meaning "to cause to feel guilty."[8] The Maryland schoolteachers sought to avoid guilt in any or all of its three meanings: deserving it, feeling it, or being made to feel it. Galo felt he had been spared guilt feelings in the second sense; he was also guilted in the third.

Unraveling the meanings of guilt requires recourse to no fewer than four intellectual disciplines: law, theology, philosophy, and psychology. Legal, religious, and moral doctrines of wrongdoing, punishment, repentance, and forgiveness entail what the law calls crime, Abrahamic religions call sin, and I call primary guilt. Roman Catholics confess to a priest and receive a penance. Jews ask forgiveness during the High Holy Days from those they have wronged. The twelve-step programs modeled on Alcoholics Anonymous (which is itself modeled on Judeo-Christian theology) exhort their members to confess their wrongs (whether or not these actions arose from their addictions), ask "God as we understand him" to correct their faults, and make amends to their victims.[9]

Primary guilt is a fact, not a feeling. It is related to what the theologian Martin Buber called "existential guilt," which "occurs when someone injures an order of the human world whose foundations he knows and recognizes as those of his own existence and of all common human existence."[10] Guilt feelings are expected of criminals and sinners. A penitentiary was a place to become and remain penitent. Buber posited a difference between the theological and psychotherapeutic views of guilt. He described a 1948 interdisciplinary conference where "it was left to the theologians to speak of guilt itself" while "the psychologists spoke of guilt feelings."[11] This difference did not surprise him, given "the negative or indifferent attitude that psychotherapy has so long taken toward the ontic character of guilt."[12] Buber urged therapists to recognize the possibility that their patients have existential guilt and, when necessary, "conduct the patient to where an existential help of the self can begin."[13] Buber's theology differs from law in a similar way. A murderer who serves her sentence has paid her debt to society, but she may continue to feel existential guilt.

The feeling I call positive guilt is related to Buber's concept of existential guilt and my concept of primary guilt. But positive guilt is a feeling, not a fact. Thoughts such as "I should have locked my car/stayed out of the bar/left him the first time he hit me" and so forth belong with "those nightmare doubts that sometimes torment us at four o'clock in the morning when we have not slept very well."[14] These thoughts need not correspond to reality. The car thief might have broken a window; the assailant might have been spoiling for a fight; the husband might have stalked and killed his wife if she had fled. Guilt feelings do not depend on reality. Some people feel guilty about the impact of their own illnesses or injuries on their families or coworkers. This acquired guilt varies with the degree of general responsibility that individuals feel for what happens to them.

People can feel guilt about things they did not do. Clinical psychology has gone a step further, regarding guilt as a symptom of pathology. Therapists may try to assuage clients' guilt about common emotions, such as sexual attraction to one's parents or children, anger at someone who has died, or envy of a new sibling. Guilt feelings can even be a product of false memory. The schizophrenic protagonist of *I Never Promised You a Rose Garden* believed she had tried to kill her infant sister until her therapist said, "The hatred was real, Deborah, and the pain also, but: you were just not big enough to do any of the things you remember doing, and the shame you say your parents felt all these years was only your guilt at wishing your sister dead."[15]

Victims, then, need not be guilty to feel guilty. Transgressors need not feel guilty to be guilty. Hannah Arendt noted that "the youth of Germany is surrounded . . . by men in positions of authority and in public office who are very guilty indeed but who *feel* nothing of the sort."[16] Secondary guilt breaks the connection between feeling and behavior. Several types of secondary guilt exist, and they differ significantly from one another. Status guilt attaches to accidental, and therefore unearned and undeserved, privilege and luck. Galo's guilt came not from what he did but from who he was: a person with more privileges than some of his fellow Cubans. The privileges Galo had and lost resulted from lucky accidents. The usual response to unlucky accidents is some variation on "Life is unfair." Somehow, this cliché does not apply to good luck. Expecting people to accept the former and agonize over the latter makes sense only if we are obliged to be as hard on ourselves as possible. Galo's guilt is not peculiar to the steadfast communist. But a perspective less compatible with liberalism would be hard to find.

People may feel guilty about actions someone else committed or omitted. Ascribed guilt can be ascribed by people to themselves or to people by others. The individual feels the emotion, but the source of the emotion is outside the individual. "In Adam's Fall / We sinned all," reads *The New-England Primer*.[17] The doctrine of original sin separates fault from action, whether interpreted literally, as shown earlier, or figuratively, as deriving from human nature.[18]

Survivor guilt can affect those who escape disasters when others were not so lucky: "Why me?" connotes not "poor me" but "lucky me." Collective guilt attaches remorse to wrongs committed by groups to which individuals belong, even if these events occurred before they were born. Germans born after World War II have expressed guilt feelings about the Nazi regime. Some Americans have similar feelings about slavery, Jim Crow laws, the internment of people of Japanese descent during World War II, or the bombing of Hiroshima and Nagasaki. An Episcopal priest described the 1961 freedom rides as "a kind of prayer—a kind of corporate confession of sin."[19]

Ascribed guilt implies a unity of humankind through history, a collective responsibility. Feminist theorists who view women as "essentially connected, not essentially separate, from the rest of human life," or prioritize "a network of relationships that extends over time" over individual autonomy, could move from unity to shared guilt.[20] Edmund Burke's vision of an "eternal society" composed of the living, the dead, and the unborn clashes with liberal principles but no more so than this statement from the twentieth-century Christian left: "I *was* there [at the crucifixion], Jesus, as you know. I am a part of mankind. . . . I am involved in your murder, Jesus, as in the lives and deaths of countless Jews."[21] These authors do not speak for all conservatives or all radicals any more than John Stuart Mill speaks for all liberals. Some conservatives equal or surpass liberals in their devotion to the "separation thesis." But the thinkers I quote here start not with the individual, as liberals do, but with society, community, and interpersonal relationships.

Collective guilt differs from what Germans who helped vote the National Socialists into power in 1933 or Southern politicians who instituted "white primaries" might (or might not) have felt. These are instances of shared positive guilt. Collective guilt is easy for the powerful to assign downward: consider "everyone stays after school unless I find out who erased the board." People disagree about the legitimacy of the concept. Arendt, for example, dismissed collective guilt as "cheap sentimentality."[22] I wonder, too, whether these young Germans substituted collective guilt for the difficult process of examining their own consciences to correct their own transgressions.

The Marriage and Divorce of Guilt and Shame

Would *collective shame* be a better term than *collective guilt*? This question makes us distinguish between two "emotions of self-assessment."[23] While *guilted* prompts spell-checking software, *shamed* is unremarkable. The verb, meaning "to cause to feel shame; make ashamed," is in common usage. The meanings of the noun *shame* include "disgrace" and "a painful emotion caused by consciousness of guilt, shortcoming, or impropriety."[24] Shame is similar, but not identical, to guilt. Might one feel guilt about overindulgence and shame about its visible results? Julie Ellison cites an account of a student who reveals that her uncle is a slumlord and "is told in no uncertain terms that he is guilty and that she should be ashamed of him."[25]

Like guilt, shame can be either a fact or a feeling. The woman who gave up her Rolls-Royce may have done so not out of guilt but to avoid the shame of such "conspicuous consumption."[26] Thorstein Veblen's tone in *The Theory of the Leisure Class* does not convey moral outrage. Does it make a difference if we label the woman's behavior "showing off"? Whether or not guilt belongs where wrongdoing or responsibility is absent, shame can exist and has existed without them. Collective shame may be self-limiting. Some Americans are ashamed of acts they had nothing to do with, but do men feel collective shame about rape? Should they?

The Hebrew Bible's account of the origin of sin is also about the origin of shame. In the Garden of Eden, Adam and Eve "were both naked, and they were not ashamed."[27] After they ate the fruit of knowledge, "they knew that they were naked" and "sewed fig leaves together, and made loincloths for themselves."[28] The story of the Fall is problematic for feminists because it sentences women to childbirth pain and male dominance. It is also problematic for liberals: ignorant obedience is blissful, while knowledge brings punishment. But Adam and Eve are ashamed of their exposure, not their disobedience. The ancient author perceives that shame is connected with knowledge. Infants are not born self-conscious about their bodies; children learn to be.

Modern philosophers have developed insightful and nuanced analyses of shame and its relation to guilt. Two British scholars, Gabriele Taylor and Bernard Williams, draw from the classics in distinguishing guilt from shame. While their observations may not correspond to ordinary usage, they enlighten. According to Taylor, "Shame requires an audience," even if the only observer is the judging self.[29] Williams points out that in several languages, including Greek, the word for shame has the same roots as words for genitals: "The basic experience connected with shame is that of being seen inappropriately, by the wrong people, in the wrong conditions. It is straightforwardly connected with nakedness, particularly in sexual connections."[30] Both authors discuss the hypothetical example of a model who feels shame when she realizes that the artist for whom she poses is sexually attracted to her.[31] Might she not feel anger instead?

"Guilt, unlike shame," Taylor writes, "is a legal concept."[32] Like shame, it can be a feeling; while shame may be but need not be, guilt is "something thought to be felt essentially about harm to others."[33] Williams surmises that "guilt is rooted in hearing, the sound in oneself of the voice of judgment; it is the moral sentiment of the word."[34] He concludes that "each emotion involves an internalized figure": shame entails "a watcher or witness"; guilt, "a victim or an enforcer."[35]

Jennifer Manion writes about the ways in which the concept of shame is gendered. She cites findings that men are most ashamed by "failure in some task deemed important . . . and failure related to sexual potency" and women by "physical unattractiveness, and most significantly, failure in maintaining interpersonal relationships."[36] Erin Taylor and Lora Ebert Wallace give the hypothetical example of a mother feeding her baby in public. She may or may not feel shame, but however she feels, she may be shamed by observers—whether she is breastfeeding or bottle-feeding![37] Shame may not be a "woman's disease" like guilt, but women seem to be ashamed of not being exemplars of womanly virtues—even when virtues such as modesty and nurturance make conflicting demands.

Guilt and shame, then, can be facts, feelings, or symptoms. They can also be facts, feelings, and symptoms: A and B but not C and any combination. People can do wrong without feeling ashamed and vice versa. The same is true of guilt. Both emotions can be either individual or collective. I have identified several types of guilt and shame that exist independently of behavior. Men and women can feel these emotions for the same reasons or for different reasons. Status guilt is about perceived privilege and is particularly powerful for liberals of either sex. Women's guilt, equally powerful, combines privilege with responsibility. Liberal guilt is status guilt. Women's guilt combines status guilt with (self-)ascribed guilt.

Why Liberal Guilt?

In liberal democracies, privilege entails not guilt but duty. Socialist states collect taxes from the advantaged to help the disadvantaged. Capitalist systems do the same, although reluctantly, and encourage charity from the advantaged. These arrangements are liberal versions of a principle that is not liberal in origin: the nineteenth-century British conservatives' idea that "the governing class ought to care for the welfare and happiness of the people."[38] Conservatives abandoned welfare paternalism long ago. Liberals have rejected paternalism but prioritize welfare.

Abrahamic religions go further. Jews, Christians, and Muslims are obliged to give to the poor, not as penance for their sins but as a fulfillment of duties their faiths impose on them. One purpose of the Ramadan fast is to help Muslims identify with the poor. Many Catholic religious orders require vows of poverty. Not giving, or not giving enough, would be an occasion for guilt. But neither politics nor religion expects people to feel guilty for relative advantage, any more than they encourage self-pity in response to relative disadvantage.

People who take identification with the poor to extremes exist in both capitalist and socialist societies. Committing oneself to poverty is no more peculiar than committing oneself to celibacy. Peter Singer's argument that those who fail to give all they can spare to the poor share the responsibility for poverty is an atheistic variation on this theme that goes even further than religious doctrine.[39]

Lay Catholics, such as Dorothy Day and Peter Maurin, who founded the Catholic Worker movement in the 1930s, have been honored by their church. Two scholars, writing about Gandhi, observed that "self-restraint may be and has been another way of mastering the environment, including the human environment."[40] When was the last time somebody suggested that the balance of Gandhi's mind was disturbed? The frequency with which terms such as *liberal guilt*, *class guilt*, and *white guilt* recur in American discourse indicates that status guilt is a common conception among liberals. *Male guilt*, however, is rare. Perhaps men feel no guiltier about gender privilege than they feel ashamed about rape.

A 2001 op-ed column in the *Minneapolis Star-Tribune* criticized a liberal Democratic senator's statement after the 2000 election that "a Republican president ought to be able to appoint people of strong conservative ideology."

The author, David Morris, wrote, "Conservatives are driven by rage, liberals by guilt."[41] The senator's attitude could not have been more diametrically opposed to the Republicans' approach to Bill Clinton's appointments. The conservatives attacked; the liberals caved in. The 2008 presidential campaign prompted one pundit on the left to write "in praise of liberal guilt."[42] This author reviewed several conservative essays opining that liberal guilt about American racism explained the widespread support for Obama. So liberals think liberals feel guilty, conservatives think liberals feel guilty, and commentators think liberals feel guilty. As in the Sorensen cartoon, liberal mea culpa follows conservative j'accuse!

Awareness of relative advantage is a partial explanation. Public reading, writing, and ruminating require that one either gets paid for these activities (like the previously mentioned authors and their academic counterparts) or has spare time to devote to them. People who work at two or three jobs (and/or) care for dependents (and/or) fall asleep exhausted on the couch every night lack opportunity to join in. Scholars and activists are privileged relative to most people. The lucky advantage most middle-class professionals possess is not having affluence handed to them but having the opportunity to acquire it. Far fewer people are born with silver spoons in their mouths than with silver keys in their hands.

Those keys do not distinguish liberals from conservatives, radicals, or the apolitical. William F. Buckley was in no position to accuse anyone of elite condescension. He was an erudite man who did not utter a sentence without letting everybody know it. Today's conservative-populist alliance avoids this mistake. Contemporary conservatives have been known to make verbal curtseys such as "the smartest person I know never finished high school" and "the wisdom of the man who works with his hands." Antonin Scalia's dissents in gay-rights cases criticize "a Court, which is the product of a law-profession culture, that has largely signed on to the so-called homosexual agenda . . . promoted by some homosexual activists."[43] His dissent in *Romer v. Evans* accused the majority of siding "with the knights rather than the villeins—and more specifically with the Templars, . . . the lawyer class from which the Court's members are drawn."[44] *Obergefell v. Hodges* provoked him to bemoan the fact that all nine justices graduated from Harvard or Yale Law School and that southwesterners, westerners ("California does not count"), and Protestants, especially Evangelical Christians, were absent on the court. He characterized the majority opinion as "couched in a style that is as pretentious as its content is egotistic."[45] A belief that some people are better than others is compatible with conservatism. But liberals, conceding that they are no better than the people without the keys, have a hard time justifying their advantages. Once recognized, privilege is fertile ground for status guilt.

Chapter 2 provides ground for a hypothetical illustration.[46] Suppose the women's faculty organization proposes a program that allows paid leaves and extension of the tenure clock for parents of infants and small children. Helen emerges from retirement to oppose this plan, arguing that people choose to have children and that, therefore, the responsibility belongs to the family, not the institution. Rose and Violet support the idea, but Violet changes her mind. Perhaps staff members persuade her, but her objections could be self-generated. She turns against the plan because it does not include the staff members. She convinces enough colleagues so that the opposition wins and the plan is defeated. Nobody asks what decision would expedite the inclusion of staff members: the faculty burying the proposal or the university adopting it and facing pressure from the staff, encouraged by faculty. Good girls cooperate with the system again. Gender equality is sacrificed for economic equality.

Actual status guilt manifests itself in a variety of ways. Liberals begin channeling Karl Marx and turn against one another.[47] The efforts of the Episcopal Church to persuade its parent organization, the Anglican Communion, to accept homosexual clergy and bishops, met with just this reaction. A reporter and former Episcopal priest who views the world as "pretty much divided between people who have a pot to piss in and people who don't" described this controversy as just one more "political dispute between bourgeois conservatives and bourgeois liberals," among other "cosmetically differentiated versions of the same earnest quest for moral rectitude in the face of one's collusion in an economic system of gross inequality."[48] Does the author think economic injustice is the only kind that matters or that economic equality will remove all other inequalities or both?[49] There is no reason why economic injustice must override all inequalities. Who says poverty is worse than heterosexism, sexism, or racism? For that matter, who says these factors are separate entities in any other than an analytical sense?

When the National Organization for Women (NOW) became a mainstay of second-wave feminism in the United States, critics tried to make these activists feel guilty by characterizing them and their constituency as "women lawyers" and asking, in effect, "Why are you complaining when there are so many women worse off than you?" The fact that women lawyers won employment discrimination cases on behalf of blue-collar workers escaped the notice of liberal critics, who forced feminists to expend resources on defending themselves that might have been better used for improving the situation of women.[50]

The liberal guilt David Morris wrote about has little to do with class. On the surface, it looks less like status guilt than like what its advocates might call humility or its critics might call timidity. Why should the losing party cede its share of the appointment power to the president? Because that is what a majority of the people want? Morris was writing after the 2000 election, which was decided by a vote of 5–4.[51] Because the losers feel positive guilt about having lost—as well they might, in some instances? But timidity characterizes liberals even when they have power or share it. The Democrats, who controlled at least one house of Congress from 1953 to 1995, strove to placate and accommodate the Republicans: witness the Democratic Leadership Council, the firing of Surgeon General Joycelyn Elders, the withdrawal of Lani Guinier's nomination as Assistant Attorney General for Civil Rights, the appointment of moderates Ruth Bader Ginsburg and Stephen Breyer to the Supreme Court, the indifference to civil liberties, and the "war on crime" examined in Chapter 4. The Democratic majority that accompanied Barack Obama into office in 2009 showed unusual gumption.

Liberalism is committed to the idea of what James Madison called "reason in her progress toward perfection."[52] Liberalism entails the obligation to recognize that your reasoning may not yet have reached this goal. Whether or not this duty applies to public officials whose constituencies expect them to represent their interests, freelance liberals try to remember to "think it possible you may be mistaken."[53] Liberal thinkers have a hard time saying, "I'm right and you're wrong," even when they word it in gentler terms. Awareness of privilege adds status guilt to humility. Self-conscious about using their advantages to win arguments, liberals bend over backward to accommodate those who disagree with them. But bending over backward is no more productive than is falling flat on your face.[54]

Liberal diffidence has had dire results for civil liberties, especially the rights of the accused. One conventional liberal view that went by the wayside was opposition to the death penalty, which had already taken a hit in response to victim's rights advocates and the fear of crime. Support for capital punishment had risen from a low of 47 percent in 1966 to 66 percent shortly after Ronald Reagan took office. By 1994, it was at a high of 80 percent. Support declined as successive news stories about exonerated death row inmates made the headlines. A 2017 Gallup poll found that 55 percent of respondents supported capital punishment.[55] The liberal retreat from opposition removed a safeguard against a result nobody wanted: the execution of the innocent.

If secondary guilt helps explain why liberals got tough on crime, the recent history of the death penalty may call for some primary guilt. Liberals share responsibility for the debacle, at least for letting it happen. One reason public support for criminal procedure rights declined after the 1960s was that liberals seemed to have lost the ability to defend them. In the milieu in which I grew up, anyone who questioned whether suspects' rights must take priority over safety and security, or even distinguished between rights that protected the innocent and rights that helped the guilty, was considered too stupid to understand. In college, the rights of the accused were never questioned. Liberals, never having "thrown themselves into the mental position of those who think differently from them and considered what those persons may have to say," did not know "the doctrine which they themselves profess."[56]

Status Guilt, Liberalism, and Feminism

Women liberal activists, feminist or not, are disadvantaged relative to their male counterparts, but they too are privileged relative to most men and women. So are feminists, whether or not they are liberals. The liberal moment within feminism means that guilt over privilege is available to feminists. The overlap between feminists and women, and the fact that the proper subject of feminism is women, exposes feminists to the charge that they are an "elite" that has "lost touch with the real concerns of women."[57] Asking whether a particular instance is an example of liberal, women's, or feminist guilt would be a useless exercise; trying to locate and identify varieties of guilt would not be.

Should feminists hire domestic workers?[58] Should they eat meat, formalize work relationships, or compete against other women in the workplace?[59] Should Western feminists criticize Third World practices?[60] Questions such as these obsess feminist thinkers and their critics. That "no" is often the answer to questions such as these is predictable but is not nearly as problematic as the threshold question: Why are they asked at all? "Guilt, thy name is 'should have.'"[61] The popularity of discussions about what feminists should do suggests a moral scrutiny that provides frequent opportunities for negative judgments. The feminist movement that reemerged in the last third of the twentieth century included among its goals the critical analysis and discouragement of women's guilt. But feminists are as vulnerable as anyone else to internalizing guilt.

An early source of this guilt was the then prevailing orthodoxy of parenting, which maintained that healthy child development required a mother who was a full-time homemaker. Feminists recognized this a staple of child-rearing advice as a "form of antifeminism in which men—under the guise of exalting maternity—are tying women more tightly to their children than has been thought necessary since the invention of bottle feeding and baby carriages."[62] Early second-wave feminists insisted that women's liberation re-

quired a redistribution of responsibility for household labor. They encouraged their audience, which at the time consisted of middle-class, college-
educated women, to put these ideas into practice. But the early years of the
second feminist wave were "a very bad time to be in need of domestic help."[63]
Because antidiscrimination laws had created new employment opportunities for members of minority groups, African American women who had
done this work moved on. Redistribution of domestic labor within families
meant, in theory, that men and women should share housework and child
care equally.

Today, men do more domestic work than their fathers did. Most mothers
work outside the home. Some want to, but even more have to, because most
families now require two incomes to survive. Women's "second shift" remains
"the problem that won't go away."[64] Women who hire help, or who do the
work themselves, take on burdens that enable men to avoid responsibility.
But equalizing domestic labor between men and women would do nothing
for single parents, same-sex couples, or people living alone. They do the work
themselves or hire others to do it if they can afford to. Feminists do not try
to instill guilt feelings among women who leave their children in the care of
others and go to work. But guilt has entered the picture again, and feminists
are prominent participants in the dialogue.

Hiring people to do housework and/or child care usually means hiring
women. The largest employers of domestic workers are cleaning services such
as Merry Maids, Maid Brigade, and the Maids International; these corporations exploit both their employees and their customers.[65] Independent local
contractors must reduce costs to compete. Wages are low, hours long, conditions unpleasant, and tenure precarious in domestic work. Even households
that hire workers to clean a few times a month are taking advantage of unfair
market conditions.[66] Both feminists and their critics have challenged the ethics and morality of women's exploiting women in this way. Feminists strive to
eradicate the gendered division of labor. A feminist post-liberalism must take
class-based exploitation as seriously as gender-based exploitation.

Most of the native-born women for whom domestic work is a permanent
occupation are poor, African American or Hispanic, and badly educated.
Household labor is an international issue as well as a domestic one. Since
about 1990, women from Southeast Asia, Central America, and the Carib-
bean have immigrated to the West to fill the gap in the labor market left by
women who had seized better opportunities. Many of these immigrants left
children at home and got jobs as nannies, housekeepers, or cleaners.

What happens when we consider these issues from the workers' point of
view? In what sense is a woman who finds care for her own children, moves
from a poor country to the West, and gets a job as a nanny or a cleaner not

"choosing"? Yes, she is being exploited, but it does not follow that she and her family are worse off than they would be otherwise. She has probably made the best available choice. While this choice is forced on her by economic circumstances, she exercises the individual responsibility praised by both liberals and conservatives. Should feminists reject it? How does it help any workers, native-born or foreign, to maintain one's own moral purity by refusing to hire them? Most workers do not want to be stuck in underpaid, under-rewarding jobs with hard physical labor. They want to earn more, to have benefits and job security, and to have opportunities for advancement, benefits, and job security. How can household workers get there?

Women leave the domestic labor market when better jobs are available. This happened during World War II, when women replaced men at skilled labor, and in the 1960s and 1970s, when clerical jobs opened to minority women. Feminists would do better to direct their energies toward making this happen again—not by starting wars but by political activity aimed at influencing their own countries' foreign policy and distribution of resources—than to doing their own housework when they need not. Employers can help domestic workers by patronizing independent contractors rather than giant corporations and by facilitating the workers' training and education—in other words, by working against their own short-term economic interests.[67] The situation of foreign household workers is more resistant to change since much of it results from conditions outside of the United States. But why not pay for English classes, avoid hiring from large corporations, encourage and support workers' efforts to organize, and learn what factors are limiting their employment opportunities? This activism should not be the responsibility of women or feminists alone.

Much writing by and on behalf of Third World women and children has criticized feminists and liberals for condemning practices such as female genital mutilation (FGM), child prostitution, and sexual slavery. These critics rarely defend FGM and never for children; some work through local power structures to eradicate it.[68] But they have accused Westerners of trying to force their own moral standards on others, making little, if any, effort to understand the role of the tradition where it exists, voyeuristically emphasizing sex-related practices instead of the rampant poverty, disease, and violence that afflict people in these societies and ignoring the role of their own governments in perpetuating these conditions.[69]

This critique contains two distinct guilt-inducing components: a charge of cultural imperialism and one more call to replace j'accuse! with mea culpa. The Western critics of FGM and their African responders kept the dialogue spirited but calm.[70] Western critics of the critics took the attitude that Jeane

Kirkpatrick once caricatured as "Blame America first."[71] The dispute got downright nasty. It got even nastier when the dialogue turned from practice, such as FGM and honor killings, for which nobody blames the West, to trafficking, forced prostitution, and sexual slavery. Alexander Cockburn blamed child prostitution in Asia not on parents who sold their children or pimps who bought them but on neoliberal "reforms" by the World Trade Organization that have destroyed Third World industries.[72]

Some radicals have proved as reluctant to censure culture and family as conservatives are. The latter idealize the two, while the former consider them irrelevant, asserting that the cause of child prostitution and sexual slavery is economic necessity. Feminists who have scrutinized the gendered components of their own culture may have little respect for its norms or those of other societies. Anyone who has read Nicholas Kristof's accounts of Asian family behavior, let alone radical feminist analyses of the family, may hesitate in accepting Cockburn's interpretation.[73]

On analysis, much of the debate over multiculturalism turns out to be a debate about anger versus guilt. Western feminists and liberals get angry; their critics admonish them to feel guilty: "Don't criticize us; look at yourselves." But anger energizes when guilt paralyzes. Sexual slavery, child prostitution, and FGM, at least for children, are customs that all sides of the debate want to end. These customs are entrenched by the vested interests of procurers, practitioners, and clients who are silent in the debate. The practices continue while the opponents attack one another instead of working together to achieve the goals they share.

We have seen how guilt can make liberals reluctant and even unable to defend their beliefs. The feminist controversies over domestic work and Third World practices encourage modest, humble, self-critical, and conciliatory behavior among the participants. Western feminists have learned a lot about the relative merits of, and the times and places for, conciliation and confrontation. This information could be useful in other places and circumstances. But feminist guilt, like liberal guilt, confounds and weakens.

Conclusion

Guilt has a place in both individual and collective life. The capacity for guilt is part of what makes us human. Guilt feelings can motivate us to examine our consciences, recognize our faults, mend our ways, improve our health, make amends, correct our behavior, and consider the effects of our actions on others. Even when the guilt we feel has no relationship to anything we did, the emotion might still lead us to try to rectify, or at least lessen, the damage done and to make things better in the future. Unlike conservatives, neither feminists nor liberals can rationalize relative privilege by attributing it to innate superiority to others or to the luck of the market.

A liberal cannot feel guilty about relative privilege without recognizing that she is privileged. Self-knowledge is better for herself and others than ignorance. The internalized responsibility that encourages feminist guilt could motivate efforts to produce change. Do the people in Jen Sorensen's cartoon look ready to make such efforts? The instances of guilt examined here show that secondary guilt inhibits social and political change by encouraging timidity and self-doubt. This guilt turns people inward onto themselves, not outward into the public sphere. Clearing one's conscience involves relinquishing individual privileges, not working to make it possible for one's advantages to be shared.

Guilt feelings are not necessarily spontaneous. All too often, guilt is imposed from above and outside. In the political arena, guilt becomes a weapon. The freedom from guilt that Galo and other Cubans got from the Castro regime came at the price of being told to feel guilty for any advantages they retained. Liberal guilt over privilege has often been encouraged by conservatives, especially those who purport to speak for the less privileged. A feminist post-liberal approach will try both to reduce guilt and turn it into activity rather than passivity.

7

Binaries and Hierarchies

Beyond Either-Or Thinking

The human mind loves to sort. Distinguishing one thing from another is an ancient skill. We classify tangible things by color, shape, height, weight, length, width, texture, and other variables. We also classify intangibles like ideas, feelings, and opinions. Sorting requires choosing categories to sort things into. Variables, such as color and size, are complex, as children learn when they move from the small to the large box of crayons or encounter a measuring stick and a scale. The mind simplifies, dividing colors into the seven on the spectrum. This division provides a cognitive map. But it also omits things that look like colors and are called colors in ordinary speech: black, white, brown, and their combinations. While recognizing order, categories impose it. While clarifying reality, categories confuse it. Herein lie the difficulties inherent in classification.

The number of categories chosen might reflect the natural world. The color spectrum resembles the colors of the rainbow. Reasoning by analogy from Psych-et-Po feminist theory and its critics lets us posit, although not presume or conclude, that some divisions reflect the visible human body.[1] Divisions by two (from the limbs, eyes, ears?), three (from the male genitals? Would women, given the power of naming, have divided things into threes?), and ten (from the fingers or toes?) are common. Like most psychoanalytic theories, these interpretations can be neither proved nor disproved. The converse, however, is not true: abstract categories about intangibles do not mirror the human body. The soul may have two or three parts, but the brain has four lobes.

Sorting does not require rating. We distinguish among colors without deciding that red is better than violet or that green is better than blue and among animals without deciding that cats are superior to dogs or horses superior to pigs. But rating requires sorting. When we divide, we make comparisons possible. Charles Darwin did rank-order primates; later scientists ranked racial groups.[2] Plato divided the soul into three parts that he arranged in hierarchical order.[3] Later classifiers developed similar, although not identical, schema.

Gender is the oldest and most obvious distinction among living things. Therefore, here, I concentrate on divisions into twos: binaries, dichotomies, and bifurcations—what statisticians call dummy variables.[4] These divisions are so common that the theory behind them has its own name: dualism. Its opposite is monism, derived from the Greek for *one*. Rene Descartes's dualism separated the mind from the body.[5] Aristotle not only separated the mind and the body but also rank-ordered them. Monists view the mind and the body as a whole. I do not take sides on this question, still a matter of dispute. We know much more about ways in which mind and body are integrated than Aristotle and Descartes did. We may be going through a similar learning process with gender difference.

I focus on two entrenched binaries: human thought, and the mix of gender, sex, and sexuality. Ideas are often classified as rational or emotional. Gender is the first division into "us" and "them."[6] Sexual preference is a late arrival. "According to some scholars the concept of the homosexual as a distinct category of person did not emerge until the late 19th century."[7] Sex looks like a binary to the naked eye. Most human beings can be identified as female or male at birth. This fact, rather than the structure of the body, may have been the source of dualism. But the naked eye deceives. Sex and gender are not dummy variables.

A feminist scholar once asked me if an emphasis on gender equality, a central theme of my scholarship, might reinforce the gender binary. She wondered if "women and men are equal" implied that only men and women matter. Considering her query has led to this chapter. I agree that the risk she identified exists and that theorists must devote intellectual effort to avoiding it. So why not discuss human beings? Why not think like a monist? I, and others, have argued that if we do not classify and specify, we default to the dominant racial and sexual groups. *People* in Western culture too often means white men. Members of the dominant groups stand for the whole.[8] I argue not that binary thinking causes the problem but that the connection between classification and power does. Free men imposed the distinction between citizens and slaves. Adult males exploited the differences between themselves and women.

"When we use dichotomies," Jacques Derrida writes, "the two terms are . . . arranged in a hierarchical order, which gives the first term priority."[9] There are two problems with this observation: it is not always true, and it is not true only of dichotomies. Is fat superior to thin or young to old? Derrida's observation also applies to divisions of more than two; consider "men, women, and children." But binaries do encourage either-or thinking. An opinion becomes either rational or emotional; a person, either male or female, either heterosexual or homosexual. Dividing the soul, psyche, or mind into parts imposes an order that has no counterpart in the natural world. Every idea is not either rational or emotional; nor is every person either a woman or a man, either homosexual or heterosexual. Gore Vidal did not convince everyone that "there is no such thing as a homosexual or a heterosexual person. There are only homo- or heterosexual acts."[10] Experience suggests he was more right than wrong. "LGBTQ" (lesbian, gay, bisexual, transgender, queer) is replacing the homo-hetero binary, and even the new formula may exclude too much. Mimi Marinucci describes "queer theory" as an approach that "avoids binary and hierarchical reasoning in general, and in connection with gender, sex, and sexuality in particular."[11] The division of humankind into two categories by sex fits most people most of the time, but enough exceptions exist to create a contradiction between the classification and the real world. How does feminist post-liberal thought cope with this knowledge?

The Soul Divided against Itself

Mind and heart. Head, heart, and gut. Rational and irrational. Thought and feeling. Reason and emotion. These terms mix the abstract and the concrete, fact and metaphor. "Mind," "soul" and "psyche" are concepts. The brain, influenced by other organs, is the site of ideas, feelings, and reactions. "Heart" and "gut" are both real and imaginary. "In your heart you know he's right" meets "In your guts you know he's nuts."[12]

Plato divided the soul first into two parts, then into three. The "calculating" part reasoned. The "irrational" or "desiring" part "loves, hungers, thirsts and is agitated by other desires." Then, Socrates and Glaucon arrive at the idea of a "third, the spirited, by nature an auxiliary to the calculating part."[13] This part enables people to feel guilt and anger. It is proper "for the calculating part to rule" but not to tyrannize: the just person "harmonizes the three parts."[14]

Plato's pupil, Aristotle, described the soul as "consisting of two parts, the rational and the irrational."[15] When you label things X and not-X, you impose hierarchy more abruptly than Plato did. Chapter 5 shows how Aristotle used this distinction to justify the rule of masters over slaves, adults over youths, and men over women.[16] Two thousand years later, Sigmund Freud divided the soul again, into three parts. The ego (Latin for *I*) is "a coherent organization of mental processes" that mediates between the id ("it"), the unconscious source of instincts and desires, and the superego, the conscience, a "higher nature . . . the representative of our relation to our parents."[17] This formula does not mimic Plato's framework. While *The Republic* emphasized a balance among the parts of the soul, *Civilization and Its Discontents* saw perpetual tension among them. People "strive after happiness," but the greatest pleasure was "that derived from the sating of crude and primary instinctual impulses; civil society requires us to substitute 'higher pleasures' for these."[18]

Neither the ancient Greek philosophers nor the modern founder of psychoanalysis *discovered* these parts; each *created and imposed* order. We use these concepts today because they serve our purposes, but the concepts are useful because they identify what we have learned to look for. "There is no reason to believe that the psyche organizes itself in this tripartite, oppositional fashion, the ancients, or Freud, to the contrary notwithstanding."[19] I wrote this sentence in my first book, prompted by a critique of an early draft.

Aristotle, but not Plato, found women lacking in intelligence.[20] Freud found them lacking in conscience:

> For women the level of what is ethically normal is different from what it is in men. Their super-ego is never so inexorable, so impersonal, so independent of its emotional origins as we require it to be in men. Character-traits which critics of every epoch have brought up against women that they show less sense of justice than men, that they are less ready to submit to the great exigencies of life, that they are more often influenced in their judgements by feelings of affection or hostility all these would be amply accounted for by the modification in the formation of their super-egos which we have inferred above. We must not allow ourselves to be deflected from such conclusions by the denials of the feminists, who are anxious to force us to regard the two sexes as completely equal in position and worth.[21]

Feminists have dealt with Aristotle's and Freud's sexism both by refuting them and by asking, in effect, "If they're right, so what? Who says wisdom and conscience are superior to emotion?" Freud has never been a hero to feminists. Nor are Plato and Aristotle heroes to liberals. But liberalism did adopt their commitment to reason over emotion.[22] This commitment has not always worked in liberals' favor in the twentieth and twenty-first centuries.

Suppose, for the purposes of argument, that liberalism is dead. Where and when might it have died? My choice for time and place would be October 13, 1988, in Los Angeles. The occasion was the second presidential debate between the major parties' presidential candidates, Vice President George H. W. Bush and Massachusetts governor Michael Dukakis. CNN's Bernard Shaw opened the debate with this question: "Governor, if Kitty Dukakis were raped and murdered, would you favor an irrevocable death penalty for the killer?" Dukakis replied, "No, I don't, Bernard. And I think you know that I've opposed the death penalty during all of my life. I don't see any evidence that it's a deterrent, and I think there are better and more effective ways to deal with violent crime. We've done so in my own state."[23] This emotionless response may have cost Dukakis the election, if he had not already lost it.

There are satisfactory *intellectual* answers to Shaw's question, the best of which speak to the injustice of allowing people to be judges in their own causes. John Locke identified this principle as a primary reason for forming civil society.[24] Dukakis did not need Locke; he could have responded without sounding like the Swarthmore graduate he was. He might have reminded his audience, in language a child could understand, that we do not get to decide what happens to those who harm us. But the candidate's failure to answer the question well was not as disturbing from a liberal viewpoint as the fact that the answer mattered so much. Passion had preempted reason as a guide to policy making. Worse still was the fact that the question was asked at all. Privacy and good taste aside, the question presumed that the appropriate way to think about crime is to inquire how victims and survivors feel, to give over public decisions to those least able to make them objectively. While there is no obvious reason that a legal system could not be organized around such questions, the result would not resemble Anglo-American jurisprudence, and the underlying principles would not be liberal. The commitment to reason over emotion had evaporated, at least with respect to criminal justice.

Public attitudes about crime and punishment had toughened between the 1960s and the 1980s. Public opinion polls showed that support for the death penalty for murder had reached 70 percent by 1985.[25] (Dukakis was the last major party nominee for national office to oppose it.) The "victim's rights" movement had won significant victories, the most prominent being the recall of three members of California's supreme court in 1986 for voting to reverse death penalty decisions.[26]

People who remained opposed to capital punishment—and 30 percent of the population was thirty million in real numbers—seemed incapable of responding to appeals to emotion. The death penalty became so popular that prosecutors sought it in cases where evidence of guilt was weak, juries imposed it with minimal analysis of the evidence, and courts relaxed their vigilance. As a result, defendants have been sentenced to death for crimes they did not commit. The debate over capital punishment no longer presumes that verdicts are accurate. The fact that support for the death penalty now ranges between 49 and 55 percent indicates a greater awareness of these problems.[27]

Among feminists, no consensus exists either on criminal justice or on the relative importance of reason and emotion. Women might fear becoming victims more than they fear becoming suspects and might consider private violence a greater danger than public punishment, but feminists were not prominent in the twentieth-century victims' rights movement.[28] Feminists have also found reason a useful tool for exposing the irrationality of male supremacy. But feminists rarely discount emotion. Feminists are well equipped to teach liberals how to answer feeling with feeling.

Feminist scholars have discussed ways in which reason has been used to set logical traps for women.[29] One of these ways is by making a calm, rational reply to an emotional statement and refusing to respond to the speaker's feelings. This is what Dukakis did in the debate. He changed the subject, turning a question about grief and anger into a question about deterrence. His performance resembled the game of Corner from transactional analysis:

> Little girl: "Mommy, do you love me?"
> Mother: "What is love?"
> This answer leaves the child with no direct recourse.
> She wants to talk about mother, and mother switches the subject to philosophy, which the little girl is not equipped to handle.[30]

The game is not limited to interchanges between adults and children. Dukakis's response was liberal in two important respects. It not only ranked reason above emotion as a tool for deciding policy issues but also implied that engaging with emotions was be beneath his dignity. Dukakis implied that he handled the question in the right way and that supporters of the death penalty handled it in the wrong way. Whatever the effect of this maneuvering on the results of the 2016 election, this common liberal practice of assuming intellectual superiority has proved fatal to liberal causes.[31]

Nothing is inherently masculine about Corner, but I venture a guess that most women recognize this game from the viewpoint of the victim. The mother's superior knowledge enables her to play Corner, just as Dukakis's skills and resources enabled him to change the subject to one he was better equipped to handle. I sympathize with him. But my career ambitions have not required the approval of voters who insist that I feel their pain, even their vicarious pain. Why have liberals not learned how to appeal to the emotions? This skill is not difficult to acquire. High school debaters learn it. If families of victims got to tell their stories, why did families of death row inmates not tell about futile efforts to get help for them? Feminists might have been able to convince liberals that this strategy was worth the effort; it beat giving up.

Art, Literature, and Cultural Appropriation

My discussion of capital punishment shows how emotion took over reason in political discourse and how defenders of reason failed to respond to emotions. But aesthetic discourse recognizes that texts can have meanings other than what their creators intend. Novelists, artists, and poets do not rank-order thought, feeling, and impulse and need not distinguish among them. They use their egos to reach the id and superego, their calculating minds to reach spirit and desire. Their audiences and their critics expect them to. The creator's identity matters in a way that it does not in the social sciences. But cultural discourse suffers from the failure to make distinctions. Thought and feeling become confused in art and literature as they do in politics. The dispute over cultural appropriation gives ample evidence of this confusion.

In ordinary language, to "appropriate" something is to "to take or make use of" it "without authority or right."[32] The corresponding tort, "misappropriation," is the use of another's name or likeness without permission. These definitions presume the existence of private property. The idea of cultural appropriation breaks that nexus. The *Cambridge English Dictionary* defines cultural appropriation as "the act of taking or using things from a culture that is not your own, especially without showing that you understand or respect this culture."[33]

What do we know about cultural appropriation? Like sexual harassment, it existed long before it was named. Any creation that deals with human beings—dead or alive, real or fictional—other than the creator appropriates. There is a long history of appropriation without respect or understanding of the culture in question. One-ups have appropriated from one-downs: colonists from natives, free people from slaves, Caucasians from African and Native Americans, men from women. After all, it is the privileged who get to do most of the creating.[34]

Helen Bannerman, a Scotswoman who had lived in South India, published the children's book *Little Black Sambo* in 1899. The book provoked controversy as early as 1932, when Langston Hughes called it a typical "pickaninny" story, "amusing undoubtedly to the white child, but like an unkind word to one who has known too many hurts to enjoy the additional pain of being laughed at."[35] Joel Chandler Harris, a white southerner, created Uncle

Remus, a plantation slave who told stories about B'rer Rabbit and B'rer Fox.[36] The 1946 film *Song of the South* was based on these stories. *Amos and Andy*, broadcast on radio from 1928 to 1960, featured two white writer-actors, Freeman Gosden and Charles Correll, who voiced working-class black characters.

The children's stories remain popular, but Sambo became Babaji.[37] *Amos and Andy* became a television show with an African American cast between 1951 and 1953. Ezra Jack Keats, a twentieth-century author and illustrator, earned praise for his portrayals of African American children.[38] Web searches turned up no accusations against him. Since his death in 1983, his reputation has not suffered, and his books are still popular. Would a twenty-first-century white author be as free or as lucky?

Men writing from women's viewpoints, and women from men's, is so common that it long ago ceased to surprise readers. But consider D. H. Lawrence's description of a woman's orgasm:

> She could only wait, wait and moan in spirit as she felt him withdrawing, withdrawing and contracting, coming to the terrible moment when he would slip out of her and be gone. Whilst all her womb was open and soft, and softly clamouring, like a sea-anemone under the tide, clamouring for him to come in again and make a fulfillment for her. She clung to him unconscious in passion, and he never quite slipped from her, and she felt the soft bud of him within her stirring and strange rhythms flushing up into her with a strange rhythmic growing motion, swelling and swelling till it filled all her cleaving consciousness, and then began again the unspeakable motion that was not really motion, but pure deepening whirlpools of sensation swirling deeper and deeper through all her tissue and consciousness, till she was one perfect concentric fluid of feeling, and she lay there crying in unconscious inarticulate cries.[39]

Lady Chatterley's Lover is a classic of erotic fiction. Its author died in 1930, so readers cannot find out what he intended to do. Lawrence, a champion of the id, aroused lust and empathy. But he also combined "the myth of the vaginal orgasm" and the myth of the "sacred penis."[40] We know better now, thanks to feminists and sexologists. Writing in a woman's voice, Lawrence set up a false ideal against which women might compare themselves. Male readers might do the same, but the author lacks the authority over them that men have over women in male supremacist society.

Unlike Lawrence, Philip Roth faced charges of misogyny in his lifetime. He denied them and expressed empathy for characters "whom [he] identified with strongly and, as it were, imagined [himself] into, while [he] was working."[41] These characters include a single mother who thinks "she was not mean, bitchy, immoral, selfish, stupid, and dishonest . . . it could not be she who was the betrayer of their children—not so long as she was as harried and unhappy as she was."[42] Readers have found this portrayal sympathetic, but it can also be read as self-imposed martyrdom. Cultural appropriation can be good or bad, but it is not new. I examine three twenty-first-century examples involving a white novelist, a white artist, and a white poet. Two of these creators are women. So are most of their critics.

Kathryn Stockett published *The Help* in 2009. The novel became a best seller and a hit Academy Award–winning film. Both book and film won the acclaim of the critical establishment but produced passionate attacks from African Americans. It is not hard to see why. Set in Jackson, Mississippi, in the 1960s, the book is narrated in the first person by two black domestic workers and one white aspiring writer. The workers speak black vernacular; the writer, Standard English. Stockett implies that she identifies with all three women, but she did not convince her critics. The characters' names— Aibiline, Minny, and Miss Skeeter—imply that she assumes the viewpoint of the workers, but her alter ego is the white narrator. She displayed a tin ear in interviews: "My own maid didn't really care for it too much, she said it hit a little too close to home for her." Duchess Harris quotes this remark in her article "Kathryn Stockett Is Not My Sister and I Am Not Her Help."[43] What I read as empathy, others read as condescension.

Open Casket, an abstract painting by Dana Schutz, depicts a notorious lynching. Emmett Till, a fourteen-year-old visiting Mississippi from Chicago, was maimed and murdered in 1955 for allegedly whistling at a white woman, who later admitted she lied. His mother, Mamie Mobley, had an open-casket funeral. The painting was hung at the 2017 Whitney Biennial in New York. Schutz said, "I don't know what it is like to be black in America. But I do know what it is like to be a mother. Emmett was Mamie Till's only son. The thought of anything happening to your child is beyond comprehension. Their pain is your pain."[44]

Some critics would have none of it. Hannah Black, a British artist of African descent, demanded that the painting be destroyed. "The subject matter is not Schutz's. The painting must go."[45] A white observer insisted, "'Being a mother' doesn't hold water. Schutz may carry a concern for her children's safety, but has she had 'The Talk' about what to do if stopped by a police officer?"[46] Josephine Livingstone and Lovia Gyarkye "pointed out that black suffering is not a material that white artists can just make use of, like oil paint or videotape." Schutz, they insisted, showed "not only a tone-deafness toward the history of his murder, but an ignorance of the history of white women's speech in that murder."[47]

Poets are more vulnerable than novelists and artists. No one gets rich or even makes a living selling poetry. Anders Carlson-Wee, an M.F.A. candidate in poetry at Vanderbilt University, has published his first book of poems and has won several awards. Here is an excerpt from "How-To," published in a radical magazine, the *Nation*: "Don't say homeless, they know you is. . . . If you're crippled don't flaunt it."[48] The outcry was immediate. A tweet from Roxane Gay, a prominent African American scholar-writer, told white authors to "stay in their lane."[49] Another reader found the poem's "sloppy handling of disability . . . demeaning to those who daily inhabit these bodies and circumstances." A third called the *Nation* "a place so white in its leadership and readership it blinds" without "accountability for the history of how those words appear on the page."[50]

Carlson-Wee issued a public apology, as did Stephanie Burt and Carmen Gimenez Smith, the editors who accepted "How-To": "We made a serious mistake by choosing to publish" it. "When we read the poem, we took it as a profane, over-the-top attack on the ways in which the members of many groups are asked—or required—to perform the work of marginalization. We can no longer read the poem in that way."[51] They revisited this theme in the next issue: "We listened, and we saw the ways in which this poem might be read by physically disabled, or displaced, or chronically ill readers."[52] Emotion defeated reason.

Accusations of cultural appropriation are easy to dismiss, to mock, and to nitpick to death. At its worst, the charge is a crude claim to intellectual property: this subject matter and this style belong to *us*, not *you*. Livingston and Gyarkye begged the crucial question by assuming rather than arguing that Emmett Till's mother is not a proper subject for a white artists. These authors assumed the authority to tell Schutz whom she should identify with and what her attitude should be. Duchess Harris refuted her own thesis that *The Help* "isn't for Black women at all" by discussing the insights she got from the novel.[53]

Historian Joan Scott condemned the *Nation*'s "craven apology," while Katha Pollitt, a *Nation* insider, called it "histrionic and self-abasing and embarrassing."[54] A former poetry editor of the magazine "was deeply disturbed by this episode, which touches on a value that is precious to me and to a free society: the freedom to write and to publish views that may be offensive to some readers."[55]

Skeptics can ask hostile questions: How much must creator and subject have in common to legitimize appropriation? Race alone, race and gender, or race, gender, and motherhood? How inclusive must the staff and readership of a journal be to allow whites to write from African American viewpoints or able-bodied people to assume the identity of a disabled person? If we factor in class, are claims of ownership weakened? The author of "Kathryn Stockett Is Not My Sister" signed her article "Duchess Harris, PhD, JD." Roxane Gay has never been homeless.

What can we learn from the long-run results of cultural appropriation? Whatever we think of Lawrence's assuming Lady Chatterley's voice, he helped set in motion a process that enabled authors of all genders and preferences to write explicitly about sex. Mammy's dialect in *Gone with the Wind*—"Yo kain sho yo buzzom befo' three o'clock an' dat dress ain' got no neck an' no sleeves"—is painful to read and hear now. Margaret Mitchell assumed Scarlett O'Hara's voice, not Mammy's.[56] But Hattie McDaniel became the first African American actor to win an Academy Award. McDaniel and Mitchell joined Bannerman, Harris, Gosden, and Correll in setting in motion a process that resulted in more opportunities for members of racial and ethnic minorities. *Gone with the Wind* enabled Alice Randall to write *The Wind Done Gone.*[57] Literature and art are not zero-sum games. Alice Childress published *Like One of the Family*[58] fifty years before *The Help* appeared. Childress did not get nearly the attention Stockett did; gatekeepers, representing the Establishment, decide what can and cannot be published and sold to film or television and how it will be received.[59] But markets and audiences now exist for authors and artists who are black, Hispanic, Asian, LGBTQ, feminist, and disabled. If critics identify Dana Schutz with the woman who lied about Emmett Till, why not work from that viewpoint themselves or encourage others to do so? If teachers bemoan white male monopolies, why not diversify their assignments?

I recognize the damage that white and male authors and artists have done by their appropriations. But I think these condemned works produced collateral benefits, the opposite of collateral damage.[60] Commitment to rehabilitation of the disabled was a collateral repair of the Civil War and World War I, the GI Bill was a collateral benefit of World War II, and if Émile Durkheim was right, social solidarity is a collateral benefit of crime.[61] The benefits of racist and sexist art and literature do not outweigh the results any more than the benefits of crime compensate for its effects, but failure to acknowledge collateral benefits will limit our analysis.

No critic has yet made a persuasive case against cultural appropriation. Pointing out errors in these arguments is the intellectual duty of the active reader. To refrain from doing so would be condescending and patronizing. But, as with the death penalty, abstract reasoning is not enough. The notion that whites should not assume black viewpoints in a racist culture is an opinion. The anger, alienation, and disgust these works have produced are facts. Defenders of cultural appropriation must deal with these facts and engage with the critics. Playing Corner, with its premise of intellectual superiority, is a move to avoid. However we may answer the critics, we may not convince them.

The poetry editors of the *Nation* were right to revisit "How-To." But they were wrong to apologize. That action was a retreat similar to the retreat of the neoliberals who got tough on crime, weakening their own political base and abandoning the defense of human rights.[62]

The disability issues raised in the discussion of the poem provide more insight into the tangled relationship of reason and emotion. Chapter 2 suggests a hypothetical example. Adam, an assistant professor, uses a wheelchair, lives independently, and works in an accessible building. He is offered more help than he needs. Faculty, staff, and students like him. He rarely mentions his disability except to make a joke. Many praise his "positive attitude," his lack of self-pity, and the absence of a chip on his shoulder. Far from fancying slights, he ignores real ones. Parents, teachers, and therapists taught him to hold himself to high standards, not to use his disability as an excuse, and not to allow the possibility of biased treatment to enter his head. They acted as gatekeepers presenting the "right" approach to disability. Adam learned to focus on what he could change. He learned to let emotion dictate what he allowed himself to think. He became a liberal capitalist hero.

Adam is up for tenure and promotion this year. His chances look good. His teaching meets department norms. His publication record is at least as good as recent successful candidates and better than some. He got a strong majority vote in the department and the head's approval. But the college vetoed the department's decision. Adam will lose his job. Some department faculty accept the dean's explanation that the times call for more rigorous review. Some never question power. But Rose and Violet believe his disability influenced the decision and have told Adam so. To convince a lawyer to take his case, he must go back over the last five years and think with a chip on his shoulder, asking questions he has refused to ask—for example, "Would my teaching evaluation scores have been higher if I were not disabled?" and "Should I have asked for help to attend events at inaccessible sites?" The placidity that has served his interests now looks like denial.

A factual version of this quandary appeared in a 2017 *New York Times* column. A former Southern Baptist minister recalled the first time someone called him a "nigger" at church camp. "I complained to a counselor who suggested I pray for the ability to turn the other cheek. Since then, I have done just that and more." But when the Southern Baptist Convention defeated a resolution denouncing "the racial bigotries of the so-called 'alt-right'" and expelled activists for LGBTQ rights, he resigned his ordination.[63] His assumption of responsibility had expired in the face of repeated insults. His intellect defeated his attitude. He had done the same thing again and again, but he stopped expecting different results.

Gender, Sex, and Sexuality

Sex and *gender* are not synonyms, but their meanings overlap. *Female* and *male* are not synonyms for *feminine* and *masculine*. The first pair indicates sex; the second, gender. Purists and scientists insist that *sex* means the biological facts that make a person female or male, while *gender* indicates the behaviors and attitudes that show that a person is feminine or masculine. The word *gender* is often followed by words such as *roles*, *attributes*, or *expectations*. But in ordinary language, phrases such as *sex roles* are common. Confusion abounds.

"The Story of X," which dates from the 1970s, may help clarify matters.

> Once upon a time, a Baby named X was born. It was named X so that nobody could tell whether it was a boy or a girl. Its parents could tell, of course, but they couldn't tell anybody else. . . . You see, it was all part of a very important Secret Scientific Xperiment. . . . Long before Baby X was born, the smartest scientists had to work out the secret details of the Xperiment and to write the Official Instruction Manual in secret code for Baby X's parents, whoever they were. These parents had to be selected very carefully.[64]

These parents, Ms. and Mr. Jones, called the baby "X" and referred to the baby as "it." They "promised to take turns holding X, feeding X, and singing X to sleep." When X started school, things went badly until the child's friendliness and androgynous skill set won over its classmates and teachers. "Really funny things began to happen." A girl classmate insisted on wearing red-and-white-checked overalls like X's. An athletic boy "started wheeling his little sister's doll carriage around the football field."[65]

The parents of opposite-sex twins insisted

> that X was a 'bad influence.' The Joneses, they said, should be forced to tell whether X was a boy or a girl. . . . If the Joneses refused to tell, the parents said, then X must take an Xamination. An Impartial Team of Xperts would Xtract the secret. Then X would start obeying all the old rules. Or else. And if X turned out to be some kind of mixed-up misfit, then X must be Xpelled from school. Immediately![66]

This successful demand backfired. The team of experts found X "just about the *least* mixed-up child we've ever Xamined! . . . [B]y the time it matters which sex X is, it won't be a secret anymore!"[67]

What if? This story is utopian science fiction written for adults to read to children. Most science fiction for children targets readers, not listeners. The advanced reproductive technology and pervasive official control are familiar themes of adult dystopian fiction; Aldous Huxley's *Brave New World* is the obvious example. But Ursula LeGuin dissociated reproduction from sex in *The Left Hand of Darkness*, a classic of feminist science fiction published three years before this story.[68] The roles and expectations seem outdated now; twenty-first-century children in North America wear pants more often than dresses.

X has sex but not gender. Cynics can imagine other scenarios. X might be ordinary, and the class bullies might attack, strip, and expose it. Not everyone would agree that people do not need gender until they are sexually mature. The Baby X story encourages us to imagine a future where society accommodates gender fluidity. But gender is not infinitely flexible. Arbitrary sexual reassignment has been tried, with disastrous results. A few boys whose penises were damaged were raised as girls. The most notorious case involved David Reimer, who fell into the hands of psychologist John Money. He arranged for the infant to have reassignment surgery and instructed his parents to treat him like a girl and reward feminine behavior. Money "published fraudulent articles about the great success of this experiment, thereby encouraging others to attempt similar therapies which damaged thousands of people." After a childhood "filled with rage and misery," Reimer had penile reconstruction and lived as a man until he committed suicide.[69] One more example of expert abuse that taught a needed lesson at a formidable price.[70]

Usually, a newborn's sex is obvious. But intersex, a condition in which an individual combines female and male DNA and/or primary and/or secondary sexual characteristics, does occur. In ambiguous cases, karyotyping, a blood test, will identify chromosomes. Most females have two X chromosomes. Most males, including the reassigned boys, have one X and one Y. Karyotyping also reveals any of several variations, rarely evident at birth. Women with Turner Syndrome have only one X chromosome or a healthy X and a damaged X. Most do not menstruate and are infertile. Women with XXX, or trisomy, may have no abnormalities. Klinefelter Syndrome affects men with XXY, who often have small testes and are infertile. These conditions carry heightened risks of physical and mental impairment. They are usually not diagnosed until symptoms appear—for example, when an adolescent girl does not start puberty. A man with Klinefelter Syndrome who does not try to father a child may never know he has it. These conditions are rare. Fewer than two hundred thousand cases of Turner Syndrome are diagnosed in the United States a year; the numbers for Klinefelter Syndrome are similar.[71] What are the social, psychological, and political costs of branding so many people, some too young to function sexually, as "abnormal"?

Some people whose biological sex is unambiguous reject their gender assignment, wholly or in part. Genderqueer people identify with neither sex. Genderfluid people vary the way they present themselves, perhaps wearing a skirt one day and slacks the next.[72] Cross-dressers or transvestites sometimes dress to confuse onlookers and sometimes not, as in drag shows. Gender dysphoria or gender identity disorder (GID), a feeling that one has been assigned to the wrong sex despite contrary anatomical evidence, is usually self-diagnosed. Some people seek medical treatment to become transgender.[73] When GID is defined as a mental illness, health insurance may pay for treatment.

Hormones can raise or lower the pitch of the voice or produce body hair and male-pattern baldness. Electrolysis can remove body hair. Breasts can be enlarged or reduced. Surgery can remove organs and construct new ones—for example, a clitoris from the skin of the penis. Complex construction enables trans men to have erections and trans women to have orgasms.[74] Some trans people forgo bottom surgery. Sex reassignment is not obvious to the casual observer unless the reassigned person wants it to be.

Reassignment procedures, especially surgery and medication, are painful, debilitating, and risky. We do not yet know what the effects of long-term hormone doses of the strength required to feminize men or masculinize women are. But many other things people do, such as bear children, run marathons, study ballet, or climb mountains, carry risk and cause pain, suffering, and weakness. Society does not consider these activities unhealthy. The relationship between transsexualism and capitalism is problematic. People without funds or insurance rarely have access to treatment. Hospitals, doctors, and Big Pharma can seize opportunities to put profit ahead of patients' welfare.[75] Few Americans consider these activities signs of pathology.

Christine Jorgensen, the first American to undergo reassignment surgery, essentially became a professional trans woman after she returned to the United States from Denmark in 1952. Many regarded her as a freak, but she did not internalize that judgment. Ophthalmologist and tennis player Richard Raskind, who became Renee Richards in 1975, was barred from competition after she refused to take the test required of all women players. She sued and won reinstatement. Like Jorgensen, she was ridiculed. Both women wrote their memoirs, inviting exposure that benefited later trans people.[76] Unlike the first homosexuals who came out, the first transgender people lacked a supportive community. Those transgender communities exist now. Some trans people, like some homosexuals, reject activism, when they can, and prefer to lead ordinary lives. They still face condemnation and ostracism. "Bathroom bills" requiring people to use the facilities for their biological sex reflect a fear that trans women would assault girls. This outcome is no more likely than gay teachers' assaulting their pupils.[77]

There are more trans women than trans men. My first reaction to this knowledge from my cisgender perspective was that something must be wrong with any man who wanted to be a woman. Then I began reading. Primary and secondary sources tell a similar story. A boy wants to dress and behave like a girl. There are still enough girlish outfits and practices for boys to imitate. This desire does not go away. Deirdre McCloskey did this in secret,[78] other boys and men got caught, but Andrew Solomon interviewed twenty-first-century parents who accepted it, sometimes with misgivings. Their children seemed happier after they took girls' names and wore girls' clothing.[79] Reading these sources and getting to know trans women convinced me that they were neither sicker nor healthier than anyone else.

Transgender people may be heterosexual, gay, lesbian, queer, or any combination. Some reject labels like dysphoria and GID, with their connotations of pathology. Living in the "wrong" gender has led to diagnosable mental illness, addiction, and suicide, but we do not know how much pathology comes from within and how much from without: punishment, alienation, ridicule, ostracism, discrimination, and so on. Some people who undergo reassignment regret it later. The psychotherapeutic establishment is divided on whether trans people are normal or deviant. There is no evidence of any physical characteristic that trans people share and no cisgender people have. Given the politics involved, research is not likely. Even if transgender status were abnormal, what would be lost by stigmatizing it or gained by accepting it?

Some feminists distrust transsexualism. Janice G. Raymond's influential book *The Transsexual Empire* was first published in 1979. In her introduction to the second edition, she writes, "The title was meant to convey the primary thesis that transsexualism constitutes a sociopolitical program that is undercutting the movement to eradicate sex-role stereotyping and oppression in this culture."[80] It also conveys a suspicion of what we now call cultural appropriation. The tendency of trans women to conform to gender stereotypes that many feminists reject reinforces this position, which has neither been supported or refuted. Some question the authenticity of a woman who was not a girl, who never had "the Talk" with her mother about avoiding sexual assault.[81] But, on the other hand, cisgender women might have something to learn from people who have lived as men.

"There is no reason to believe that homosexuality itself would ever have kept anyone from full participation in society."[82] But bigotry, fear, and ignorance have and often still do. Chapter 1 discusses how feminists and liberals accepted homosexuality as normal and increased their political strength. I wrote the quoted sentence in 1983, when the hetero-homosexual binary was still dominant and the recurring estimate of homosexuals in the population was 10 percent. The LGBTQ spectrum has made this estimate obsolete, but that transgender people, intersexuals, and people with atypical chromosomes account for a much smaller number is worth noting. It can be traumatic for people to learn that a family member, friend, or anyone they see often is transitioning. Sometimes it destroys relationships: love becomes rejection, friendship becomes enmity, indifference becomes alienation. It is easy to blame individual trans people for the way they handle it, just as "uppity" black activists, "strident" feminists, "whiny" disabled people, and "flamboyant" homosexuals were blamed by people who proclaimed their tolerance.

But what is better for society: to condemn members of these groups or to accept them? Advances in knowledge confirm Judith Butler's statement that "it is important not only to understand how the terms of gender are . . . established as presuppositional but to trace the moments where the binary system of gender is disputed and challenged, where the coherence of the categories are put into question, and where the very social life of gender turns out to be malleable and transformable."[83] A utilitarian approach best fits feminist and liberal values.

How can we make gender less important? Suppose we phased out urinals and replaced them with stalls. In a generation or two we might not need sex-specific bathrooms. We might want to keep some single-occupancy bathrooms for those who fear assault or embarrassment and/or some family bathrooms for infant and child care. But the adjustments are no more difficult than those required to accommodate disabilities.

Baby X used the pronoun *it*, but the word's neuter connotation is unacceptable to some trans people, who may prefer *they*. This combination of a plural pronoun and a singular antecedent is a grammatical error that bothers some people more than it does others. I dislike it; I remain unconvinced by the radical argument that grammar is nothing but a proxy for class. But multicultural sensitivity may have to override correct usage until purists come up with an acceptable substitute. Why not avoid the construction altogether?

Conclusion

Binary thinking divides the world into "them" and "us," "we" and "they," "ours" and "theirs," "normal" and "abnormal," "usual" and "unusual." Hierarchical thinking accompanies binary thinking. Liberals ranked reason over emotion when thinking about crime, thus weakening their political impact;

they now risk doing it again over cultural appropriation. Early second-wave feminists preferred heterosexuals to lesbians, thus limiting the movement's appeal.[84] They risk doing it again by excluding trans women.[85] Men were the superior "subject," women the inferior "other."[86] The problem is not dichotomy but hierarchy. The feminist post-liberal task is to separate the first from the second.

8

Conclusion

A Feminist Post-liberal Future?

The right-wing domination of the U.S. government peaked on October 5, 2018, and collapsed on January 3, 2019. The Senate's confirmation of Brett Kavanaugh to replace Anthony Kennedy on the Supreme Court was a victory for Donald Trump's supporters. The midterm election of a Democratic majority in the House of Representatives brought back divided government. But the executive and judicial branches remain in the control of Trump's coalition of conservatives, capitalists, and evangelical Christians. *Planned Parenthood v. Casey*, one of the "perfectly liberal" decisions discussed in Chapter 3, may be reversed along with *Roe v. Wade*. The Affordable Care Act (ACA) will not be repealed—but a federal judge has ruled it unconstitutional.[1] Even before Kavanaugh solidified the pro-business majority on the court, it ruled that public-sector workers who did not join unions could not be required to pay fees to them.[2]

There are hopeful signs. The Me Too movement has deprived notorious sexual predators of their powerful positions. If this development acts as a general deterrent, ambitious men will stop their aggressive behavior or never exhibit any. Amazon has raised its minimum wage to $15 per hour for all employees, including part-time and temporary workers. If the economy works the way capitalists think it does, Amazon will have an advantage in the labor market. Schoolteachers are no longer good girls. In 2018, "a groundswell of teacher walkouts" occurred in six states, all of which achieved some success.[3] The word *socialism*, freed from its association with communism, has lost its sting.

A bipartisan victory occurred even before the 116th Congress convened. The president signed the First Step Act on December 21. This criminal justice reform bill addresses many of the problems discussed in Chapter 4. It affects only federal crimes, but it presents a model for the states to emulate. This cooperation was a welcome change from Senate debates on Supreme Court nominations. The Republican majority fought dirty, refusing to hold hearings on Barack Obama's nominee to replace Antonin Scalia but expediting the confirmation of Trump's nominees. Kavanaugh was confirmed despite credible accusations of sexual assault. He won his seat by a vote of 50–48. He received two fewer votes than Clarence Thomas, a Republican nominee who faced a sexual harassment accusation, got in 1991. The Democrats held the majority then. Eleven of them voted for Thomas, while two Republicans voted against him. Kavanaugh prevailed with one defector from each party.

Senator Susan Collins of Maine voted with her fellow Republicans. She surprised and angered many Americans; after all, she was one of two Republican senators to vote to save the ACA. Nobody yet knows how her vote will affect her career if she runs again in 2020 (and if she does not, that may be a partial answer). Her speech on the Senate floor emphasized her commitment to the liberal values of due process and presumption of innocence. Never mind that millions of people in the United States are deprived of liberty without due process of law every day. Never mind that due process and presumption of innocence apply only in criminal cases. Compare the Head Start employee who was fired because of an accusation to the official solicitude shown to many men accused of sexual assault.[4]

I do not identify the Republicans with the baddies or the Democrats with the goodies, as we used to say in nursery school. Republicans have no monopoly on sexual abuse, corruption, or dirty politics. Liberals helped create the carceral state. Read critically, Collins's speech reveals two problems of liberalism I discuss in this book: its benefits do not extend to all, and it does not protect the vulnerable from arbitrary power.[5]

I devote much of this book to defending liberal values such as equality, fairness, freedom of expression, and due process. I insist that they should apply to all. But liberal theory has best satisfied the interests of people who are free from the obligation to perform maintenance work. Men had women to do it for them. Saying that women had equal rights with men was all very well, but the division of labor and distribution of resources had already taken away their opportunities to exercise those rights.[6]

Liberal theory works for fewer and fewer men, too. The middle class is shrinking. For a generation after World War II, a man did not even need college to find a stable job, support a family, buy a home, afford transportation, and get health and retirement benefits. Now the family wage has disappeared except in the case of highly paid professionals. College is a necessary but not a sufficient condition for financial security; new schoolteachers in my county cannot afford to buy lunch. The power of organized labor has declined to the point that at-will employment is the near-universal reality. Where it is not, as with academic tenure, permanent faculty are replaced by adjuncts. At all levels of the economy, aging workers' jobs are increasingly vulnerable.

These developments were under way before the Republicans won the presidency and the Senate in 1980. From then on, the Reaganites emphasized personal responsibility, limited government, and unfettered capitalism, while the New Deal Democrats and their successors sought to extend government's provisions for the general welfare and to restrain corporate power. There were victories and defeats on both sides. Party control of the executive and legislative branches fluctuated. Divided government was the rule, not the exception. Neither party formed a voting bloc. Bipartisan cooperation was common. The Republicans moved to the right, emulating Ronald Reagan and Margaret Thatcher, not Dwight Eisenhower and Richard Nixon. The Democrats also moved rightward, becoming neoliberals, abandoning civil liberties, and supporting the Personal Responsibility and Work Opportunity Reconciliation Act (PRWORA) to "end welfare as we know it."[7] The 2008 election ended Democratic passivity.

The Republicans won it all eight years later. They got control of the federal government and most state governments. There is no better evidence of how partisan the Senate has become than a comparison between the vote on Kavanaugh and the vote on Thomas twenty-seven years earlier.[8] This episode also teaches the grim lesson that, despite the Me Too movement, women accusers get scant respect. The Trump administration thwarts environmental protection to accommodate industries, jeopardizing the entire planet. The Republicans may have benefited from the Kavanaugh episode not only by getting a conservative majority on the court but by strengthening their majority in the Senate. By accusing women protestors of "screaming," "shrieking," and "yelling," they reinforce the lesson of 2016: more is expected of, and less is tolerated from, women than of men. Whatever the results of the midterm election, at least two of three branches will be controlled by foes of feminism and liberalism.

The Kavanaugh hearings reminded us once again that violence against women is one of the most formidable obstacles they face. Intimate injustice and sexual assault are barriers to full participation. Chapter 5 argues that encouraging alternatives to the conventional family, the site of so much male dominance, could help women break a cycle of domestic violence. But that is not enough. The woman who can support her household can leave her abusive partner. Generous benefits that are taken for granted in industrial European countries are necessary conditions for women's autonomy.

Violence against women is the extreme form of male dominance. Some women and children never experience it. But no women escape gendered expectations. Hillary Clinton is an obvious example. Susan, the new mother from Chapter 2, faces conflicting work and family demands. Paid maternity leave would make these obligations easier to reconcile. Anita performs hard physical labor, experiences continual pain and fatigue, and must moonlight to support herself. Her condition will only get worse. What happens if her rent goes up or her car breaks down? Will public transportation get her to work at 2:00 A.M.? She lives on the edge of ruin. Medicaid enables her to afford treatment, but her ailments may have worsened because of poor nutrition and bad medical care. There are millions of women like her in this country. Working-class men, too, are injured by maldistribution of resources. The family wage may never come back, but redistribution will help the needy.

Government activism is one potential source of improvement. An economy organized around meeting needs rather than enabling profits would improve women's lives. The free markets loved by conservatives, libertarians, and plutocrats have worked for people like Hillary Clinton and me but not for people like Susan and Anita. It would be nice if they did, but they have not at least since the Industrial Revolution, if ever. Sellers charge what the traffic will bear; employers pay the lowest possible wages. A welfare state is necessary for equality, whether we call it socialist or capitalist, however it combines the two systems, and whether the public sector or the private sector drives it. So far, the private sector has failed to provide decent living conditions and health care. Providing adequate food, clothing, and shelter for all will reward some lazy people. The "free-rider problem" of people getting things without paying for them will get worse.[9] Taxes must rise, at least in the short run. And, yes, waste will happen, as it always has. But these risks are worth the benefits of ending poverty.

Male dominance and plutocracy are collateral damage from liberal values. The right of privacy combined with the premise of mutual consent to affirm aggressors' power over victims. Liberals' emphasis on individual freedom combined with conservatives' emphasis on individual responsibility created a conventional theory that allowed capitalism to run riot and ride roughshod. Capitalism superseded jurisprudence and theology, but male supremacy superseded capitalism.[10]

A third source of women's oppression is the American political system itself. The United States is not a democracy. The framers did not found a democracy but a federal constitutional republic. The Constitution was adopted by men who valued state sovereignty over popular sovereignty. Federalism preempted democracy. The question Americans must ask now is whether the system now frustrates government of, by, and for the people. More and more Americans answer yes to that question.

Certain constitutional amendments might be a partial solution. Overturning *Citizens United v. FEC* and imposing limits on campaign spending would weaken the nexus between money and power. Term limits on members of Congress was a popular cause until the Republicans won both houses in 1994 and the Supreme Court invalidated them a year later.[11] They are problematic because even if a majority wants them, they limit the people's power to choose the representatives they want. But term limits on federal judges, or at least on Supreme Court justices, would further democratize the system by allowing no party to control a branch in perpetuity. I am uneasy about this prospect because the debate can descend into ageism. But we older Americans vote; we are not an out-group. Is this a question for the extraordinary majority required to amend the Constitution to decide?

Congress could institute programs that help people get into the middle class. The military draft is a lost cause,[12] but why not institute voluntary public service with a civilian version of the GI Bill? Many high school graduates who are not ready for college might be after a few years. Would the beneficiaries of such a program reject their backgrounds and join the elite or work to further the interests of those they left behind? That would be up to them, would it not? Education would give them a choice.

A democratic system would apportion its legislature on an equal population basis. But every state has two senators and at least one representative. There is no realistic possibility of abolishing the states, however attractive that idea was to those who remember the twentieth-century civil rights movement. In fact, Article V of the Constitution forbids depriving any state of equal representation in the Senate without its permission. Hopeless? Not quite.

Congress can regulate the size of the House. Article I of the Constitution limits its size to one member for every thirty thousand inhabitants. Congress could set the membership almost as high as eleven thousand—not an appealing idea without radical restructuring that I, for one, cannot imagine. But why not 650, like the House of Commons, or 700? A constitutional amendment might create some interstate districts; Texas might share with Oklahoma, Louisiana, and/or Arkansas; California with Arizona or Nevada; New York with Connecticut or New Jersey; and so on. The shared districts could be created by the two legislatures acting in cooperation. This change might weaken federalism in the long run, but would that be so bad? Two-state gerrymandering would not be impossible, but it would be difficult.

While Article V puts states' equal representation in the Senate beyond the power of the amending process, nothing prevents amending the Constitution to add more members selected by other constituencies. Election from national at-large seats? Appointment by a federal commission? Lot? Choice among volunteers? The possibilities are many.

The presidential election system was another victory for the states over the people. Each state's number of electoral votes equals its membership in Congress, so every state has at least three. Restructuring Congress as I have suggested would also restructure the Electoral College and strengthen the power of voters vis-à-vis states. Direct popular vote is long overdue. This change would not transform the United States into a democracy, but it would make it more nearly democratic.

Constitutional amendments are not the quickest way to produce change. The process militates against ratification. State governments can reverse policies that inhibit voting and participation. Congress and the executive have the power to establish governmental benefits—maybe slowly, one at a time— without amendments. I do not assume that enhanced majority rule will aid feminist and liberal causes. If a majority of the people support the status quo, we will have to keep on fighting our battles one by one.

Male dominance, plutocracy, and minority rule limit women's freedom and threaten their well-being. The rights that liberals value cannot, by themselves, create equality. Instead of limited government, we need the government to use its power to enhance possibilities.

I have spent much of my career studying the ways class, race, disability, and sexuality divide women who have common interests. Now I must add age to this list. I joined a discussion on social media about using the pronoun *they* for people who prefer not to identify themselves by gender. I made the arguments I discuss in Chapter 7. All hell broke loose. I was told to "stick to poli sci" ("stay in your lane?") and "keep your prescriptivism to yourself." A prescriptivist believes that one variety of language is superior to others. I was informed that grammar is indeed a proxy for class. In some circles, this is apparently a fact, not an opinion. The message I got was that social scientists in their seventies had no business entering this debate. Several participants identified as women. Disputes over cultural appropriation also pit women against women. The scholars who oppose the carceral state ignore or dismiss crimes against women. Instead of recognizing our common enemies, we turn on one another. This division elected Donald Trump.

Hillary Clinton's detractors on the left insisted that the election of a woman president would not be a radical change. Now we know they were wrong. A Clinton victory would not have ended poverty or violence, reined in big business, or freed women. But it would have signaled and spurred the weakening of asymmetrical gendered expectations. The alternative was reactionary change, and that is what we got.[13]

In the twentieth century, feminists and liberals showed their powers of adaptation by rejecting homophobia. Now we are called on to combat intimate violence, reduce binary thinking, and control capitalism. Feminist influence can purge liberalism of male supremacy.

Notes

PREFACE AND ACKNOWLEDGMENTS

1. Guttenplan 2016, 3.
2. Graves 2016.
3. Baer 1999.
4. See, for example, Allen and Parnes 2017.
5. C. Kennedy 2008.
6. E. Kennedy 2008.
7. Zeleny and Hulse 2008.
8. Baer 2018.
9. Baer 1999, 192–200.
10. See, for example, Spaeth and Segal 1999.
11. Baer 2014b.
12. Baer 2014a.
13. Frost 1941.

CHAPTER 1

1. Sophia 1739. The identity of the author is unknown, but the tract is variously attributed to Lady Mary Wortley Montagu and Lady Sophia Fermor.
2. S. Harris 1995, 3–14, 15–43. For a pre-liberal comparison of male and female intelligence, see Aristotle, *The Politics*, bk. 1.
3. Koch and Peden 1944, 248–66.
4. Baer 2002b, 19.
5. Rousseau (1762) 2002.
6. Wollstonecraft (1792) 1929, 39. See also Sapiro 1992.

7. Condorcet (1790) 1912; Gouges 1791.

8. Hufton 1989; Roudinescu 1992; Scott 1996.

9. Burke (1790) 1955.

10. Hufton 1989, chap. 3.

11. Friedan 1963; Wolf 2011.

12. But liberal feminists devoted considerable time and energy to defending women's rights to blue-collar jobs. See Mayeri 2011.

13. Bentham (1817) 1843; Mill 1869.

14. Kirchberg v. Feenstra 1981.

15. Flexner 1971, 46.

16. S. Davis 2008, chap. 4.

17. Baer 1999, 11, 40.

18. Baer and Goldstein 2006, 18–19.

19. See Mill 1859; Fromm 1941; Riesman, Glazer, and Denny 1950; and Riesman 1954.

20. See Mill 1869, Riesman 1964; Fromm 1984.

21. Goodman 1960, 12–13 (emphasis in original).

22. Jackson 2007.

23. Schlesinger 2007.

24. Weeks 2007.

25. Schlesinger 2007, 452, 706–7, 477, 741. On Marilyn Monroe, see Reeves 1991, 319–27.

26. See Hartz 1955.

27. See Harper v. Virginia State Board of Elections 1966; South Carolina v. Katzenbach 1966; and Griswold v. Connecticut 1965.

28. Carcasson 2006.

29. Baer 2002b, 12–13. See also Harrison 1988.

30. Moynihan 1965, 30, 29, 19.

31. Moynihan 1965, 19, 29.

32. Kristof 2015, A25.

33. See Alexander 2010; Hinton 2016.

34. Baer 2002b, 56–63; Mansbridge 1986.

35. Jay 1999.

36. Altman 1982, 17–21, 223–24.

37. Massachusetts was the first state to legalize it; see Goodridge v. Commissioner of Public Health 2003. See also McCarthy 2014; and Pew Research Center 2015.

38. Jones, Cox, and Navarro-Rivera 2014.

39. Obergefell v. Hodges 2015.

40. M. Goldberg 2014, 13.

41. M. Goldberg 2014, 14.

42. A mini-convention at the University of Maryland Law School in February 2015 may have arrived at a resolution: use the "clear and convincing evidence" standard on campus and "guilty beyond a reasonable doubt" in criminal trials.

43. Ward 2000.

44. "Ecofeminism" was popular in the late twentieth century. See, for example, Gaard 1993 and Griffin 1978.

45. Mannheim 1954, 35, 38, 57, 122, 225–36, 238, 278.

46. Marx (1848) 1959, 22.

47. Lenin (1917) 1990, 180.

48. See Baer 1999, 30–38; 2005, 101–3.

49. Okin 1989, 61.

50. Okin 1989, 94; Pateman 1989. Similar arguments have made their way into mainstream American political theory. See R. Smith 1989, 238; 1993, 556, 562–63.

51. Rothman 1989, 249 (emphasis in original); MacKinnon 1989, 248.

52. MacKinnon 1987, 1989; Dworkin 1987. But some scholars persist in assuming consent.

53. Fineman 1995, 8.

54. J. Williams 1992, 2000.

55. Sen 1985; Nussbaum and Sen 1993; Nussbaum 2000.

56. Eisenstein 1981, 3

57. West 1988, 1, 2, 14.

58. Mill 1859, chap. 2, chap. 4.

59. MacKinnon 1987, 93–102; 1989, 184–94.

60. Lochner v. New York 1905; Muller v. Oregon 1908. See also Baer 1978, chap. 2; Baer 1999, 40–41; Lemons 1973; and Offen 1988.

61. Baer 1999, 41.

62. West 1988, 1, 2, 14, 10.

63. West 1988, 13.

64. MacKinnon 1987, 40, 51.

65. Baer 1999, 41.

66. Eisenstein 1994, 6.

67. Goldstein 1992.

68. Baer 1999, 42–52.

69. These ideas fit Mills's definition of grand theory, but he might not have classified them as such. He associated grand theory with Talcott Parsons, whom he criticized for "a level of thinking so general that its practitioners cannot logically get down to observation" and for a tacit "ideological meaning" that "legitimate[s] stable forms of domination." Mills 1959, 23, 33, 49. Although liberal and psychoanalytic theory can legitimize domination, these criticisms do not strictly apply to the theories I discuss.

70. See, for example, Hartsock 1983 (Marxism) and A. Harris 1990 (feminist jurisprudence).

71. See Wittgenstein 1958.

72. This may be what Eisenstein means. See Eisenstein 1994, 40.

73. Koestler (1941) 2006, 162.

74. Chang 2003, chap. 10.

75. Demick 2010, 48.

76. Guillermoprieto 2004, 102.

77. Roosevelt 1937; Lenin (1917) 1990, 180.

78. Calhoun 1851, 52.

79. Mill 1859, chap. 4; Stephen 1874, 162.

80. Devlin 1959, 9.

81. Sandel 1998.

82. C. Taylor 1989; MacIntyre 2007. But John Rawls, a frequent subject of these critiques, suggests that the notion of a human being as an unencumbered subject may

apply only to the individual in relation to politics (1993, 30–32). See also Sandel 1998, 191–95. I agree with Rawls as far as he goes but would substitute a term like *power relations* for *politics* to deal with the power wielded over individuals by the private sector.

83. West 1988, 1–3. See also Baer 1999, 42–47.

84. Glendon 1991, x.

85. Baer 1999, 5–8, 176–86.

CHAPTER 2

1. Baer 1999, 198.

2. Baer 2013.

3. Malinowski 1944, 37–38.

4. Maslow 1970, chap. 7.

5. Redfield 2013, 10.

6. Darwin 1871, 25, 52, 74, 96, 423.

7. Solomon 2012, 179.

8. See, for example, Irwin 2015.

9. Malinowski 1944, 23.

10. Boas 1908, 22.

11. For example, the indigenous people of the Kalahari Desert in southern Africa, usually called "Bushmen" or "San," do not have adequate access to water. Thomas 1989.

12. Malinowski 1944, 75.

13. Malinowski 1944, 75.

14. Darwin 1871, 52.

15. Some animal rights activists insist that scientists exaggerate the differences between human beings and other animal species and have coined the ugly word *speciesism* to describe this attitude. See Ryder 2010; Singer (1975) 1990. I prefer the term *human supremacy*. But my argument here is that human beings are different from animals, not superior to them.

16. Hobbes 1962, 80; see also Mead 1935, 3–161.

17. Rossiter 2003, 73.

18. A. Smith 1776, bk. 1, chap. 2.

19. Hobbes 1962; Rawls 1971.

20. See, for example, Desmond Morris 1986.

21. So, too, is the account in the Hebrew Bible of the fall from Eden. God's curse on Eve—"I will greatly multiply your pain in childbirth, in pain you will bring forth children"—legitimizes the real-life situation. Genesis 3:16 (New American Standard Bible). In the nineteenth century, this verse was cited as an argument against pain relief during childbirth. See also the discussion of Genesis in Chapter 6.

22. Okin 1999.

23. Benedict (1934) 1959, 234.

24. Mead 1935, xxii.

25. Mead 1935.

26. Friedan 1963, 147–48.

27. Benedict (1934) 1959, 26.

28. See Baer 1978, 190–93; S. Goldberg 1973; Desmond Morris 1986; Tiger 1969.

29. Desmond Morris 1986, 20.

30. Tiger 1969, 190, 182.

31. See Solnit 2015, 5–7.

32. Hrdy 1981, 94.

33. Bell 1992, 341.

34. Muller v. Oregon 1908, 421.

35. Muller v. Oregon 1908, 421. See also the discussion of *Muller* in Chapter 3.

36. See, for example, Barnes 1999; Brownmiller 1975, 314–18; Stross 1974; Yang 2004.

37. See Judges 21:19 (NASB). The capture of the Sabine women accompanied the founding of Rome.

38. Hudson, Bowen, and Nielson 2015, 551.

39. For definitions of *liberal* and *feminist*, see the "Women within Liberalism" section in Chapter 1 and Baer 2013, preface.

40. Sapiro 1992, xix. In fact, the eighteenth and nineteenth centuries were a particularly dangerous time for women to bear children in Western Europe and the British Isles. Most maternal deaths are caused by one or more of three factors: hemorrhage, obstruction of labor, and infection. Gawande 2007, 169–200. Transfusions and Caesarean sections have drastically reduced the incidence of maternal deaths from the first two causes in developed countries. But "a two centuries' plague of puerperal fever" began when physicians replaced midwives as birth attendants. Doctors often came to childbeds from sickbeds or even from corpses. In the absence of antisepsis and even routine hygiene, the incidence of infection rose. Rich 1976, 143. Once doctors began washing their hands, maternal death rates plummeted.

41. Desmond Morris 1986, 71.

42. Consider, for example, Maria Anna (1738–89), the second child of Empress Maria Theresa of Austria-Hungary and Holy Roman Emperor Francis I. Her disabilities and poor health kept her out of the dynastic marriage market. A respected intellectual, she served as the abbess of convents in Prague and Klagenfurt. Her youngest sister became Queen Marie Antoinette of France.

43. Benedict (1934) 1959, 263.

44. Plato 1961, 192b.

45. Smith-Rosenberg 1975, 8.

46. Devlin 1959, 9.

47. The general fertility rate in a given population is the average number of children that women between the ages of fifteen and forty-four bear in their lifetime. The term *birth rate* refers to the ratio of live births to the number of women of childbearing age. The crude birth rate is the ratio of live births to total population. Both birth rates are usually expressed as *N* per one thousand. The terms *birth rate* and *fertility rate* have been used interchangeably, but I use *fertility rate* to mean general fertility rate as defined here.

48. Mather 2012.

49. Lewin 2014. See also Basu 2002.

50. See the section "'Ahead of Whatever's in Second Place': The Case for Reconciliation" in Chapter 1.

51. Ahmed 2015; see also Sen 2015.

52. Eisenstadt v. Baird 1972. See also Griswold v. Connecticut 1965.

53. Compare *Buck v. Bell* (1927) with *Skinner v. Oklahoma* (1942). The first case upheld the court-ordered sterilization of Carrie Buck, a "feeble-minded" inmate of a Virginia institution. The second invalidated a law providing for mandatory sterilization for anyone convicted three times or more of certain crimes.

54. Baer 2002a, 178–84; Ephron 1973, 47–52; Frankfort 1973.

55. Yew 2012; Kavoussi 2012.

56. Kittay 1999.

57. Bridgestock 2014.

58. Hofverberg 2016.

59. Rich 1986, 59.

60. Austen (1816) 2004, 80.

61. Austen (1816) 2004, 8. But why should Emma be drawn to people who criticize her? Austen's novels have received feminist criticism. See, for example, Marshall 1992.

62. Patmore (1854) 1891.

63. Welter 1966.

64. Spock 1957, 570. These words also appear verbatim in Spock 1968, 563–64.

65. Mead 1954, 477.

66. Friedan 1963, 129.

67. "Spock Modifies His Ideas" 1987.

68. "Champion of Working Moms" 1995; Matishak 2015; "Navy, Marine Corps Now Offer 18 Weeks of Maternity Leave" 2015.

69. Michaux and Dunlap 2009.

70. Michaux and Dunlap 2009, 148.

71. Michaux and Dunlap 2009, 144.

72. Wolf 2011, xii, xv. See also Jung 2015.

73. Cohen 2015.

74. Cohen 2015. For my discussion of these issues, see Baer 1999, chap. 7.

75. Clinton 1996.

76. Kedrowski and Lipscomb 2007.

77. I have discussed this distribution of responsibility before; see Baer 1999, 5–8.

78. See the section "Rights without Freedom: Gender Equality versus Male Supremacy" in Chapter 1.

79. My hypothetical institution is obviously a research-oriented university. In a liberal arts college or an institution whose primary task is educating schoolteachers, Violet would be favored.

80. This generalization might not apply in Anita's case. Her male contemporaries might be homeless, incarcerated, or dead.

81. The term *Third World* has two original meanings: economically underdeveloped countries and countries outside both the industrialized capitalist world and the industrial communist bloc (Sauvy 1952). Some commentators reject the terms *Third World* and *underdeveloped* as pejorative. I reject a common substitute, *developing countries*, because it implies that industrialization is inevitable. I use *Third World* because its second meaning, although now uncommon, is value-neutral.

82. A. Harris 1990, 585.

83. Nearly 60 percent of African American mothers in the United States breastfeed their newborns. The respective figures for Anglos and Hispanics are 75 percent and 80 percent. This "lag" is a source of concern to many experts. Currie 2013.

84. The interviews conducted by Studs Terkel (1974) provide ample anecdotal evidence of the well-documented relationship between many working-class occupations and injury, illness, and even death.

85. J. Williams 2000, 2.

86. Baer 2013, 82–85; Seaman 2003.

87. Must adjunct status damage an instructor? I was an adjunct in my twenties. That is how I learned to teach. Two courses per semester earned me a living. Was I exploited? No more than my first students were by having such an inexperienced teacher. Is a little exploitation while you are young such a bad thing? Many adjuncts are not young. Some have families to support. Adjuncts who are not permanently or primarily in this market may depress wages for the rest.

88. Gilligan 1982, 74.

89. Women are expected not only to do things differently from men but also often to do more. These burdens are an unintended and ironic consequence of progress. Consider the transition from the norm that every working group must have at least one woman to the norm that half of every group must consist of women.

90. Malinowski 1944, 37–38.

91. Kay 1985.

CHAPTER 3

Early versions of this chapter were presented at the annual meeting of the Southern Political Science Association, New Orleans, January 9–11, 2014, and at the Constitutional Shmooze, College Park, Maryland, February 27–28, 2015.

1. See, for example, Article I, §§2, 3, 6, 7, and 9; Article II, §1; Article III, §3; and Amendments 4, 5, 12, and 14, §1.

2. Powell v. Alabama 1932 (right to counsel); Gideon v. Wainwright 1963 (right to counsel); Miranda v. Arizona 1966 (counsel and questioning); Brandenburg v. Ohio 1969 (First Amendment). But compare Norris v. Alabama 1935. Its prohibition of racial discrimination in jury duty had no effect on sex discrimination.

3. Brown v. Board of Education 1954 (school desegregation); Mapp v. Ohio 1961 (exclusionary rule); Murray v. Curlett 1963 (school prayer and Bible reading); Loving v. Virginia 1967 (racial intermarriage).

4. See, for example, Civil Rights Act of 1964, Title VII; Education Amendments Act of 1972, Title IX; and Pregnancy Discrimination Act of 1978.

5. Lochner v. New York 1905.

6. Muller v. Oregon 1908.

7. See Griswold v. Connecticut 1965; Eisenstadt v. Baird 1971; Lawrence v. Texas 2004; and Obergefell v. Hodges 2015.

8. Craig v. Boren 1976.

9. Marbury v. Madison 1803, 177.

10. U.S. v. Butler 1935, 62.

11. Lochner v. New York 1905, 75.

12. Griswold v. Connecticut 1965, 516.

13. Rehnquist 1987, 414.

14. Frank 1949, 161–62.

15. Spaeth and Segal 1993, 65.

16. Spaeth and Segal 1993, chaps. 6–10; Segal and Spaeth 1999.

17. Weeks v. Southern Bell 1969, 235–36.

18. Lochner v. New York 1905, 75.

19. Baer 1978, 43–51.

20. Bunting v. Oregon 1917; West Coast Hotel v. Parrish 1937.

21. Sunstein 1987, 873.

22. Rowe 1999, 223.

23. U.S. v. Lopez 1995, 605. See also U.S. v. Morrison 2000.

24. R. George 2005, 5. See also Bernstein 2005.

25. Sunstein 1987, 879.

26. Roe v. Wade 1973. See also Lusky 1975.

27. Ely 1973, 947 (emphasis in original).

28. Citizens United v. Federal Election Commission 2010; Bush v. Gore 2000.

29. I borrow the term *old constitutionalism* in this section's title from Gillman 1993, chap. 3.

30. See, for example, Epstein 1985, 277–79; Barnett 2005.

31. Rogers and Vanberg 2007.

32. Gillman 1995, 10.

33. See Baer 1983, 92–94.

34. Lochner v. New York 1905, 59.

35. Fiss 1993, 163. See also Horwitz 1992; Bernstein 2005; Baer 1978, 45–50; and Rowe 1999.

36. Lochner v. New York 1905, 61.

37. Gillman 1993, 14. See also Baer 1978, 45, 67n7; Slaughter-House Cases 1873; Munn v. Illinois 1877; Barbier v. Connolly 1884; Yick Wo v. Hopkins 1885; and Holden v. Hardy 1898.

38. U.S. v. Lopez 1995; U.S. v. Morrison 2000.

39. Griswold v. Connecticut 1965, 485.

40. Roe v. Wade 1973, 153, 163–64.

41. Rossiter 1965, 216.

42. MacKinnon 1989, 168. See also MacKinnon 1987, chap. 8; and Baer 2013, 85–89.

43. Fiss 1993, 174. I borrow the term *new realism* in this section's title from Gillman 1993, chap. 3.

44. Fiss 1993, 177.

45. Fiss 1993, 178.

46. Adkins v. Children's Hospital 1923.

47. Minor v. Happersett 1875.

48. Norgren 2013, 42.

49. Bradwell v. Illinois 1872, 141.

50. Muller v. Oregon 1908, 421–22.

51. Muller v. Oregon 1908, 421.

52. Muller v. Oregon 1908, 422.

53. Muller v. Oregon 1908, 419.

54. See Baer 1978, chap. 1.

55. Bunting v. Oregon 1917.

56. Murray and Eastwood 1965, 237.

57. Goesaert v. Cleary 1948. See also Radice v. New York 1924; Babcock et al. 1975, 277–78; Baer 1978, 111–21; and Kenney 1992, chap. 1.

58. Baer 1978, 43–51.

59. Baer 1978, 136, 149.

60. Rosenfeld v. Southern Pacific Company 1971, 1221. See also Baer 1978, 150.

61. Reed v. Reed 1971; Frontiero v. Richardson 1973; Craig v. Boren 1976, 197.

62. Weeks v. Southern Bell 1969, 235–36.

63. Brown v. Board of Education 1954, 495.

64. Kirstein v. University of Virginia 1970. See Baer 2002b, 228–29.

65. Mississippi University for Women v. Hogan 1982.

66. U.S. v. Virginia 1996, 521.

67. The gap between supply and demand is far from overwhelming. Of applicants to VMI, 51 percent were admitted in 2018, and 81 percent of those to the Citadel Military College of South Carolina were admitted. By sex, the acceptance rates were 51 percent male and 54 percent female for VMI; they were 82 percent male and 74 percent female for the Citadel. The percentages of admitted students who enrolled was 53 percent male and 51 percent female for VMI and 34 percent male and 25 percent female for the Citadel. See National Center for Education Statistics 2018a, 2018b.

68. U.S. v. Virginia 1991, 1411.

69. U.S. v. Virginia 1992.

70. Baer and Goldstein 2006, 518.

71. Mississippi University for Women v. Hogan 1982, 724.

72. U.S. v. Virginia 1996, 533, 540 (emphasis in original).

73. This is the case that declared compulsory flag salutes a violation of the First Amendment. "If there is any fixed star in our constitutional constellation, it is that no official, high or petty, can prescribe what shall be orthodox in politics, nationalism, religion, or other matters of opinion or force citizens to confess by word or act their faith therein." West Virginia State Board of Education v. Barnette 1943, 642.

74. Their staff pages are available, respectively, at https://www.vmi.edu/about/offices-a-z and http://www.citadel.edu/root/faculty-staff. The Citadel has had a woman provost.

75. See, for example, Stiehm 1981.

76. Stiehm 1981, 301.

77. Ruddick 1989.

78. Swerdlow 1993.

79. Conroy 1987, 2002.

80. Kenney 1992, 11 (emphasis in original).

81. Rosenfeld v. Southern Pacific Company 1971.

82. Phillips v. Martin-Marietta 1971.

83. The EEOC fined the corporation $10,000. But the women lost their jobs in 1980 when the plant closed.

84. Wright v. Olin Corporation 1982; Baer 2002b, 111–13.

85. United Auto Workers v. Johnson Controls 1989.

86. Kenney 1992, 15–20.

87. U.S. v. Virginia 1992, 914.

88. Kenney 1992, chap. 1.

89. United Auto Workers v. Johnson Controls 1991, 207.

90. Rosen 1991.

91. Baer 1991a, 1992, 1999; Card 1991; MacKinnon 1987, 1989; Ruddick 1990; West 1988; J. Williams 1992. But see also McClain 1992.

92. Baer 1999, 125–28.

93. Roe v. Wade 1973.

94. Roe v. Wade 1973, 153, 170, 204.

95. Planned Parenthood of Central Missouri v. Danforth 1976.

96. Beal v. Doe 1977; Maher v. Roe 1977. The court upheld the federal Hyde Amendment in Harris v. McRae 1980.

97. Kenney 1992; Akron v. Akron Center for Reproductive Health 1983.

98. Doe v. Bolton 1973.

99. Roe v. Wade 1973, 172–77.

100. Lusky 1975, 947.

101. Planned Parenthood of Southeastern Pennsylvania v. Casey 1992, 852.

102. Heagney 2013.

103. Reed v. Reed 1971. See also Baer 2002b.

104. Frontiero v. Richardson 1973.

105. Craig v. Boren 1976.

106. U.S. v. Virginia 1996.

107. "Court Upholds Texas Measure on Abortions" 2015.

108. Whole Woman's Health v. Hellerstedt 2016.

109. Heagney 2013.

110. Tribe 1990, 45–51.

111. MacKinnon 1987, 99; MacNair, Derr, and Naranjo-Buebl 1995; Derr 2002, 172–74.

112. MacKinnon 1987.

113. Wolff 1968.

114. Gonzales v. Carhart 2007, 1634.

115. Muller v. Oregon 1908, 422.

116. Baer 1978, chap. 2.

117. *Johnson Controls* is a good example. The Pregnancy Discrimination Act of 1978 was a response to *General Electric v. Gilbert*, in which the court ruled that employment discrimination on the basis of pregnancy did not violate Title VII.

118. Stanton v. Stanton 1975, 10 (age of majority); Frontiero v. Richardson 1973, 685 (military benefits); Kirchberg v. Feenstra 1981 ("head and master" law).

119. Orr v. Orr 1979 (alimony); Craig v. Boren 1976.

120. Fiallo v. Bell 1977; Rostker v. Goldberg 1981.

121. Michael M. v. Superior Court of Sonoma County 1981, 471–72.

122. Michael M. v. Superior Court of Sonoma County 1981, 499.

123. Another group of cases, involving the custody rights of unwed fathers, are pertinent to this discussion. The court has sometimes, but not always, used similar logic to reject fathers' claims. See Baer 2002b, 39–45.

124. Miller v. Albright 1998, 436.

125. Tuan Anh Nguyen v. INS 2001, 62.

126. This was not the first time the court had ignored DNA evidence. *Michael H. v. Gerald D.* (1989) upheld a ruling that removed the parental rights of a biological father.

127. Tuan Anh Nguyen v. INS 2001, 64–65.

128. Tuan Anh Nguyen v. INS 2001, 65.

129. Sessions v. Morales-Santana 2017.

130. 8 U.S.C. §§1401(a)(7), 1409(a), 1409(c).

131. Sessions v. Morales-Santana 2017, 7, 12, 13, 14n13.

132. Sessions v. Morales-Santana 2017, 10, 11, 18.

CHAPTER 4

1. See Amendments 1 and 5 of the U.S. Constitution. See also Chapter 1.

2. See U.S. Constitution, Amendments 2, 4, 5, and 8.

3. U.S. v. Rabinowitz 1950, 69.

4. See Mallory v. U.S. 1957; Mapp v. Ohio 1961; Escobedo v. Illinois 1964; and Miranda v. Arizona 1966.

5. See, for example, Dickerson v. U.S. 2000; and Missouri v. Seibert 2004.

6. Vizguerra 2017.

7. Baer 2003.

8. See M. Goldberg 2014, 13–14.

9. Barron v. Baltimore 1833.

10. Baer 1983, 57–64.

11. Palko v. Connecticut 1937, 327, 325.

12. People v. Defore 1926, 21.

13. Betts v. Brady 1942; Wolf v. Colorado 1949.

14. Brown v. Board of Education 1954.

15. Gideon v. Wainwright 1963; Mapp v. Ohio 1961.

16. Mapp v. Ohio 1961, 659.

17. Miranda v. Arizona 1966.

18. Mapp v. Ohio 1961.

19. Burns 2012; Meili 2003.

20. Armstrong 2014.

21. See Brewer v. Williams 1977; and Missouri v. Seibert 2004.

22. Nix v. Williams 1984.

23. See Darrow 1902; Quinney 1980; and Scheingold 1984.

24. As much as possible, I avoid the use of the words *guilty* and *innocent*. They confuse the discourse. An acquitted defendant is found "not guilty." Committing a crime does not entail legal guilt. Someone can be innocent of a particular act without being an innocent person.

25. National Research Council 2014, 21, 34. The statistics include all federal and state inmates in prisons and jails.

26. Murakawa 2014.

27. Gottschalk 2015, 1.

28. Hinton 2016.

29. Gottschalk et al. 2015.

30. Gottschalk 2015, 121.

31. Alexander 2010, xii.

32. Murakawa 2014, 140–87; Hinton 2016, chaps. 4–5, 7–8.

33. See Alexander 2010, chaps. 4–5; Gottschalk 2015, chaps. 6–7, 11; and Lerman and Weaver 2015, chaps. 3–5

34. Gottschalk 2015, 7, chap. 3. See also A. Davis 2011, chap. 5.
35. Alexander 2010, 1.
36. Lerman and Weaver 2015, 32, chap. 2.
37. Gottschalk 2015, 34–37; Stillman 2013.
38. A. Davis 2011, chap 3.
39. National Research Council 2014, 174. See also Lerman and Weaver 2015, chap. 3; and Murakawa 2014, 95–99.
40. Lerman and Weaver 2015, chaps. 6–8.
41. Alexander 2010, 191.
42. Hinton 2016, 336.
43. Lerman and Weaver 2015: 199.
44. Gottschalk 2015, chap. 9.
45. Baer 2002b, 180–84; Baer 2002a, 83–84, 194–96; Roberts 1997; Threadcraft 2016.
46. Moynihan 1965, 30; 1970, 7. See also Alexander 2010, 44, 175; and Hinton 2016, 249.
47. Nathan 2016.
48. Lerman and Weaver, 2015, 115–16.
49. Gottschalk et al. 2015, 807.
50. Gottschalk 2015, 196.
51. Gottschalk 2006, 115.
52. Hinton 2016, 27–30.
53. R. Harris 1969, 68–69.
54. Hinton 2016, 94–95.
55. Gottschalk 2015, 88.
56. Federal Bureau of Prisons 2019.
57. See U.S. Constitution, Article I, §2 and Amendments 15, 19, 24, and 26.
58. His effort was futile, since New York had no death penalty in 1989.
59. Richardson v. Ramirez 1974. See also Gottschalk 2015, 246; Hinton 2016, 335–36; and Lerman and Weaver 2015, 201.
60. McCleskey v. Kemp 1987.
61. Lerman and Weaver 2015, 9, 24.
62. National Research Council 2014, 135; Hinton 2016, chap. 9. A "three strikes and you're out" ("in?") law establishes a minimum mandatory prison sentences for repeat offenders. Sixteen states have these. Washington and California enacted these laws by ballot initiative in 1993 and 1994. The peak year was 1995, after the Republicans took over Congress, when ten states passed similar laws.
63. Gilmore 2007, 87 (emphasis in original).
64. Solomon 2012, 495.
65. Murakawa 2015, chap. 4.
66. National Research Council 2014, 130.
67. National Research Council 2014, 155.
68. Feinberg 2008, 624.
69. Feinberg 2008.
70. The term *incapacitation* is misleading. Only death incapacitates prisoners from injuring employees and fellow prisoners.
71. Gottschalk 2015, 184–86.

72. For works that do, see A. Davis 2011 and Drape and Tracy 2016.

73. Baum 2016, 22.

74. Hinton 2016, 250.

75. Kolbert 2016, 68; Daley 2016.

76. Baer 2013, 12.

77. Durkheim 1984, 58.

78. Durkheim 1982, 98.

79. Shils and Young 1953.

80. Menninger 1966, 203, 153 (emphasis in original).

81. Foucault 1979, part iv. Marx defined the *lumpenproletariat* as "decayed roués with dubious means of subsistence and of dubious origin, alongside ruined and adventurous offshoots of the bourgeoisie, were vagabonds, discharged soldiers, discharged jailbirds, escaped galley slaves, swindlers, mountebanks, lazzaroni (pickpockets), tricksters, gamblers, maquereaux [pimps], brothel keepers, porters, literati, organ grinders, ragpickers, knife grinders, tinkers, beggars—in short, the whole indefinite, disintegrated mass, thrown hither and thither, which the French call la bohème." This group of people lacked class consciousness and were incapable of achieving it. Marx 1852, 38.

82. Gilmore 2007, 26.

83. De Beauvoir 1952, xvi.

84. Gottschalk 2015, 196.

85. Gottschalk 2015, 200.

86. Gottschalk 2015, 214.

87. Corrigan 2006, 297–300.

88. Threadcraft 2014, 735–60.

89. Another problem with Megan's Laws is that they do not work. Adults can tell children to avoid a certain dwelling and even show them photographs of registered offenders. But predators can change their appearance and approach victims in other locations. Data support what common sense suggests. Studies have shown that sex offender registries have no effect on the incidence of child sexual abuse. See, for example, Neyfahk 2015. The apparent purpose of these laws is to reassure parents—misleadingly, if Gottschalk and Rose Corrigan are correct.

90. Gottschalk 2015, 212.

91. Stillman 2016.

92. It is also not good drama criticism. My colleague Marian Eide pointed out that William Shakespeare did not intend to portray a typical teenage romance.

93. None of the books I discuss cite radical feminist scholarship. This omission does not prove that the authors are unfamiliar with it—only that they do not consider it relevant to their research.

94. Michael M. v. Superior Court of Sonoma County 1981, 483–485, 488n.

95. Gottschalk 2006, 121–33.

96. Gottschalk 2006, 121.

97. Forman 2017.

98. Muhammad 2017, 20.

99. Gottschalk 2006, 139.

100. Gottschalk et al. 2015. But in 2018, a consensus may be emerging on support of victim impact statements. See Lepore 2018.

101. Gottschalk 2006, 149. See also Gest 2014; Hirschel et al. 2007; Hyden 2014; and Novisky and Peralta 2015.

102. Carson 2014.

103. National Incident-Based Reporting System data are available at https://www .fbi.gov/services/cjis/ucr/nibrs. National Crime Victimization Survey data are available at https://www.bjs.gov/index.cfm?ty=dcdetail&iid=245. Since any one perpetrator may be charged with more than one rape, and any one victim may have been raped by more than one perpetrator, these statistics are not exact. The Department of Justice collects crime statistics in two ways. The National Incident-Based Reporting System gathers data from police jurisdictions nationwide. The Bureau of Justice Statistics in the Office of Justice Programs collects survey data from the general population.

104. Rape, Abuse, and Incest National Network 2015.

105. Rape, Abuse, and Incest National Network 2015.

106. Dobie 2016.

107. Brownmiller 1975, chap. 9.

108. LeBlanc 2003, 405–6. For a twentieth-century fictional example of a heroic rapist, see Kesey 1962.

109. Oliver 2016. See also Bray, n.d.

110. Stack 2016.

111. "Stanford Sexual Assault Case" 2016.

112. Astor 2018.

113. Cleary 2016.

114. Sanchez and Watts 2016.

115. Chokshi 2016; "Montana Judge" 2016; Sanchez and Watts 2016; J. Smith 2016. Sources do not reveal what Blake's job was, so we have no way of judging his class status.

116. Clark 2016.

117. In January 2017, Turner was listed on Ohio's sex offender registry as living in Bellbrook. In July 2017, Blake was listed as living in Glasgow, Montana.

118. Ford 1974. This parallel raises some troubling questions. What did we lose when Ford pardoned the worst upperworld criminal in American history? Are the dirty tricks now common in apportionment, districting, and voting regulations traceable to that pardon? Will a future president make the same mistake? Did the idea that some corporations are too big to fail stem from the idea that some offenders are too big to punish?

119. "Stanford University Statement" 2016.

120. Gibbs 2016.

121. Drape and Tracy 2016.

122. See the section "Familism, Law, and Bureaucracy" in Chapter 5.

123. See Baer 2002b, 256–64.

124. See Brownmiller 1975, chap. 7.

125. Davis and Schenwar have personal and familial experience with incarceration. Davis, whose membership in the Communist Party cost her a faculty position at the University of California, Los Angeles, was accused of kidnapping and murder because of her involvement with the Black Panther Party. She spent several months in jail in 1971 and 1972 before she was acquitted. Schenwar's sister has been in and out of correction facilities for drug offenses since 2012. These books are not memoirs. Davis

presents Marxist theory, while Schenwar produces "what anthropologists term an 'intimate ethnography,' a work that explores the lives of family members while . . . 'linking the individual stories to larger social processes.'" Campbell 2015, 1043.

126. A. Davis 2003, 16–17.

127. Critical Resistance, n.d.

128. A. Davis 2003, 14.

129. A. Davis 2003, 16.

130. W. Clinton 1996.

131. Schenwar 2014, 152 (emphasis in original).

132. Schenwar 2014, 142.

133. Schenwar 2014, 153.

134. San Antonio Independent School District v. Rodriguez 1973; Washington v. Davis 1976; Personnel Administrator of Massachusetts v. Feeney 1976.

135. Baum 2016.

136. See Baer 2013, 42–49.

137. Stolberg and Eckholm 2016.

138. I have discussed this possibility elsewhere. See Baer 2002b, 256–64.

CHAPTER 5

1. Universal Declaration of Human Rights, Article 16(3).

2. Fineman 1995, 143.

3. Reynolds v. U.S. 1878, 165.

4. Public Law 104-199, §3.7; U.S. v. Windsor 2013.

5. See the discussion of anthropology in Chapter 2.

6. Engels 1972.

7. Universal Declaration of Human Rights, Article 16(3).

8. U.S. Citizenship and Immigration Services Form I-485, "Application to Register Permanent Residence or Adjust Status," is available at https://www.uscis.gov/i-485. This preference now applies to the children, parents, and siblings of citizens and legal residents. President Donald Trump and some members of Congress are working to curb chain migration by limiting this preference to children of legal residents.

9. Jordan 2019.

10. Desmond Morris 1986, 71.

11. Obergefell v. Hodges 2015. See also Griswold v. Connecticut 1965; Loving v. Virginia 1967; and Roe v. Wade 1973.

12. Henderson 2014.

13. See the section "One at a Time: Choice and Tradition" in Chapter 2.

14. Lasch 1977.

15. Elshtain 1996, 37. See also Baer 1999, 36.

16. *Merriam-Webster Dictionary*, s.v. "familism," available at https://www.merriam-webster.com/dictionary/familism.

17. See Wisconsin v. Yoder 1972. Courts have established exceptions to this rule. Cassandra C., a seventeen-year-old diagnosed with lymphoma, did not want chemotherapy. Her mother, Jackie Fortin, accepted her wishes. Legally, Fortin had the power to make the decision—until the Connecticut Department of Children and Family Services took the case to court. Cassandra became a ward of the state but stopped

chemotherapy when she turned eighteen. In conflicts between parent and child, parent wins. But in conflicts between experts and patients, experts win. See Baer 2015, 244–45.

18. Devlin 1959, 9.

19. See the section "Gender Roles, Male Supremacy, and Society" in Chapter 2.

20. Plato, 1968, 455c.

21. Aristotle 1946, 1.5.1254b2, 1.12.1259b.

22. Plato 1968, 458d.

23. Plato 1968, 461d, 461e.

24. Plato 1968, 380.

25. Aristotle 1946, 2.3.1261b.

26. Fineman 1995, 228.

27. Aristotle 1946, 1.5.1254a.

28. Aristotle 1946, 1.8.1259b.

29. Aristotle 1946, 7.16.1335a.

30. Cartwright 2016.

31. The first African slaves in North America did look different from their owners. But how did two centuries of white male sexual predation affect the slaves' appearances?

32. Aristotle 1946, 1.2.1252b.

33. Aristotle 1946, l.

34. But Europe—and Britain, as Thomas Jefferson pointed out in his first draft of the Declaration of Independence—participated in the transatlantic slave trade, the kidnapping, purchase, transportation, and sale of Africans to the Americas.

35. Cott 1978; Rosenberg 1982.

36. See Griswold v. Connecticut 1965; Loving v. Virginia 1967; Roe v. Wade 1973; Obergefell v. Hodges 2015. See also Baer 1999, 30–38.

37. MacKinnon 1989, 190–91.

38. Sophia 1739. See also the discussion of this text in Chapter 1.

39. Kulikoff 2000, 228.

40. See Rousseau (1762) 2002.

41. See the "Feminists Confront Liberalism" section in Chapter 1.

42. Desmond Morris 1986; Tiger 1969.

43. Bierstedt 1963, 364.

44. See, for example, Nochlin 1971.

45. See Patmore (1854) 1891.

46. Goodman 1960; Fromm 1941; Moynihan 1965.

47. See the "Feminists Confront Liberalism" section in Chapter 1.

48. Fikkert et al. 2014, 16.

49. Lupton 2011, 5.

50. Lupton 2011, 28.

51. Fikkert et al. 2014, 28–29.

52. See Kristof and WuDunn 2009.

53. Cockburn 2006, 8.

54. Cockburn 2006, 8.

55. Belluck 2017. However, no reliable evidence of honor killings in the United States exists. Singal 2017.

56. Kristof 2017.

57. See the section "Privilege and the Limits of Leniency" in Chapter 4.

58. Weiser 2017.

59. Woods 2017; Shepherd 2017.

60. Silver 2014.

61. Tatum 2017.

62. Hartocollis and Capecchi 2017.

63. Hager 2017. Jones is now a graduate student at New York University.

64. Heyword 2017.

65. Balakar 2017; Kavoussi 2014.

66. Yew 2012.

67. Hill 1991, 355.

68. Solomon 2012, 688–97. I have expressed negative opinions about surrogacy. I do not see how a gestational surrogate can be fairly compensated. See Baer 2013, 90–95. This objection does not apply to egg donors or to unpaid surrogates, such as Laura. I have also argued that the gestational mother should have the unilateral right to cancel the contract. Baer 1999, 55. I still hold these positions. I use surrogacy here as an introduction to rethinking family status.

69. In the Matter of Baby M 1988; Baer 2013, 101–2.

70. Peltz 2017; Weinberger 2017.

71. Cardozo 1921, 21.

72. Few-Demo et al. 2017, 89.

73. Reynolds v. U.S 1878, 164.

74. Cleveland v. U.S. 1946, 26.

75. "Polygamist Wife" 1997; Joseph 1991, A31.

76. K. Butler 2011.

77. Baer 1991b, 297–98; 1996, 318–19; 2002, 315–16.

78. Rossiter 2003.

CHAPTER 6

1. J. Williams 2017.

2. Baer 2013, 103–7.

3. Guillermoprieto 2004, 102.

4. See Chang 2003, chap. 10; King 1958, 85.

5. Demick 2009. See also the section "Ahead of Whatever's in Second Place: The Case for Reconciliation" in Chapter 1.

6. Dominus 2009.

7. Friedman 2009.

8. *Dictionary.com*, s.v. "guilt," available at https://www.dictionary.com/browse/guilt?s=t (accessed August 31, 2019). See also *Merriam-Webster Dictionary*, s.v. "guilt," available at https://www.merriam-webster.com/dictionary/guilt (accessed August 31, 2019).

9. Alcoholics Anonymous 2001, steps 3, 5, 7–9.

10. Buber 1965, 127.

11. Buber 1965, 121, 123.

12. Buber 1965, 127.

13. Buber 1965, 148.

14. Sayers 1958, 6.

15. Greenberg 1964, 238. Psychology has popularized the term *false memory syndrome*—but it does not apply to cases such as this, fictional or real. Instead, the concept has been psychology's gift to the criminal defense bar, a rejoinder to accusations of child sexual abuse when these charges are based on memories that the alleged victims repressed and recovered. Loftus and Ketcham 1994. The resulting controversy shows no signs of abating. Reconciliation is unlikely because both sides base their conclusions on presumptions that have been proved true: people can repress and recover memories, and they can honestly believe they remember something that did not happen. We do not need science to teach us that people also can and do lie. Both false accusations and false denials are common types of lies.

The use of false memory syndrome as a defense to criminal charges can result in the acquittal of abusers. But the concept itself is a sign that psychology and the law are taking child sexual abuse seriously. Psychotherapy has a history of denying and trivializing accounts of child sexual abuse. Sigmund Freud came to believe that his patients' memories of sexual abuse by their fathers were the product of unconscious fantasies. Malcolm 1984; Masson 1984. The founder of transactional analysis quoted a patient who remembered that "an adolescent uncle got sexy with her, and made her feel sexy, too"; "I knew I liked it under all the other feelings." Berne 1972, 129. The feminist assault on the status quo that began in the 1970s and continues to the present day in psychology and the law has upended the early tolerance. The discovery that boys, too, are vulnerable to abuse has intensified the struggle. A defense is necessary because people are being held to answer for these crimes.

16. Arendt 1964, 251 (emphasis in original).

17. *The New-England Primer* 1777 (1991), n.p.

18. Genesis 3; Romans 5:12–21; 1 Corinthians 22:15 (New American Standard Bible); United Methodist Church 1992, Article VII.

19. Boyd 1965, 3.

20. West 1988, 1–3; Gilligan 1982, 59. See also Baer 1999, 41–55.

21. Wolfe 2016; Boyd 1965, 37 (emphasis in original).

22. Arendt 1964, 117.

23. G. Taylor 1985.

24. *Merriam-Webster Dictionary*, s.v. "shame," available at https://www.merriam-webster.com/dictionary/shame (accessed August 31, 2019). See also *Dictionary.com*, s.v. "shame," available at https://www.dictionary.com/browse/shame (accessed August 31, 2019).

25. Ellison 1999, 367n32, citing P. Williams 1991, 17–28.

26. Veblen 1953, chap. 4.

27. Genesis 2:25 (NASB).

28. Genesis 3:7 (NASB).

29. G. Taylor 1985, 59.

30. B. Williams 1993, 78.

31. G. Taylor 1985, 60–61; B. Williams 1993, 220–21.

32. G. Taylor 1985, 85.

33. G. Taylor 1985, 86.

34. B. Williams 1993, 89.

35. B. Williams 1993, 219.

36. Manion 2003, 24–25.

37. Taylor and Wallace 2012, 76–77.

38. Beer 1969, 268.

39. Singer 1972, 1999, 2006.

40. Rudolph and Rudolph 1967, 185.

41. David Morris 2001.

42. Rosenbaum 2008.

43. Lawrence v. Texas 2003, 602.

44. Romer v. Evans 1996, 652.

45. Obergefell v. Hodges 2015, 6–7. If Scalia thought homosexual activists are privileged, he was probably right; most activists are. If he thought homosexuals were a privileged group, he was wrong; they exist in every class and socioeconomic status.

46. See the section "Where Are We Now? Some Stories" in Chapter 2.

47. And not for the first time. Liberals once defended the practice of paying men more than women for the same work on the (inaccurate) assumption that only the men had families to support. But even Marx reserved the application of the principle— "From each according to his ability; to each according to his needs"—to societies where the proletarian revolution had succeeded.

48. Keizer 2008, 43.

49. See Baer 2013.

50. Mayeri 2011.

51. Bush v. Gore 2000.

52. Padover 1953, 296–97

53. Cromwell 1650.

54. See Baer 2013, 106–7.

55. J. Jones 2017. See also J. Jones 2016. But a 2016 poll from the Pew Research Organization put the figure at 49 percent. Oliphant 2016.

56. Mill 1869, chap. 2. I discuss this more fully in the section "The War on Crime: Civil Liberties Meets Law and Order" in Chapter 4.

57. Fox-Genovese 1996.

58. Ehrenreich 2001, 2002; Flanagan 2004.

59. Adams 1990; K. George 1994; S. Gordon 1991; Meece 2009.

60. Dawit and Mekuria 1993; James and Robertson 2002; Okin 1999; Walker and Parmar 1993; Baer 2013. I explain my use of the term *Third World* in Chapter 2.

61. Greenfeld 1970, 87.

62. Mead 1954, 477.

63. Flanagan 2004, 112.

64. Hochschild 1989; Baer 2002b, 315.

65. Ehrenreich 2001, 51–119; 2002.

66. Ehrenreich 2002; Flanagan 2004.

67. Or by paying for the housecleaner's child's tutoring, as a colleague did. The cleaner's acceptance of help was as praiseworthy as the employer's offer.

68. Parekh 1999, 71, does defend FGM but only for adults.

69. My concern here is with the moral acceptability of Western criticism of these practices, not with its efficacy. The reaction of local residents to criticism may well render it ineffective. Aimee Molloy, in *However Long the Night: Molly Melching's Journey to Help Millions of African Women and Girls Triumph* (2013), recounts a different Western approach to reform. Melching lived in Senegal for more than thirty years; learned Wolof, the native language; and cofounded Tostan, an organization devoted to improving the socioeconomic status of girls and women, furthering their education, and ending FGM. Organizations such as these welcome financial contributions.

70. Dawit and Mekaria 1993; Walker and Parmar 1993.

71. James and Robertson 2002; Kirkpatrick 1984.

72. The discussion of domestic labor and Third World practices draws on Baer 2013, chaps. 3, 6.

73. See Song 2007.

CHAPTER 7

1. Baer 1999, 23–24.

2. Darwin 1871, 25, 52, 74, 96, 423; Sullivan 2018.

3. Plato 1968, 439d–442b.

4. Gujarati 2003, 1002.

5. Descartes (1641) 1911.

6. See Dickerson v. U.S. 2000; Escobedo v. Illinois 1964; Mallory v. U.S. 1957; Mapp v. Ohio 1961; Miranda v. Arizona 1966; Missouri v. Seibert 2004; U.S. v. Rabinowitz 1950, 69; and Vizguerra 2017.

7. Lawrence v. Texas 2003, 568.

8. Baer 1999, chaps. 1 and 2. I do not know if or how this generalization applies where the dominant group is not Caucasian. From 1974 to 1976, I lived on Oahu, Hawaii, where whites were neither a majority nor a plurality. No racial or ethnic group was dominant. The majority of the population was Asian, but the Chinese, Japanese, and Korean residents did not act as a unified group and were not perceived that way. Being a haole in Hawaii did not seem much different from being an Anglo on the mainland.

9. Derrida 1981, viii.

10. Vidal 1990, 48.

11. Marinucci 2016, 43.

12. The first slogan was used by supporters of Barry Goldwater during the 1964 presidential campaign; the second as a response to them by supporters of Lyndon Johnson.

13. Plato 1968, 439d–442b.

14. Plato 1968, 441c, 443d.

15. Aristotle 1953, 52.

16. See the section "Patriarchy and Male Supremacy" in Chapter 5.

17. Freud (1923) 1960, 7, 26.

18. Freud (1930) 2010, 23–26.

19. Baer 1978, 191.

20. See the section "Patriarchy and Male Supremacy" in Chapter 5.

21. Freud 1925.

22. See the section "Feminists Confront Liberalism" in Chapter 1.

23. "Presidential Debate" 1988.

24. Locke 1690, chap. 2, §§7–8; chap. 7, §§87–89.

25. Newport 2007.

26. See Kenney 2013, chap. 7.

27. See the section "The Growth of the Carceral State" in Chapter 4; J. Jones 2017; Oliphant 2016.

28. A twenty-first-century consensus between feminists and victims' rights advocates may be emerging with respect to sexual assault. See Lepore 2018.

29. Baer 1999, 74–78.

30. Berne 1964, 95.

31. See Baer 2013, 103–7; Sorensen 2017; J. Williams 2017.

32. *Merriam-Webster Dictionary*, s.v. "appropriate," available at https://www .merriam-webster.com/dictionary/appropriate (accessed September 1, 2019).

33. *Cambridge English Dictionary*, s.vv. "cultural appropriation," available at https://dictionary.cambridge.org/us/dictionary/english/cultural-appropriation.

34. See the section "Why Liberal Guilt?" in Chapter 6.

35. Pilgrim 2012.

36. J. Harris 2002.

37. Bannerman 2002.

38. I did not know Keats was white until I started working on this chapter. My ignorance may have resulted from my child-free status.

39. Lawrence 1959, 125.

40. Koedt 1970; Ellis 2008, 109.

41. Roth 1975, 110.

42. Roth 1962, 218.

43. D. Harris 2011.

44. R. Kennedy 2017.

45. R. Kennedy 2017.

46. Monroe 2017.

47. Livingstone and Gyarkye 2017.

48. Carlson-Wee 2018, 35.

49. Gay 2018.

50. "Letters to the Editor" 2018, 26–28.

51. Griswold 2018.

52. Burt and Smith 2018.

53. Bannerman 2002.

54. "Letters to the Editor" 2018, 26, 27.

55. Schulman 2018.

56. Mitchell 1936, 78.

57. Randall 2001.

58. Childress 1956.

59. But Childress wrote the young adult novel *A Hero Ain't Nothin' but a Sandwich* (1978) and the screenplay for the film.

60. See Malinowski 1944, 23; Boas 1908, 22.

61. See the section "Punishment: Its Purposes and Consequences" in Chapter 4.

62. See the section "The Growth of the Carceral State" in Chapter 4.

63. Ware 2017.
64. Gould 1972.
65. Gould 1972.
66. Gould 1972.
67. Gould 1972.
68. Huxley 1932; LeGuin 1969.
69. Solomon 2012, 614. See also J. Butler 2004, 59–74. The primary source is Money and Ehrhardt 1972. For Reimer's account, see Colapinto 2000. For a fictional version, see Eugenides 2002.
70. See Baer 2013, 75–77, 82–85.
71. National Organization for Rare Disorders, n.d.a, n.d.b.
72. Solomon 2012, 612.
73. J. Butler 2004, 76; McBride 2018; McCloskey 1999; Singal 2018; Solomon 2012, chap. 11. I use the term *transsexualism* for the condition but *transgender* or *trans* for individuals who transition.
74. A trans man who still has a uterus can bear a child with artificial insemination. See Grady 2018.
75. Ware 2017.
76. Jorgensen 1967; Richards 1984, 2007.
77. See Baer 1983, 246–49.
78. McCloskey 1999, 12–16.
79. Solomon 2012, 627–32. Sexual reassignment for children raises special issues. Solomon quoted an expert who said that a boy's desire to "'be a girl because only girls want to do these things' is not showing evidence of being transgender; he's showing evidence of sexism" (609). This book's account of a first grader who tried to cut off his penis (644) does not reassure the reader about the child's mental health. The brain's rational capacity is not fully developed until age twenty-five. While any eighteen-year-old who has the means and finds a cooperative medical team can transition, parents and professionals should hesitate to offer this treatment to minors.
80. Raymond 1994, xii.
81. Monroe 2017.
82. Baer 1983, 226.
83. J. Butler 2004, 216.
84. See Jay 1999.
85. McCloskey 1999.
86. De Beauvoir 1952, xvi.

CHAPTER 8

1. Goodnough and Pear 2018.
2. Janus v. AFSCME 2018.
3. Karp and Sanchez 2018.
4. See Chapters 4 and 5.
5. Mill 1859, chaps. 2, 4.
6. Okin 1989, 94; Pateman 1988; R. Smith 1989, 238; 1993, 556, 562–63.
7. W. Clinton 1993.

8. I intend no nostalgia here. "Bipartisanship" often became code for "deference to the president." Bipartisan cooperation got Thomas on the Supreme Court. Bipartisan foreign policy got us into Vietnam.

9. Baumol 1952.

10. Baer 1999, chap. 8.

11. U.S. Term Limits v. Thornton 1995.

12. Baer 2013, 41, 49–55.

13. Baer 2018, 756.

References

Adams, Carol J. 1990. *The Sexual Politics of Meat: A Feminist-Vegetarian Critical Theory*. London: Continuum.

Adkins v. Children's Hospital. 1923. 261 U.S. 525.

Ahmed, Azam. 2015. "In Cuba, an Abundance of Love but a Lack of Babies." *New York Times*, October 27. Available at https://www.nytimes.com/2015/10/28/world/americas/in-cuba-an-abundance-of-love-but-a-lack-of-babies.html.

Akron v. Akron Center for Reproductive Health. 1983. 462 U.S. 416.

Alcoholics Anonymous. 2001. *Alcoholics Anonymous*. 4th ed. New York: Alcoholics Anonymous World Services. Available at https://www.aa.org/bigbookonline.

Alexander, Michelle. 2010. *The New Jim Crow: Mass Incarceration in the Age of Colorblindness*. New York: New Press.

Allen, Jonathan, and Amie Parnes. 2018. *Shattered: Inside Hillary Clinton's Doomed Campaign*. New York: Penguin Random House.

Altman, Dennis. 1982. *The Homosexualization of America, the Americanization of the Homosexual*. New York: St. Martin's Press.

Arendt, Hannah. 1964. *Eichmann in Jerusalem: A Report on the Banality of Evil*. New York: Penguin Books.

Aristotle. 1946. *The Politics*. Translated by Ernest Barker. New York: Oxford University Press.

———. 1953. *The Nicomachean Ethics*. Translated and edited by J.A.K. Thomson. Baltimore: Penguin Books.

Armstrong, Ken. 2014. "Dollree Mapp, 1923–2014: 'The Rosa Parks of the Fourth Amendment.'" *Marshall Project*, December 8. Available at https://www.themarshallproject.org/2014/12/08/dollree-mapp-1923-2014-the-rosa-parks-of-the-fourth-amendment#.CFJksgROZ.

Astor, Maggie. 2018. "California Voters Remove Judge Aaron Persky, Who Gave a 6-Month Sentence for Sexual Assault." *New York Times*, June 6. Available at https://www.nytimes.com/2018/06/06/us/politics/judge-persky-brock-turner -recall.html.

Austen, Jane. (1816) 2004. *Emma*. New York: Barnes and Noble Books.

Babcock, Barbara A., Ann E. Freeman, Eleanor H. Norton, and Susan C. Ross, eds. 1975. *Sex Discrimination and the Law: Cases and Remedies*. Boston: Little, Brown.

Baer, Judith A. 1978. *The Chains of Protection: The Judicial Response to Women's Labor Legislation*. Westport, CT: Greenwood Press.

———. 1983. *Equality under the Constitution: Reclaiming the Fourteenth Amendment*. Ithaca, NY: Cornell University Press.

———. 1991a. "Nasty Law or Nice Ladies? Jurisprudence, Feminism, and Gender Difference." *Women and Politics* 11 (1): 1–31.

———. 1991b. *Women in American Law: The Struggle for Equality from the New Deal to the Present*. New York: Holmes and Meier.

———. 1992. "How Is Law Male? A Feminist Perspective on Constitutional Inter-pretation." In *Feminist Jurisprudence: The Difference Debate*, edited by Leslie F. Goldstein, 160–87. Savage, MD: Rowman and Littlefield.

———. 1999. *Our Lives before the Law: Constructing a Feminist Jurisprudence*. Prince-ton, NJ: Princeton University Press.

———, ed. 2002a. *Historical and Multicultural Encyclopedia of Women's Reproductive Rights in the United States*. Westport, CT: Greenwood Press.

———. 2002b. *Women in American Law: The Struggle for Equality from the New Deal to the Present*. 3rd ed. New York: Holmes and Meier.

———. 2003. "Compromising Rights: How Does a Constitution Mean?" Paper pre-sented at the annual meeting of the IPSA Research Committee on Comparative Judicial Studies, Parma, Italy, June 16–18.

———. 2006. "Five Minutes of Global Feminism." *Thomas Jefferson Law Review* 28:111–22.

———. 2013. *Ironic Freedom: Personal Choice, Public Policy, and the Paradox of Reform*. New York: Palgrave MacMillan.

———. 2014a. "Guilt and What to Do about It: A Feminist Post-liberal Analysis." Paper presented at the annual meeting of the Midwest Political Science Associa-tion, Chicago, April 3–6.

———. 2014b. "Liberal and Feminist Theory on the Supreme Court: Between *Lochner* and *Muller*." Paper presented at the annual meeting of the Southern Political Sci-ence Association, New Orleans, January 9–11.

———. 2015. "Privacy at 50: The Bedroom, the Courtroom, and the Spaces in Be-tween." *Maryland Law Review* 75 (1): 233–46.

———. 2018. "Can Feminist Postliberalism Survive the 2016 Election?" *Journal of Politics* 80 (3): 751–756.

Baer, Judith, and Leslie Friedman Goldstein, eds. 2006. *The Constitutional and Legal Rights of Women*. New York: Oxford University Press.

Balakar, Nicholas. 2017. "U.S. Fertility Rate Reaches a Record Low." *New York Times*, July 3. Available at https://www.nytimes.com/2017/07/03/health/united-states -fertility-rate.html.

Bannerman, Helen, with Fred Marcellino. 2002. *The Story of Little Babaji*. New York: HarperCollins.

Barbier v. Connolly. 1884. 113 U.S. 27.

Barnes, J. H. 1999. "Marriage by Capture." *Journal of the Royal Anthropological Society* 5 (March): 57–73.

Barnett, Randy E. 2005. "What's So Wicked about Lochner?" *NYU Journal of Law and Liberty* 1:325–33.

Barron v. Baltimore. 1833. 32 U.S. 243.

Basu, A. M. 2002. "Why Does Education Lead to Lower Fertility? A Critical Review of Some of the Possibilities." *World Development* 30 (10): 1779–90.

Baum, Dan. 2016. "Legalize It All: How to Win the War on Drugs." *Harper's*, April, pp. 22–32.

Baumol, William J. 1952. *Welfare Economics and the Theory of the State*. Cambridge, MA: Harvard University Press.

Beal v. Doe. 1977. 439 U.S. 438.

Beer, Samuel H. 1969. *British Politics in the Collectivist Age*. New York: Vintage Books.

Bell, Diane. 1992. "Considering Gender: Are Human Rights for Women, Too? An Australian Case." In *Human Rights in Cross-Cultural Perspective*, edited by Abdullah An'Naim, 339–62. Philadelphia: University of Pennsylvania Press.

Belluck, Pam. 2017. "Michigan Case Adds U.S. Dimension to Debate on Genital Mutilation." *New York Times*, June 10. Available at https://www.nytimes.com/2017/06/10/health/genital-mutilation-muslim-dawoodi-bohra-michigan-case.html.

Benedict, Ruth. (1934) 1959. *Patterns of Culture*. Boston: Houghton Mifflin.

Bentham, Jeremy. (1817) 1843. *A Plan for Political Reform*. Vol. 3 of *The Works of Jeremy Bentham*, edited by John Bowring. Edinburgh, UK: William Tait.

Berne, Eric. 1964. *Games People Play: The Psychology of Transactional Analysis*. New York: Grove Press.

———. 1972. *What Do You Say after You Say Hello?* New York: Grove Press.

Bernstein, David. 2005. "*Lochner v. New York*: A Centennial Retrospective." *Washington University Law Quarterly* 85 (5): 1469–1528.

Betts v. Brady. 1942. 366 U.S. 545.

Bierstedt, Robert. 1963. *The Social Order: An Introduction to Sociology*. 2nd ed. New York: McGraw-Hill.

Boas, Franz. 1908. *Anthropology*. New York: Columbia University Press.

Boyd, Malcolm. 1965. *Are You Running with Me, Jesus?* New York: Holt, Rinehart and Winston.

Bradwell v. Illinois. 1872. 83 U.S. 130.

Brandenburg v. Ohio. 1969. 395 U.S. 444.

Bray, Ilona. n.d. "What's a Crime of Moral Turpitude According to U.S. Immigration Law?" Nolo. Available at http://www.nolo.com/legal-encyclopedia/what-s-crime-moral-turpitude-according-us-immigration-law.html (accessed June 18, 2019).

Brewer v. Williams. 1977. 430 U.S. 387.

Bridgestock, Laura. 2014. "Differences in Average Working Hours around the World." *QS Top Universities*, March 12. Available at http://www.topuniversities.com/blog/differences-average-working-hours-around-world.

Brown v. Board of Education. 1954. 347 U.S. 483.

Brownmiller, Susan. 1975. *Against Our Will: Men, Women, and Rape.* New York: Bantam Books.

Buber, Martin. 1965. *The Knowledge of Man: Selected Essays.* Edited by Maurice Friedman. Translated by Maurice Friedman and Ronald Gregor Smith. New York: Harper and Row

Buck v. Bell. 1927. 274 U.S. 2000.

Bunting v. Oregon. 1917. 243 U.S. 426.

Burke, Edmund. (1790) 1955. *Reflections on the Revolution in France.* Edited by Thomas H. D. Mahoney. New York: Bobbs-Merrill.

Burns, Sarah. 2012. *The Central Park Five: The Untold Story behind One of New York City's Most Infamous Crimes.* New York: Vintage Books.

Burt, Stephanie, and Carmen Gimenez Smith. 2018. "The Poetry Editors Reply." *The Nation,* September 10–17. Available at https://www.thenation.com/article/letters-from-the-september-10-17-2018-issue.

Bush v. Gore. 2000. 531 U.S. 98.

Butler, Judith. 2004. *Undoing Gender.* New York: Routledge.

———. 2011. *Bodies That Matter.* New York: Routledge.

Butler, Katherine. 2011. "The Feminist Polygamist Revealed." *EcoSalon,* February 1. Available at http://ecosalon.com/the-feminist-polygamist-revealed.

Calhoun, John C. 1851. *A Disquisition on Government.* In *The Works of John C. Calhoun,* vol. 1, edited by Richard K. Cralle. Columbia, SC: A. S. Johnston.

Campbell, Andrea Louise. 2015. "Family Story as Political Science: Reflections on Writing *Trapped in America's Safety Net.*" *Perspectives on Politics* 13 (4): 1043–52.

Carcasson, Martin. 2006. "Ending Welfare as We Know It: President Clinton and the Political Transformation of the Anti-welfare Culture." *Rhetoric and Public Affairs* 9 (4): 655–92.

Card, Claudia. 1991. *Feminist Ethics.* Lawrence: University Press of Kansas.

Cardozo, Benjamin N. 1921. *The Nature of the Judicial Process.* New Haven, CT: Yale University Press.

Carlson-Wee, Anders. 2018. "How-To." *The Nation,* July 20–August 6, p. 35.

Carson, E. Ann. 2014. "Prisoners in 2013." *Bureau of Justice Statistics Bulletin,* September. Available at https://www.bjs.gov/content/pub/pdf/p13.pdf.

Cartwright, Mark. 2016. "Women in Ancient Greece." *Ancient History Encyclopedia,* July 27. Available at https://www.ancient.eu/article/927.

"Champion of Working Moms: Pediatrician T. Berry Brazelton Sees a Hardening of Attitudes against the Needs of Parents." 1995. *Los Angeles Times,* November 6. Available at https://www.latimes.com/archives/la-xpm-1995-11-06-fi-386-story.html.

Chang, Jung. 2003. *Wild Swans: Three Daughters of China.* New York: Simon and Schuster.

Childress, Alice. 1956. *Like One of the Family.* Brooklyn, NY: Independence.

———. 1978. *A Hero Ain't Nothin but a Sandwich.* New York: Coward, McCann and Geoghegan.

Chokshi, Niraj. 2016. "Outrage Follows 60-Day Sentence in Incest Case against Father of Girl, 12." *New York Times,* October 21. Available at https://www.nytimes.com/2016/10/22/us/montana-judge-criticized-for-60-day-sentence-for-felony-incest.html.

Citizens United v. Federal Election Commission. 2010. 558 U.S. 50.

Clark, Naeemah. 2016. "Stanford Sexual-Assault Case Reveals the Chasm That Privilege Creates." *Chronicle of Higher Education* 62 (39): 25–26.

Cleary, Tom. 2016. "Read: Full Letter to the Judge by Dan Turner, Brock's Father." *Heavy*, August 29. Available at http://heavy.com/news/2016/06/brock-turner-father-dad-dan-turner-full-letter-statement-stanford-rapist.

Cleveland v. U.S. 1946. 329 U.S. 14.

Clinton, Hillary Rodham. 1996. *It Takes a Village: And Other Lessons Children Teach Us.* New York: Simon and Schuster.

Clinton, William Jefferson. 1993. State of the Union Address. February 17. Available at https://www.infoplease.com/homework-help/us-documents/state-union-address-william-j-clinton-february-17-1993.

———. 1996. State of the Union Address. January 23. Available at https://clinton whitehouse4.archives.gov/WH/New/other/sotu.html.

Cockburn, Alexander. 2006. "Nick Kristof's Brothel Problem." *The Nation*, February 13, p. 8.

Cohen, Elizabeth. 2015. "No Alcohol during Pregnancy—Ever—Plead U.S. Pediatricians." *CNN*, October 21. Available at http://www.cnn.com/2015/10/21/health/aap-no-alcohol-during-pregnancy.

Colapinto, John. 2000. *As Nature Made Him: The Boy Who Was Raised as a Girl.* New York: HarperCollins.

Condorcet, Nicolas de. (1790) 1912. "On the Admission of Women to the Rights of Citizenship." Translated by Alice Drysdale Vickery. In *The First Essay on the Political Rights of Women*, by Alice Drysdale Vickery, 5–11. Letchworth, UK: Garden City Press.

Conroy, Pat. 1987. *The Lords of Discipline.* New York: Random House.

———. 2002. *My Losing Season.* New York: Nan A. Talese.

Corrigan, Rose. 2006. "Making Meaning of Megan's Law." *Law and Social Inquiry* 31 (Spring): 267–312.

Cott, Nancy F. 1977. *The Bonds of Womanhood: "Women's Sphere" in New England, 1780–1835.* New Haven, CT: Yale University Press.

"Court Upholds Texas Measure on Abortions." 2015. *New York Times*, June 10, pp. A1, A16.

Craig v. Boren. 1976. 429 U.S. 190. 21

Critical Resistance. n.d. "Our Mission." Available at http://criticalresistance.org (accessed June 18, 2019).

Cromwell, Oliver. 1650. Letter to the General Assembly of the Church of Scotland. August 3. Available at http://www.olivercromwell.org/Letters_and_speeches/letters/Letter_129.pdf.

Currie, Donya. 2013. "Breastfeeding Rates for Black US Women Increase, but Lag Overall: Continuing Disparity Raises Concerns." *Nation's Health* 43 (3): 1–20.

Daley, David. 2016. *Ratf*cked: The True Story behind the Plan to Steal American Democracy.* New York: W. W. Norton.

Darrow, Clarence. 1902. "Crime and Criminals: Address to the Prisoners in Cook County Jail." Available at http://www.bopsecrets.org/CF/darrow.htm.

Darwin, Charles. 1859 (2001). *On the Origin of Species.* Edited by Jim Manis. Hazleton, PA: Pennsylvania State University. Available at http://www.f.waseda.jp/sidoli/Darwin_Origin_Of_Species.pdf.

————. 1871. *The Descent of Man, and Selection in Relation to Sex*. 2 vols. London: John Murray. Available at http://darwin-online.org.uk/EditorialIntroductions/Freeman_TheDescentofMan.html.

Davis, Angela Y. 2003. *Are Prisons Obsolete?* New York: Seven Stories Press.

————. 2011. *The Meaning of Freedom: And Other Difficult Dialogues*. San Francisco: City Lights Books.

Davis, Sue. 2008. *The Political Thought of Elizabeth Cady Stanton*. New York: New York University Press.

Dawit, Seble, and Salem Mekuria. 1993. "The West Just Doesn't Get It." *New York Times*, December 7, p. A27

De Beauvoir, Simone. 1952. *The Second Sex*. Translated and edited by H. M. Parshley. New York: Alfred A. Knopf.

Demick, Barbara. 2009. *Nothing to Envy: Ordinary Lives in North Korea*. New York: Spriegel and Grau.

————. 2010. "Letter from Yanji." *New Yorker*, July 12–19, pp. 44–49.

Derr, Mary Krane. 2002. "Pro-life Feminism." In *A Historical and Multicultural Encyclopedia of Female Reproductive Rights in the United States*, edited by Judith A. Baer, 172–74. Westport, CT: Greenwood.

Derrida, Jacques. 1981. *Dissemination*. Translated by Barbara Johnson. Chicago: University of Chicago Press.

Descartes, Rene. (1641) 1911. *Meditations on First Philosophy*. In *The Philosophical Works of Descartes*, vol. 1, translated by Elizabeth S. Haldane and G.R.T. Ross, 131–200. London: Cambridge University Press.

Devlin, Patrick. 1959. *The Enforcement of Morals*. New York: Oxford University Press.

Dickerson v. U.S. 2000. 530 U.S. 428.

Dobie, Kathy. 2016. "To Catch a Rapist." *New York Times Magazine*, January 5. Available at https://www.nytimes.com/2016/01/10/magazine/to-catch-a-rapist.html.

Doe v. Bolton. 1973. 410 U.S. 179.

Dominus, Susan. 2009. "Not the Rolls, My Good Man: These Times Demand the Station Wagon." *New York Times*, March 3. Available at https://www.nytimes.com/2009/03/02/nyregion/02bigcity.html.

Drape, Joe, and Marc Tracy. 2016. "A Majority Agreed She Was Raped by a Stanford Football Player: That Wasn't Enough." *New York Times*, December 29. Available at https://www.nytimes.com/2016/12/29/sports/football/stanford-football-rape-accusation.html.

Durkheim, Émile. 1982. *The Rules of Sociological Method*. Edited by Steven Lukes. Translated by W. D. Halls. New York: Free Press.

————. 1984. *The Division of Labor in Society*. Translated by Lewis Coser. New York: Macmillan.

Dworkin, Andrea. 1987. *Intercourse*. New York: Free Press.

Ehrenreich, Barbara. 2001. *Nickel and Dimed: On (Not) Getting By in America*. New York: Henry Holt.

————. 2002. "Maid to Order." In *Global Woman: Nannies, Maids, and Sex Workers in the New Economy*, edited by Barbara Ehrenreich and Arlie Hochschild, 85–103. New York: Henry Holt.

Eisenstadt v. Baird. 1972. 405 U.S. 438.

Eisenstein, Zillah. 1981. *The Radical Future of Liberal Feminism*. New York: Longman.

————. 1994. *The Color of Gender: Reimaging Democracy*. Berkeley: University of California Press.

Ellis, Albert. 2008. *Sex without Guilt for the 21st Century*. Fort Lee, NJ: Barricade Books.

Ellison, Julie. 1999. "A Short History of Liberal Guilt." *Critical Inquiry* 22 (2): 344–71.

Elshtain, Jean Bethke. 1996. "Suffer Little Children." *New Republic*, March 4, pp. 33–38.

Ely, John Hart. 1973. "The Wages of Crying Wolf: A Comment on *Roe v. Wade*." *Yale Law Journal* 82 (April): 920–49.

Engels, Friedrich. 1972. *The Origin of the Family, Private Property, and the State*. Edited by Eleanor Burke Leacock. Translated by Alec West. New York: International.

Ephron, Nora. 1973. *Crazy Salad*. New York: Bantam Books.

Epstein, Richard A. 1985. *Takings: Private Property and the Power of Eminent Domain*. Cambridge, MA: Harvard University Press.

Escobedo v. Illinois. 1964. 378 U.S. 478.

Eugenides, Jeffrey. 2002. *Middlesex*. New York: Farrar, Straus and Giroux.

Federal Bureau of Prisons. 2019. "Statistics." June 13. Available at https://www.bop .gov/about/statistics/population_statistics.jsp.

Feinberg, Joel. 2008. "The Classic Debate." In *Philosophy of Law*, 8th ed., edited by Joel Feinberg and Jules Coleman, 624–29. Belmont, CA: Thomson Wadsworth.

Few-Demo, April, Aine M. Humble, Melissa A. Curran, and Sally A. Lloyd. 2017. "Queer Theory, Intersectionality, and LGBT-Parent Families: Transformative Critical Pedagogy in Family Theory." *Journal of Family Theory and Review* 8 (March): 74–94.

Fiallo v. Bell. 1977. 430 U.S. 787.

Fikkert, Brian, David Platt, John Perkins, and James Corbett. 2014. *When Helping Hurts: How to Alleviate Poverty without Hurting the Poor . . . and Yourself.* 2nd ed. Chicago: Moody.

Fineman, Martha Albertson. 1995. *The Neutered Mother, the Sexual Family, and Other Twentieth-Century Tragedies*. New York: Routledge.

Fiss, Owen M. 1993. *Troubled Beginnings of the Modern State: 1888–1910*. New York: Macmillan.

Flanagan, Caitlin. 2004. "How Serfdom Saved the Women's Movement." *Atlantic Monthly*, March, pp. 109–28.

Flexner, Eleanor. 1971. *Century of Struggle: The Women's Rights Movement in the United States*. New York: Atheneum.

Ford, Gerald R. 1974. Proclamation 4311: Granting Pardon to Richard Nixon. September 8. Available at https://catalog.archives.gov/id/299996.

Forman, James, Jr. 2017. *Locking Up Our Own: Crime and Punishment in Black America*. New York: Farrar, Straus and Giroux.

Foucault, Michel. 1979. *Discipline and Punish: The Birth of the Prison*. Translated by Alan Sheridan. New York: Vintage Books.

Fox-Genovese, Elizabeth. 1996. *"Feminism Is Not the Story of My Life": How Today's Feminist Elite Has Lost Touch with the Real Concerns of Women*. New York: Anchor.

Frank, Jerome. 1949. *Courts on Trial*. Princeton, NJ: Princeton University Press.

Frankfort, Ellen. 1973. *Vaginal Politics*. New York: Bantam Books.

Freud, Sigmund. (1923) 1960. *The Ego and the Id*. Translated by James Strachey. New York: W. W. Norton.

———. 1925. "Some Psychological Consequences of the Anatomical Distinction between the Sexes." Available at http://www.aquestionofexistence.com/Aquestion ofexistence/Problems_of_Gender/Entries/2011/8/28_Sigmund_Freud_files/ Freud%20Some%20Psychological%20Consequences%20of%20the%20Ana tomical%20Distinction%20between%20the%20Sexes.pdf.

———. (1930) 2010. *Civilization and Its Discontents*. Translated by James Strachey. New York: W. W. Norton.

Friedan, Betty. 1963. *The Feminine Mystique*. New York: W. W. Norton.

Friedman, Thomas L. 2009. "Obama's Real Test." *New York Times*, March 17. Available at https://www.nytimes.com/2009/03/18/opinion/18friedman.html.

Fromm, Erich. 1941. *Escape from Freedom*. New York: Holt, Rinehart and Winston.

———. 1984. *Man for Himself: An Inquiry into the Psychology of Ethics*. New York: Holt, Rinehart and Winston.

Frontiero v. Richardson. 1973. 411 U.S. 677.

Frost, Robert. 1941. "The Lesson for Today." Available at https://ddink55.wordpress .com/2011/03/24/the-lesson-for-today.

Gaard, Greta, ed. 1993. *Ecofeminism: Women, Animals, Nature*. Philadelphia: Temple University Press.

Gawande, Atul. 2007. *Better: A Surgeon's Notes on Performance*. New York: Henry Holt.

Gay, Roxane. 2018. Twitter post, August 2. Available at https://twitter.com/rgay/ status/1025078752726769664.

George, Kathryn Paxton. 1994. "Should Feminists be Vegetarians? *Signs* 19 (Winter): 405–34.

George, Robert P. 2005. "Judicial Usurpation and the Constitution: Historical and Contemporary Issues." Heritage Foundation, April 11. Available at https:// www.heritage.org/report/judicial-usurpation-and-the-constitution-historical -and-contemporary-issues.

Gest, Ted. 2014. "Do Mandatory Domestic Violence Arrests Hurt Victims?" *Crime Report*, May 21. Available at https://thecrimereport.org/2014/05/21/ 2014-05-domestic-violence-policing-for-wed-icj.

Gibbs, Lindsay. 2016. "USA Swimming Bans Stanford Rapist Brock Turner for Life." *Think Progress*, June 10. Available at https://thinkprogress.org/usa-swimming -bans-stanford-rapist-brock-turner-for-life-52456129e3d0#.t73j3olas.

Gideon v. Wainwright. 1963. 372 U.S. 335.

Gilligan, Carol. 1982. *In a Different Voice*. Cambridge, MA: Harvard University Press.

Gillman, Howard. 1993. *The Constitution Besieged: The Rise and Demise of Lochner Era Police Power Jurisprudence*. Durham, NC: Duke University Press.

Gilmore, Ruth Wilson. 2007. *Golden Gulag: Prisons, Surplus, Crisis, and Opposition on Globalizing California*. Berkeley: University of California Press.

Glendon, Mary Ann. 1991. *Rights Talk: The Impoverishment of Political Discourse*. New York: Basic Books.

Goesaert v. Cleary. 1948. 335 U.S. 464.

Goldberg, Michelle. 2014. "Campus Rape Crisis: The System Is Broken; Can It Be Fixed?" *The Nation*, June 23–30, pp. 12–16.

Goldberg, Steven. 1973. *The Inevitability of Patriarchy*. New York: William Morrow.

Goldstein, Leslie F., ed. 1992. *Feminist Jurisprudence: The Difference Debate*. Lanham, MD: Rowman and Littlefield.

Gone with the Wind. 1939. Directed by Victor Fleming, George Cukor, and Sam Wood. Beverly Hills, CA: Metro-Goldwyn-Mayer.

Gonzales v. Carhart. 2007. 550 U.S. 124.

Goodman, Paul. 1960. *Growing Up Absurd: Problems of Youth in the Organized Society*. New York: Random House.

Goodnough, Abby, and Robert Pear. 2018. "Texas Judge Strikes Down Obama's Affordable Care Act as Unconstitutional." *New York Times*, December 14. Available at https://www.nytimes.com/2018/12/14/health/obamacare-unconstitutional -texas-judge.html.

Goodridge v. Commissioner of Public Health. 2003. 440 Mass. 309.

Gordon, Suzanne. 1991. *Prisoners of Men's Dreams: Striking Out for a New Feminine Future*. Boston: Little, Brown.

Gottschalk, Marie. 2006. *The Prison and the Gallows: The Policy of Mass Incarceration in America*. New York: Cambridge University Press.

———. 2015. *Caught: The Prison State and the Lockdown of American Politics*. Princeton, NJ: Princeton University Press.

Gottschalk, Marie, Naomi Murakawa, Amy Lerman, and Vesla Weaver. 2015. "Critical Trialogue: The Carceral State." *Perspectives on Politics* 13 (September): 798–814.

Gouges, Olympe de. 1791. "Declaration of the Rights of Woman." Available at https:// csivc.csi.cuny.edu/americanstudies/files/lavender/decwom2.html.

Gould, Lois. 1972. "The Story of X." *Ms.*, July. Available at https://waylandbrown.files .wordpress.com/2011/03/x-story.pdf.

———. 1978. *X: A Fabulous Child's Story*. New York: Daughters.

Grady, Denise. 2018. "A Family in Transition: Two Fathers and the Baby Girl They Never Expected." *New York Times*, June 16. Available at https://www.nytimes .com/2018/06/16/health/transgender-baby.html.

Graves, Lucia. 2016. "You Liked Bernie Sanders: So Why Didn't You Vote Hillary Clinton?" *The Guardian*, November 13. Available at https://www.theguardian.com/ commentisfree/2016/nov/13/you-liked-sanders-so-why-didnt-you-vote-clinton.

Greenberg, Joanne [Hannah Green]. 1964. *I Never Promised You a Rose Garden*. New York: Holt McDougal.

Greenfeld, Josh. 1970. *A Child Called Noah: A Family Journey*. New York: Warner Books.

Griffin, Susan. 1978. *Woman and Nature: The Roaring inside Her*. New York: Harper and Row.

Griswold, Alex. 2018. "'The Nation' Apologizes for Publishing Poem with 'Disparaging and Ableist' Language." *Washington Free Beacon*, July 31. Available at https://freebea con.com/culture/nation-apologizes-publishing-poem-disparaging-ableist-language.

Griswold v. Connecticut. 1965. 381 U.S. 479.

Guillermoprieto, Alma. 2004. *Dancing with Cuba*. New York: Pantheon.

Gujarati, Damodar N. 2003. *Basic Econometrics*. New York: McGraw Hill.

Guttenplan, D. D. 2016. "Mourn, Resist, Organize." *The Nation*, November 28, pp. 3–4.

Hager, Eli. 2017. "From Prison to Ph.D.: The Redemption and Rejection of Michelle Jones." *New York Times*, September 13. Available at https://www.nytimes.com/2017/09/13/us/harvard-nyu-prison-michelle-jones.html.

Harper v. Virginia State Board of Elections. 1966. 383 U.S. 301.

Harris, Angela. 1990. "Race and Essentialism in Feminist Legal Theory." *Stanford Law Review* 42 (February): 581–616.

Harris, Duchess. 2011. "Kathryn Stockett Is Not My Sister and I Am Not Her Help." *Feminist Wire*, August 12. Available at http://www.thefeministwire.com/2011/08/kathryn-stockett-is-not-my-sister-and-i-am-not-her-help.

Harris, Joel Chandler. 2002. *The Complete Tales of Uncle Remus.* Boston: Houghton Mifflin.

Harris, Richard. 1969. *The Fear of Crime.* New York: Praeger.

Harris, Sharon M., ed. 1995. *Selected Writings of Judith Sargent Murray.* New York: Oxford University Press.

Harrison, Cynthia. 1988. *On Account of Sex: The Politics of Women's Issues, 1945–1968.* Berkeley: University of California Press.

Harris v. McRae. 1980. 448 U.S. 297.

Hartocollis, Anemona, and Christina Capecchi. 2017. "'Willing to Do Everything,' Mothers Defend Sons Accused of Sexual Assault." *New York Times*, October 22. Available at https://www.nytimes.com/2017/10/22/us/campus-sex-assault-mothers.html.

Hartsock, Nancy. 1983. *Money, Sex, and Power: Toward a Feminist Historical Materialism.* New York: Longman.

Hartz, Louis. 1955. *The Liberal Tradition in America: An Interpretation of American Political Thought since the Revolution.* New York: Harcourt, Brace, Jovanovich.

Heagney, Meredith. 2013. "Justice Ruth Baer Ginsburg Offers Critique of Roe v. Wade during Law School Visit." University of Chicago Law School, May 15. Available at https://www.law.uchicago.edu/news/justice-ruth-bader-ginsburg-offers-critique-roe-v-wade-during-law-school-visit.

Henderson, Tim. 2014. "More Americans Living Alone, Census Says." *Washington Post*, September 28. Available at https://www.washingtonpost.com/politics/more-americans-living-alone-census-says/2014/09/28/67e1d02e-473a-11e4-b72e-d60a9229cc10_story.html.

Heyward, Anna. 2017. "Since Trump's Victory, Democratic Socialists of America Has Become a Budding Political Force." *The Nation*, December 21. Available at https://www.thenation.com/article/in-the-year-since-trumps-victory-democratic-socialists-of-america-has-become-a-budding-political-force.

Hill, John L. 1991. "What Does It Mean to Be a 'Parent'? The Claims of Biology as the Basis for Parental Rights." *New York University Law Review* 66:353–420.

Hinton, Elizabeth. 2016. *From the War on Poverty to the War on Crime: The Making of Mass Incarceration in America.* Cambridge, MA: Harvard University Press.

Hirschel, David, Eve Buzawa, April Pattavina, and Don Faggiani. 2007. "Domestic Violence and Mandatory Arrest Laws: To What Extent Do They Influence Police Arrest Decisions?" *Journal of Criminal Law and Criminology* 98 (Fall): 255–98.

Hobbes, Thomas. 1962. *Leviathan.* Edited by Michael Oakeshott. New York: Macmillan.

Hochschild, Arlie, with Anne Machung. 1989. *The Second Shift.* New York: Avon.

Hofverberg, Elin. 2016. "Sweden: Single Women Receive Legal Right to Insemination Assistance." *Global Legal Monitor*, January 29. Available at http://www.loc.gov/law/foreign-news/article/sweden-single-women-receive-legal-right-to-insemination-assistance.

Holden v. Hardy. 1898. 169 U.S. 366.

Horwitz, Morton J. 1992. *The Transformation of American Law, 1870–1960.* New York: Oxford University Press.

Hrdy, Sarah Blaffer. 1981. *The Woman That Never Evolved.* Cambridge, MA: Harvard University Press.

Hudson, Valerie M., Donna Lee Bowen, and Perpetua Lynne Nielsen. 2015. "Clan Governance and State Stability: The Relationship between Female Subordination and Political Order." *American Political Science Review* 109 (August): 535–55.

Hufton, Olwen H. 1989. *Women and the Limits of Citizenship in the French Revolution.* Toronto: University of Toronto Press.

Huxley, Aldous. 1932. *Brave New World.* London: Chatto and Windus.

Hyden, Margareta. 2014. "What Social Networks Do in the Aftermath of Domestic Violence." *British Journal of Criminology* 55 (September): 1040–57.

In the Matter of Baby M. 1988. 109 N.J. 396; 537 A2d 1227.

Irwin, Neil. 2015. "How Germany Prevailed in the Greek Bailout." *New York Times*, July 29. Available at https://www.nytimes.com/2015/07/30/world/europe/how-germany-prevailed-in-the-greek-bailout.html.

Jackson, Harold. 2007. "Arthur M. Schlesinger, Jr." *The Guardian*, March 1. Available at https://www.theguardian.com/world/2007/mar/01/usa.booksobituaries.

James, Stanlie M., and Claire C. Robertson, eds. 2002. *Genital Cutting and Transnational Sisterhood: Disputing U.S. Polemics.* Urbana: University of Illinois Press.

Janus v. AFSCME. 2018. 588 U.S. ___.

Jay, Karla. 1999. *Tales of the Lavender Menace: A Memoir of Liberation.* New York: Basic Books.

Jones, Jeffrey M. 2016. "U.S. Support for Death Penalty at 60%." Gallup, October 25. Available at http://www.gallup.com/poll/196676/death-penalty-support.aspx.

———. 2017. "U.S. Death Penalty Support Lowest since 1972." Gallup, October 26. Available at https://news.gallup.com/poll/221030/death-penalty-support-lowest-1972.aspx.

Jones, Robert P., Daniel Cox, and Juhem Navarro-Rivera. 2014. "A Shifting Landscape: A Decade of Change in American Attitudes about Same-Sex Marriage and LGBT Issues." Public Religion Research Institute, February 26. Available at https://www.prri.org/wp-content/uploads/2014/02/2014.LGBT_REPORT-1.pdf.

Jordan, Miriam. 2019. "No More Family Separations, Except These 900." *New York Times*, July 31. Available at https://www.nytimes.com/2019/07/30/us/migrant-family-separations.html.

Jorgensen, Christine. 1967. *Christine Jorgensen: A Personal Autobiography.* New York: Paul S. Eriksson.

Joseph, Elizabeth. 1991. "My Husband's Nine Wives." *New York Times*, May 23, p. A31.

Jung, Courtney. 2015. *Lactivism: How Feminists and Fundamentalists, Hippies and Yuppies, and Physicians and Politicians Made Breastfeeding Big Business and Bad Policy.* New York: Basic Books.

Karp, Stan, and Adam Sanchez. 2018. "The 2018 Wave of Teacher Strikes: A Turning Point for Our Schools?" *Rethinking Schools* 32 (4). Available at https://www .rethinkingschools.org/issues/volume-32-no-4-summer-2018.

Kavoussi, Bonnie. 2012. "U.S. Birth Rate Not High Enough to Keep Population Stable." *Huffington Post*, August 15. Available at http://www.huffingtonpost .com/2012/08/15/us-birth-rate_n_1779960.html.

Kay, Herma Hill. 1985. "Equality and Difference: The Case of Pregnancy." *Berkeley Women's Law Journal* 1:1–37.

Kedrowski, Karen M., and Michael E. Lipscomb. 2007. *Barely There: Breastfeeding Rights in the United States.* Westport, CT: Praeger.

Keizer, Garret. 2008. "Turning away from Jesus: Gay Rights and the War for the Episcopal Church." *Harper's*, June, pp. 39–50.

Kennedy, Caroline. 2008. "A President like My Father." *New York Times*, January 27. Available at https://www.nytimes.com/2008/01/27/opinion/27kennedy.html.

Kennedy, Edward M. 2008. "Senator Kennedy's Obama Endorsement Speech." Edward M. Kennedy Institute, January 28. Available at https://www.emkinstitute .org/resources/obama-endorsement-speech.

Kennedy, Randy. 2017. "White Artist's Painting of Emmett Till at Whitney Biennial Draws Protests." *New York Times*, March 21. Available at https://www.nytimes .com/2017/03/21/arts/design/painting-of-emmett-till-at-whitney-biennial-draws -protests.html.

Kenney, Sally J. 1992. *For Whose Protection? Reproductive Hazards and Exclusionary Policies in the United States and Britain.* Ann Arbor: University of Michigan Press.

———. 2013. *Gender and Justice: Why Women in the Judiciary Really Matter.* New York: Routledge.

Kesey, Ken. 1962. *One Flew over the Cuckoo's Nest.* New York: Viking Press.

King, Martin Luther, Jr. 1958. *Strive toward Freedom.* New York: Harper and Row.

Kirchberg v. Feenstra. 1981. 450 U.S. 455.

Kirkpatrick, Jeane. 1984. Republican Party Convention speech. August 20. Available at https://speakola.com/political/jeane-kirkpatrick-blame-america-first-gop-1984.

Kirstein v. University of Virginia. 1970. 309 F. Supp. 184 (E.D. Va.)

Kittay, Eva Feder. 1999. *Love's Labor: Essays on Women, Equality, and Dependency.* New York: Routledge.

Koch, Adrienne, and William Peden, eds. 1944. *The Life and Selected Writings of Thomas Jefferson.* New York: Modern Library.

Koedt, Ann. 1970. *The Myth of the Vaginal Orgasm.* Boston: New England Free Press.

Koestler, Arthur. (1941) 2006. *Darkness at Noon.* New York: Simon and Schuster.

Kolbert, Elizabeth. 2016. "Drawing the Line: How Redistricting Turned America from Blue to Red." *New Yorker*, June 27, pp. 68–71.

Kristof, Nicholas. 2015. "When Liberals Blew It." *New York Times*, March 12, p. A25.

———. 2017. "11 Years Old, a Mom, and Pushed to Marry Her Rapist in Florida." *New York Times*, May 26. Available at https://www.nytimes.com/2017/05/26/ opinion/sunday/it-was-forced-on-me-child-marriage-in-the-us.html.

Kristof, Nicholas, and Sheryl WuDunn. 2009. *Half the Sky: Turning Oppression into Opportunity for Women Worldwide.* New York: Knopf Doubleday.

Kulikoff, Allan. 2000. *From British Peasant to Colonial American Farmers.* Chapel Hill: University of North Carolina Press.

Lasch, Christopher. 1977. *Haven in a Heartless World: The Family Besieged*. New York: W. W. Norton.

Lawrence, D. H. 1959. *Lady Chatterley's Lover*. New York: Penguin Books.

Lawrence v. Texas. 2003. 539 U.S. 558.

LeBlanc, Adrian Nicole. 2003. *Random Family*. New York: Scribner.

LeGuin, Ursula K. 1969. *The Left Hand of Darkness*. New York: Ace Books.

Lemons, J. Stanley. 1973. *The Woman Citizen: Social Feminism in the 1920s*. Urbana: University of Illinois Press.

Lenin, V. I. (1917) 1990. "The State and Revolution." In *The Human Rights Reader*, edited by Walter Laqueur and Barry Rubin, 179–83. New York: Meridian.

Lepore, Jill. 2018. "Sirens in the Night." *New Yorker*, May 21, pp. 48–55.

Lerman, Amy E., and Vesla M. Weaver. 2015. *Arresting Citizenship: The Democratic Consequences of American Crime Control*. Chicago: University of Chicago Press.

"Letters to the Editor." 2018. *The Nation*, September 10–17, pp. 26–29.

Lewin, Tamar. 2014. "U.S. Birthrate Declines for Sixth Consecutive Year; Economy Could Be a Factor." *New York Times*, December 4. Available at http://www.nytimes.com/2014/12/05/us/us-sees-decline-in-births-for-sixth-year.html.

Livingstone, Josephine, and Lovia Gyarkye. 2017. "The Case against Dana Schutz." *New Republic*, March 22. Available at https://newrepublic.com/article/141506/case-dana-schutz.

Lochner v. New York. 1905. 198 U.S. 45.

Locke, John. 1690. *Two Treatises of Government*. London: Awnsham Churchill.

Loftus, Elizabeth F., and Katherine Ketcham. 1994. *The Myth of Repressed Memory*. New York: St. Martin's Press.

Loving v. Virginia. 1967. 388 U.S. 1.

Lupton, Robert D. 2011. *Toxic Charity: How Churches Hurt Those They Help and How to Reverse It*. New York: HarperCollins.

Lusky, Louis. 1975. *By What Right? A Commentary on the Supreme Court's Power to Revise the Constitution*. Charlottesville, VA: Michie.

MacIntyre, Alasdair. 2007. *After Virtue: A Study in Moral Theory*. 3rd ed. Notre Dame: University of Indiana Press.

MacKinnon, Catharine A. 1987. *Feminism Unmodified*. Cambridge, MA: Harvard University Press.

———. 1989. *Toward a Feminist Theory of the State*. Cambridge, MA: Harvard University Press.

MacNair, Rachel, Mary Krane Derr, and Linda Naranjo-Huebl, eds. 1995. *Prolife Feminism: Yesterday and Today*. New York: Sulzburger and Graham.

Maher v. Roe. 1977. 432 U.S. 464.

Malcolm, Janet. 1984. *In the Freud Archives*. New York: Alfred A. Knopf.

Malinowski, Bronislaw. 1944. *A Scientific Theory of Culture and Other Essays*. Chapel Hill: University of North Carolina Press.

Mallory v. U.S. 1957. 354 U.S. 449.

Manion, Jennifer C. 2003. "Girls Blush, Sometimes: Gender, Moral Agency, and the Problem of Shame." *Hypatia* 18 (3): 21–41.

Mannheim, Karl. 1954. *Ideology and Utopia: An Introduction to the Sociology of Knowledge*. Translated by Louis Werth and Edward Shils. New York: Harcourt, Brace.

Mansbridge, Jane J. 1986. *Why We Lost the ERA*. Chicago: University of Chicago Press.

Mapp v. Ohio. 1961. 367 U.S. 643.

Marbury v. Madison. 1803. 5 U.S. 137.

Marinucci, Mimi. 2016. *Feminism Is Queer: The Intimate Connection between Queer and Feminist Theory.* 2nd ed. London: Zed Books.

Marshall, Christine. 1992. "'Dull Elves' and Feminists: A Summary of Feminist Criticism of Jane Austen," *Persuasions* 14 (1992): 39–45. Available at http://www.jasna.org/persuasions/printed/number14/marshall.pdf.

Marx, Karl. (1848) 1959. *The Communist Manifesto.* In *Marx and Engels: Basic Writings on Philosophy and Politics,* edited by Lewis S. Feuer, 2–41. Garden City, NY: Doubleday.

———. 1852. "The Eighteenth Brumaire of Louis Napoleon." Available at https://www.marxists.org/archive/marx/works/download/pdf/18th-Brumaire.pdf.

Maslow, Abraham. 1970. *Motivation and Personality.* 2nd ed. New York: Harper and Row.

Masson, Jeffrey Moussaieff. 1984. *The Assault on Truth: Freud's Suppression of the Seduction Theory.* New York: Farrar, Straus and Giroux.

Mather, Mark. 2012. "The Decline in U.S. Fertility." Population Reference Bureau, July 18. Available at https://www.prb.org/us-fertility.

Matishak, Martin. 2015. "Navy Triples Maternity Leave to 18 Weeks." *The Hill,* July 6. Available at http://thehill.com/policy/defense/246909-us-navy-triples-maternity-leave-to-18-weeks.

Mayeri, Serena. 2011. *Reasoning from Race: Feminism, Law, and the Civil Rights Revolution.* Cambridge, MA: Harvard University Press.

McBride, Sarah. 2018. *Tomorrow Will Be Different: Love, Loss, and the Fight for Trans Equality.* New York: Crown Archetype

McCarthy, Justin. 2014. "Same-Sex Marriage Support Reaches New High at 55%." Gallup, May 21. Available at https://news.gallup.com/poll/169640/sex-marriage-support-reaches-new-high.aspx.

McClain, Linda C. 1992. "'Atomistic Man' Revisited: Liberalism, Connection, and Feminist Jurisprudence." *Southern California Law Review* 65 (March): 1171–1264.

McCleskey v. Kemp. 1987. 481 U.S. 279.

McCloskey, Deirdre. 1999. *Crossing: A Memoir.* Chicago: University of Chicago Press.

Mead, Margaret. 1935. *Sex and Temperament in Three Primitive Societies.* New York: William Morrow.

———. 1954. "Some Theoretical Considerations on the Problem of Mother-Child Separation." *American Journal of Orthopsychiatry* 24 (July): 471–83.

Meece, Mickey. 2009. "Backlash: Women Bullying Women at Work." *New York Times,* May 9. Available at https://www.nytimes.com/2009/05/10/business/10women.html.

Meili, Trisha. 2003. *I Am the Central Park Jogger: A Story of Hope and Possibility.* New York: Simon and Schuster.

Menninger, Karl. 1966. *The Crime of Punishment.* New York: Viking Press.

Michael H. v. Gerald D. 1989. 491 U.S. 110.

Michael M. v. Superior Court of Sonoma County. 1981. 450 U.S. 464.

Michaux, Melissa Buis, and Leslie Dunlap. 2009. "Baby Lit: Feminist Response to the Cult of True Motherhood." In *You've Come a Long Way, Baby,* edited by Lilly Goren, 137–58. Lexington: University Press of Kentucky.

Mill, John Stuart. 1859. *On Liberty*. London: John W. Parker.

———. 1869. *The Subjection of Women*. London: Longmans, Green, Reader, and Dyer.

Miller v. Albright. 1998. 523 U.S. 420.

Mills, C. Wright. 1959. *The Sociological Imagination*. New York: Oxford University Press.

Miranda v. Arizona. 1966. 384 U.S. 436.

Mississippi University for Women v. Hogan. 1982. 458 U.S. 718.

Missouri v. Seibert. 2004. 542 U.S. 600.

Mitchell, Margaret. 1936. *Gone with the Wind*. New York: Macmillan.

Molloy, Aimee. 2013. *However Long the Night: Molly Melching's Journey to Help Millions of African Women and Girls Triumph*. New York: HarperCollins.

Money, John, and Anke Ehrhardt. 1972. *Man and Woman, Boy and Girl*. Baltimore: Johns Hopkins University Press.

Monroe, Irene. 2017. "Emmett Till Painting Raises Concerns of Cultural Appropriation." *Huffington Post*, April 1. Available at https://www.huffpost.com/entry/emmett-till-painting-raises-concerns-of-cultural-appropriation_b_58dfd0c9e4b0d804fbbb735b.

"Montana Judge Sparks Outrage with Light Sentence for Man Who Raped 12-Year-Old Daughter." 2016. *Chicago Tribune*, October 21. Available at http://www.chicagotribune.com/news/nationworld/ct-montana-judge-rape-sentence-20161021-story.html.

Morris, David. 2001. "Commentary: Conservative Rage vs. Liberal Guilt." Institute for Local Self-Reliance, January 21. Available at https://ilsr.org/16846.

Morris, Desmond. 1986. *The Illustrated Naked Ape: A Zoologist's Study of the Human Animal*. New York: Crown.

Moynihan, Daniel Patrick. 1965. *The Negro Family: A Call for National Action*. Washington, DC: U.S. Department of Labor.

———. 1970. Letter to President Richard Nixon. January 16. Available at https://www.nixonlibrary.gov/sites/default/files/virtuallibrary/documents/jul10/53.pdf.

Muhammad, Khalil Gibran. 2017. "Power and Punishment." *New York Times Book Review*, April 16, pp. 1, 20.

Muller v. Oregon. 1908. 208 U.S. 412.

Munn v. Illinois. 1877. 94 U.S. 113.

Murakawa, Naomi. 2014. *The First Civil Right: How Liberals Built Prison America*. New York: Oxford University Press.

Murray, Pauli, and Mary Eastwood. 1965. "Jane Crow and the Law: Sex Discrimination and Title VII." *George Washington Law Review* 34:232–56.

Murray v. Curlett. 1963. 374 U.S. 203.

Nathan, Debbie. 2016. "What Happened to Sandra Bland?" *The Nation*, April 21. Available at https://www.thenation.com/article/what-happened-to-sandra-bland.

National Center for Education Statistics. 2018a. "Citadel Military College of South Carolina." *College Navigator*. Available at http://nces.ed.gov/collegenavigator/?q=Citadel&s=SC&id=217864#admsns.

———. 2018b. "Virginia Military Institute." *College Navigator*. Available at http://nces.ed.gov/collegenavigator/?q=virginia+military+institute&s=VA&id=234085#admsnsnces.ed.

National Organization for Rare Disorders. n.d.a. "Klinefelter Syndrome." Available at https://rarediseases.org/rare-diseases/klinefelter-syndrome (accessed September 13, 2019).

————. n.d.b. "Turner Syndrome." Available at https://rarediseases.org/rare-diseases/turner-syndrome (accessed September 13, 2019).

National Research Council. 2014. *The Growth of Incarceration in the United States: Exploring Causes and Consequences.* Washington, DC: National Academies Press.

"Navy, Marine Corps Now Offer 18 Weeks of Maternity Leave." 2015. *National Public Radio*, July 8. Available at https://www.npr.org/2015/07/08/421083589/navy-marine-corps-now-offer-18-weeks-of-maternity-leave.

The New-England Primer. (1777) 1991. Reprint, Aledo, TX: WallBuilder Press.

Newport, Frank. 2007. "Sixty-Nine Percent of Americans Support Death Penalty." Gallup, October 12. Available at https://news.gallup.com/poll/101863/sixtynine-percent-americans-support-death-penalty.aspx.

Neyfakh, Leon. 2015. "California's Sane New Approach to Sex Offenders." *Slate*, April 2. Available at https://slate.com/news-and-politics/2015/04/californias-sane-new-approach-to-sex-offenders-and-why-no-one-is-following-its-example.html.

Nochlin, Linda. 1971. "Why Are There No Great Women Artists?" In *Woman in Sexist Society: Studies in Power and Powerlessness*, edited by Vivian Gornick and Barbara K. Moran, 480–510. New York: Basic Books.

Norgren, Jill. 2013. *Rebels at the Bar: The Fascinating, Forgotten Stories of America's First Women Lawyers.* New York: New York University Press.

Norris v. Alabama. 1935. 294 U.S. 587.

Novisky, Meghan A., and Robert L. Peralta. 2015. "When Women Tell: Intimate Partner Violence and the Factors Related to Police Intervention." *Violence against Women* 21 (January): 65–86.

Nussbaum, Martha C. 2000. *Women and Human Development: The Capabilities Approach.* New York: Cambridge University Press.

Nussbaum, Martha C., and Amartya Sen. 1993. *The Quality of Life.* New York: Cambridge University Press.

Obergefell v. Hodges. 2015. 576 U.S. ___.

Offen, Karen. 1988. "Defining Feminism: A Comparative Historical Approach." *Signs* 14 (Autumn): 119–57.

Okin, Susan Moller. 1989. *Justice, Gender, and the Family.* New York: Basic Books.

————, ed. 1999. *Is Multiculturalism Bad for Women?* Princeton, NJ: Princeton University Press.

Oliphant, J. Baxter. 2016. "Support for Death Penalty Lowest in More Than Four Decades." Pew Research Center, September 29. Available at http://www.pewresearch.org/fact-tank/2016/09/29/support-for-death-penalty-lowest-in-more-than-four-decades.

Oliver, Bill. 2016. "Texas A&M Tenured Professor Loses His Endowed Position after He Is Convicted and Sentenced for Assaulting His Wife." *WTAW News Talk 1620*, April 1. Available at http://wtaw.com/2016/04/01/texas-tenured-professor-loses-his-endowed-position-after-he-is-convicted-sentenced-assaulting-wife.

Orr v. Orr. 1979. 440 U.S. 268.

Padover, Saul K., ed. 1953. *The Complete Madison: His Basic Writings.* New York: Harper and Brothers.

Palko v. Connecticut. 1937. 302 U.S. 319.

Parekh, Bhikhu. 1999. "A Varied Moral World." In *Is Multiculturalism Bad for Women?*, edited by Susan Moller Okin, 69–75. Princeton, NJ: Princeton University Press.

Pateman, Carole. 1988. *The Sexual Contract*. Stanford, CA: Stanford University Press.

Patmore, Coventry. (1854) 1891. *The Angel in the House*. London: Cassell.

Peltz, Jennifer. 2017. "Courts and Tri-parenting: A State-by-State Look." *Boston.com*, June 18. Available at https://www.boston.com/news/national-news/2017/06/18/courts-and-tri-parenting-a-state-by-state-look.

People v. Defore. 1926. 242 N.Y. 13.

Personnel Administrator of Massachusetts v. Feeney. 1976. 442 U.S.256.

Pew Research Center. 2015. "Support for Same-Sex Marriage at Record High, but Key Segments Remain Opposed." June 8. Available at https://www.people-press.org/2015/06/08/support-for-same-sex-marriage-at-record-high-but-key-segments-remain-opposed.

Phillips v. Martin-Marietta. 1971. 400 U.S. 542.

Pilgrim, David. 2012. "The Picaninny Caricature." Jim Crow Museum of Racist History, March 30. Available at https://ferris.edu/HTMLS/news/jimcrow/antiblack/picaninny/homepage.htm.

Planned Parenthood of Central Missouri v. Danforth. 1976. 428 U.S. 52.

Planned Parenthood of Southeastern Pennsylvania v. Casey. 1992. 505 U.S. 833.

Plato. 1961. *The Symposium*. Translated by Michael Joyce. In *The Collected Dialogues of Plato*, edited by Edith Hamilton and Huntington Cairns, 526–74. New York: Pantheon Books.

———. 1968. *The Republic*. Translated by Allan Bloom. New York: Basic Books.

Pollitt, Katha. 2017. "Dana Schutz's Right to Make Art." *The Nation*, April 6. Available at https://www.thenation.com/article/dana-schutzs-right-to-make-art.

"Polygamist Wife Contends Polygamy Is the Ultimate Feminist Lifestyle." 1997. *Las Vegas Sun*, May 5. Available at https://lasvegassun.com/news/1997/may/05/polygamist-wife-contends-polygamy-is-the-ultimate-.

Powell v. Alabama. 1932. 287 U.S. 45.

"Presidential Debate: Transcript of the Second Debate between Bush and Dukakis." 1988. *New York Times*, October 14. Available at https://www.nytimes.com/1988/10/14/us/the-presidential-debate-transcript-of-the-second-debate-between-bush-and-dukakis.html.

Quinney, Richard. 1980. *Class, State, and Crime*. 2nd ed. New York: Longman.

Radice v. New York. 1924. 264 U.S. 292.

Randall, Alice. 2001. *The Wind Done Gone*. Boston: Houghton Mifflin.

Rape, Abuse, and Incest National Network. n.d. "The Criminal Justice System: Statistics." Available at https://www.rainn.org/statistics/criminal-justice-system (accessed June 18, 2019).

Rawls, John. 1971. *A Theory of Justice*. Cambridge, MA: Belknap Press of Harvard University Press.

———. 1993. *Political Liberalism*. New York: Columbia University Press.

Raymond, Janice. 1994. *The Transsexual Empire: The Making of the She-Male*. 2nd ed. New York: Teachers College Press.

Redfield, Robert. 2013. "Introduction." In *Magic, Science and Religion and Other Essays*, by Bronislaw Malinowski, 9–13. London: Read Books.

Reed v. Reed. 1971. 404 U.S. 71.

Reeves, Richard. 1991. *A Question of Character: The Life of John F. Kennedy.* Roseville, CA: Prima.

Rehnquist, William H. 1987. "The Notion of a Living Constitution." *Harvard Journal of Law and Public Policy* 29 (2): 401–15.

Reynolds v. U.S. 1878. 98 U.S. 145.

Rich, Adrienne. 1976. *Of Woman Born: Motherhood as Experience and Institution.* New York: W. W. Norton.

———. 1986. *Blood, Bread, and Poetry: Selected Prose, 1979–1985.* New York: W. W. Norton.

Richards, Renee. 1984. *Second Serve.* New York: Stein and Day.

———. 2007. *No Way, Renee: The Second Half of My Notorious Life.* New York: Simon and Schuster.

Richardson v. Ramirez. 1974. 418 U.S. 24.

Riesman, David. 1954. *Individualism Reconsidered.* Garden City, NY: Doubleday.

———. 1964. "Two Generations." *Daedalus* 93:72–97.

Riesman, David, with Nathan Glazer and Reuel Denny. 1950. *The Lonely Crowd.* New Haven, CT: Yale University Press.

Roberts, Dorothy. 1997. *Killing the Black Body: Race, Reproduction, and the Meaning of Liberty.* New York: Pantheon Books.

Roe v. Wade. 1973. 410 U.S. 113.

Rogers, James R., and Georg Vanberg. 2007. "Resurrecting Lochner: A Defense of Unprincipled Judicial Activism." *Journal of Law, Economics and Organization* 23:442–68.

Romer v. Evans. 1996. 517 U.S. 620.

Roosevelt, Franklin Delano. 1937. Second inaugural address. Available at http://history matters.gmu.edu/d/5105.

Rosen, Ruth. 1991. "What Feminist Victory in the Court?" *New York Times*, April 1, pp. A11, A23.

Rosenbaum, Ron. 2008. "In Praise of Liberal Guilt." *Slate*, May 22. Available at www .slate.com/id/2191906.

Rosenberg, Rosalind. 1982. Beyond Separate Spheres: Intellectual Roots of Modern Feminism. New Haven, CT: Yale University Press.

Rosenfeld v. Southern Pacific Co. 1971. 444 F.2d 1219 (9th Cir.).

Rossiter, Clinton, ed. 2003. *The Federalist Papers.* New York: New American Library.

Rostker v. Goldberg. 1981. 453 U.S. 57.

Roth, Philip. 1962. *Letting Go.* New York: Random House.

———. 1975. *Reading Myself and Others.* New York: Farrar, Straus and Giroux.

Rothman, Barbara Katz. 1989. *Recreating Motherhood.* New York: W. W. Norton.

Roudinesco, Elisabeth. 1992. *Madness and Revolution: The Lives and Legends of Théroigne de Méricourt.* London: Verso.

Rousseau, Jean-Jacques. (1762) 2002. *Emile, or On Education.* Translated by Barbara Foxley. Available at http://www.gutenberg.org/cache/epub/5427/pg5427.html.

Rowe, Gary D. 1999. "Lochner Revisionism Revisited." *Law and Social Inquiry* 24 (1): 221–52.

Ruddick, Sara. 1989. *Maternal Thinking: Toward a Politics of Peace.* Boston: Beacon Press.

Rudolph, Lloyd I., and Susanne Hoeber Rudolph. 1967. *The Modernity of Tradition: Political Development in India*. Chicago: University of Chicago Press.

Ryder, Richard D. 2010. "Speciesism Again: The Original Leaflet." *Critical Society*, no. 2 (Spring). Available at https://web.archive.org/web/20121114004403/http://www.criticalsocietyjournal.org.uk/Archives_files/1.%20Speciesism%20Again.pdf.

San Antonio Independent School District v. Rodriguez. 1973. 411 U.S. 1.

Sanchez, Ray, and Amanda Watts. 2016. "Montana Judge Defends 60-Day Sentence in Child Incest Case." *CNN*, October 25. Available at http://www.cnn.com/2016/10/19/us/montana-judge-incest-case-trnd/index.html.

Sandel, Michael J. 1998. *Liberalism and the Limits of Justice*. 2nd ed. Cambridge: Cambridge University Press.

Sapiro, Virginia. 1992. *A Vindication of Political Virtue: The Political Theory of Mary Wollstonecraft*. Chicago: University of Chicago Press.

Sauvy, Albert. 1952. "Three Worlds, a Planet." *The Observer*, August 14, p. 14.

Sayers, Dorothy L. 1958. *Strong Poison*. New York: Avon Books.

Scheingold, Stuart. 1984. *The Politics of Law and Order: Street Crime and Public Policy*. New York: Longman.

Schenwar, Maya. 2014. *Locked Down, Locked Out: Why Prison Doesn't Work and How We Can Do Better*. San Francisco: Berrett-Koehler.

Schlesinger, Arthur M., Jr. 2007. *Journals, 1952–2000*. Edited by Andrew Schlesinger and Stephen Schlesinger. New York: Penguin Press.

Schulman, Grace. 2018. "The Nation Magazine Betrays a Poet—and Itself." *New York Times*, August 6. Available at https://www.nytimes.com/2018/08/06/opinion/nation-poem-anders-carlson-wee.html.

Scott, Joan Wallach. 1996. *Only Paradoxes to Offer: French Feminists and the Rights of Man*. Cambridge, MA: Harvard University Press.

Seaman, Barbara. 2003. *The Greatest Experiment Ever Performed on Women: Exploding the Estrogen Myth*. New York: Hyperion.

Segal, Jeffrey, and Harold J. Spaeth. 1999. *Majority Rule or Majority Will: Adherence to Precedent on the U.S. Supreme Court*. Cambridge: Cambridge University Press.

Sen, Amartya. 1985. *Commodities and Capabilities*. New York: Oxford University Press.

———. 2015. "Women's Progress Outdid China's One-Child Policy." *New York Times*, November 2. Available at http://www.nytimes.com/2015/11/02/opinion/amartya-sen-womens-progress-outdid-chinas-one-child-policy.html.

Sessions v. Morales-Santana. 2017. 137 S. Ct. 1678.

Shepherd, Liz. 2017. "Judge Halts Order Giving Rapist Joint Custody of Child Conceived in the Crime." *USA Today*, October 10. Available at https://www.usatoday.com/story/news/nation-now/2017/10/10/rapist-custody-case/751246001.

Shils, Edward, and Michael Young. 1953. "The Meaning of the Coronation." *Sociological Review* 1 (December): 63–81.

Silver, Moriah [pseud.]. 2014. "'The Second Rape': Legal Options for Rape Survivors to Terminate Parental Rights." American Bar Association. Available at https://www.americanbar.org/content/dam/aba/administrative/family_law/20141.pdf.

Singal, Jesse. 2017. "Here's What the Research Says about Honor Killings in the U.S." *Intelligencer*, March 6. Available at http://nymag.com/daily/intelligencer/2017/03/heres-what-the-research-says-about-american-honor-killings.html.

———. 2018. "Your Child Says She's Trans: She Wants Hormones and Surgery; She's 13." *The Atlantic*, July–August, pp. 88–107.

Singer, Peter. 1972. "Famine, Affluence, and Morality." *Philosophy and Public Affairs* 1 (1): 229–43.

———. (1975) 1990. *Animal Liberation*. New York: New York Review of Books.

———. 1999. "The Singer Solution to World Poverty." *New York Times Magazine*, September 5, pp. 60–63.

———. 2006. "What Should a Billionaire Give—and What Should You?" *New York Times Magazine*, December 17, p. 58.

Skinner v. Oklahoma. 1942. 316 U.S. 535.

Slaughter-House Cases. 1873. 83 U.S. 36.

Smith, Adam. 1776. *An Inquiry into the Nature and Causes of the Wealth of Nations*. London: W. Strahan and T. Cadell.

Smith, Jennifer. 2016. "Outrage after Man, 40, Walks Free from Court despite Admitting to Incest Rape of 12-Year-Old Girl." *Daily Mail*, October 15. Available at http://www.dailymail.co.uk/news/article-3839191/Outrage-man-40-walks-free -court-admitting-incest-rape-12-year-old-girl.html.

Smith, Rogers M. 1989. "'One United People': Second-Class Female Citizenship and the American Quest for Community." *Yale Journal of Law and Humanities* 1 (2): 229–93.

———. 1993. "Beyond Tocqueville, Myrdal, and Hartz: The Multiple Traditions in America." *American Political Science Review* 87 (September): 549–66.

Smith-Rosenberg, Carroll. 1975. "The Female World of Love and Ritual: Relations between Women in Nineteenth-Century America." *Signs* 1 (31): 1–29.

Solnit, Rebecca. 2015. "Shooting Down Man the Hunter." *Harper's*, June, pp. 5–7.

Solomon, Andrew. 2012. *Far from the Tree: Parents, Children, and the Search for Identity*. New York: Scribner.

Song, Sarah. 2007. *Justice, Gender, and the Politics of Multiculturalism*. New York: Cambridge University Press.

Song of the South. 1946. Directed by Harve Foster and Wilfred Jackson. Burbank, CA: Walt Disney Productions.

Sophia [pseud.]. 1739. *Woman Not Inferior to Man*. London: John Hawkins.

Sorensen, Jen. 2017. "A Brief History of Liberal Demonization." *The Nation*, June 1. Available at https://www.thenation.com/article/brief-history-liberal-demonization.

South Carolina v. Katzenbach. 1966. 383 U.S. 663.

Spaeth, Harold J., and Jeffrey A. Segal. 1993. *The Supreme Court and the Attitudinal Model*. Cambridge: Cambridge University Press.

Spock, Benjamin. 1957. *The Common Sense Book of Baby and Child Care*. Rev. ed. New York: Duell, Sloan, and Pierce.

———. 1968. *Baby and Child Care*. New rev. and enlarged ed. New York: Pocket Books.

"Spock Modifies His Ideas on New Moms' Work Plan." 1987. *South Florida Sun-Sentinel*, February 19. Available at https://www.sun-sentinel.com/news/fl-xpm-1987 -02-19-8701110225-story.html.

Stack, Liam. 2016. "Light Sentence for Brock Turner in Stanford Rape Case Draws Outrage." *New York Times*, June 6. Available at https://www.nytimes.com/2016/06/07/ us/outrage-in-stanford-rape-case-over-dueling-statements-of-victim-and-attackers -father.html.

"Stanford Sexual Assault Case: Victim Impact Statement in Full." 2016. *The Guardian*, June 6. Available at http://www.theguardian.com/us-news/2016/jun/06/stanford-sexual-assault-case-victim-impact-statement-in-full.

"Stanford University Statement regarding Brock Turner Case." 2016. *Stanford News*, June 16. Available at https://news.stanford.edu/2016/06/06/stanford-university-statement-regarding-brock-turner-case.

Stanton v. Stanton. 1975. 421 U.S. 7.

Stephen, James Fitzjames. 1874. *Liberty, Equality, Fraternity.* London: Smith, Elder.

Stiehm, Judith Hicks. 1981. *Bring Me Men and Women: Mandated Change at the U.S. Air Force Academy.* Berkeley: University of California Press.

Stillman, Sarah. 2013. "Taken." *New Yorker*, August 5. Available at http://www.newyorker.com/magazine/2013/08/12/taken?.

———. 2016. "The List." *New Yorker*, March 6. Available at http://www.newyorker.com/magazine/2016/03/14/when-kids-are-accused-of-sex-crimes.

Stockett, Kathryn. 2009. *The Help.* New York: G. P. Putnam's Sons.

Stolberg, Sheryl Gay, and Erik Eckholm. 2016. "Virginia Governor Restores Voting Rights to Felons." *New York Times*, April 22. Available at https://www.nytimes.com/2016/04/23/us/governor-terry-mcauliffe-virginia-voting-rights-convicted-felons.html.

Stross, Brian. 1974. "Tzeltal Marriage by Capture." *Anthropological Quarterly* 47 (July): 328–46.

Sullivan, Andrew. 2018. "Denying Genetics Isn't Shutting Down Racism, It's Fueling It." *Intelligencer*, March 30. Available at http://nymag.com/intelligencer/2018/03/denying-genetics-isnt-shutting-down-racism-its-fueling-it.html.

Sunstein, Cass R. 1987. "Lochner's Legacy." *Columbia Law Review* 87 (June): 873–919.

Sweatt v. Painter. 1950. 339 U.S. 629.

Swerdlow, Amy. 1993. *Women Strike for Peace: Traditional Motherhood and Radical Politics in the 1960s.* Chicago: University of Chicago Press.

Tatum, Sophie. 2017. "Education Department Withdraws Obama-Era Sexual Assault Guidance." *CNN*, September 22. Available at https://www.cnn.com/2017/09/22/politics/betsy-devos-title-ix/index.html.

Taylor, Charles. 1989. *Sources of the Self: The Making of Modern Identity.* Cambridge, MA: Harvard University Press.

Taylor, Erin N., and Lora Ebert Wallace. 2012. "For Shame: Feminism, Breastfeeding Advocacy, and Maternal Guilt." *Hypatia* 27 (1): 76–98.

Taylor, Gabriele. 1985. *Pride, Shame, and Guilt: Emotions of Self-Assessment.* Oxford: Clarendon Press.

Terkel, Studs. 1974. *Working: People Talk about What They Do All Day and How They Feel about It.* New York: Avon Books.

Thomas, Elizabeth Marshall. 1989. *The Harmless People.* Rev. ed. New York: Vintage Books.

Threadcraft, Shatema. 2014. "Intimate Injustice, Political Obligation, and the Dark Ghetto." *Signs* 39 (Spring): 735–60.

———. 2016. *Intimate Justice: The Black Female Body and the Body Politic.* New York: Oxford University Press.

Tiger, Lionel. 1969. *Men in Groups.* New York: Random House.

Tribe, Laurence H. 1990. *Abortion: The Clash of Absolutes.* New York: W. W. Norton.

Tuan Anh Nguyen v. INS. 2001. 553 U.S. 53.

United Auto Workers v. Johnson Controls. 1989. 866 F.2d 871 (7th Cir.).

United Auto Workers v. Johnson Controls. 1991. 499 U.S. 187.

United Methodist Church. 1992. *United Methodist Book of Discipline.* Nashville, TN: United Methodist Church.

U.S. Term Limits v. Thornton. 1995. 514 U.S. 779.

U.S. v. Butler. 1935. 297 U.S. 1.

U.S. v. Lopez. 1995. 514 U.S. 549.

U.S. v. Morrison. 2000. 529 U.S. 598.

U.S. v. Rabinowitz. 1950. 339 U.S. 56.

U.S. v. Virginia. 1991. 766 F. Supp. 1407 (W.D. Va.).

U.S. v. Virginia. 1992. 976 F.2d 890 (4th Cir.).

U.S. v. Virginia. 1996. 518 U.S. 515.

U.S. v. Windsor. 2013. 133 S. Ct. 2675.

Veblen, Thorstein. 1953. *The Theory of the Leisure Class: An Economic Study of Institutions.* New York: New American Library.

Vidal, Gore. 1990. *At Home: Essays, 1982–1988.* New York: Vintage Books.

Vizguerra, Jeannette. 2017. "Why I Will Not Leave." *New York Times,* February 24. Available at https://www.nytimes.com/2017/02/24/opinion/why-i-will-not-leave .html.

Walker, Alice, and Pratibha Parmar. 1993. *Warrior Marks: Female Genital Mutilation and the Sexual Blinding of Women.* New York: Harcourt, Brace.

Ward, Jule DeJager. 2000. *La Leche League: At the Crossroads of Medicine, Feminism, and Religion.* Chapel Hill: University of North Carolina Press.

Ware, Lawrence. 2017. "Why I'm Leaving the Southern Baptist Convention." *New York Times,* July 17. Available at https://www.nytimes.com/2017/07/17/opinion/ why-im-leaving-the-southern-baptist-convention.html.

Washington v. Davis. 1976. 426 U.S. 229.

Weeks, Linton. 2007. "A Historian Who Made the Ivory Tower Glisten." *Washington Post,* March 2, p. C01.

Weeks v. Southern Bell. 1969. 408 F.2d 228 (5th Cir.).

Weinberger, Bari. 2017. "Tri-parenting: Three's Company or Three's a Crowd?" *Law Journal Newsletters,* October. Available at http://www.lawjournalnewsletters.com/ sites/lawjournalnewsletters/2017/10/01/tri-parenting-threes-company-or-threes -a-crowd.

Weiser, Benjamin. 2017. "Anthony Weiner Says His Actions 'Crushed the Aspirations of My Wife.'" *New York Times,* September 13. Available at https://www.nytimes .com/2017/09/13/nyregion/anthony-weiner-sentencing-memo-sexting.html.

Welter, Barbara. 1966. "The Cult of True Womanhood: 1820–1860." *American Quarterly* 8 (2): 151–74.

West, Robin. 1988. "Jurisprudence and Gender." *University of Chicago Law Review* 55 (Winter): 1–72.

West Coast Hotel v. Parrish. 1937. 300 U.S. 379.

West Virginia State Board of Education v. Barnette. 1943. 319 U.S. 624.

Whole Woman's Health v. Hellerstedt. 2016. 579 U.S. ___.

Williams, Bernard. 1993. *Shame and Necessity.* Berkeley: University of California Press.

Williams, Joan. 1992. "Deconstructing Gender." In *Feminist Jurisprudence: The Difference Debate*, edited by Leslie F. Goldstein, 41–89. Savage, MD: Rowman and Littlefield.

———. 2000. *Unbending Gender: Why Family and Work Conflict and What We Can Do about It*. New York: Oxford University Press.

———. 2017. "The Dumb Politics of Elite Condescension." *New York Times*, May 27. Available at https://www.nytimes.com/2017/05/27/opinion/sunday/the-dumb -politics-of-elite-condescension.html.

Williams, Patricia J. 1991. *The Alchemy of Race and Rights*. Cambridge, MA: Harvard University Press.

Wisconsin v. Yoder. 1972. 406 U.S. 205.

Wittgenstein, Ludwig. 1958. *Philosophical Investigations*. 3rd ed. Translated by G.E.M. Anscombe. New York: Macmillan.

Wolf, Joan B. 2011. *Is Breast Best? Taking On the Breastfeeding Experts and the New High Stakes of Motherhood*. New York: New York University Press.

Wolfe, Stephen. 2016. "Edmund Burke's Eternal Society: A Philosophical Reflection." *Imaginative Conservative*, December 16. Available at https://theimaginativeconser vative.org/2016/12/edmund-burke-eternal-society-stephen-wolfe.html.

Wolff, Robert Paul. 1968. *The Poverty of Liberalism*. Boston: Beacon Press.

Wolf v. Colorado. 1949. 338 U.S. 25.

Wollstonecraft, Mary. (1792) 1929. *A Vindication of the Rights of Woman*. London: J. M. Dent and Sons.

Woods, Amanda. 2017. "Convicted Rapist Gets Joint Custody of Victim's Child." *New York Post*, October 9. Available at http://nypost.com/2017/10/09/convicted -rapist-gets-joint-custody-of-victims-child.

Wright v. Olin Corporation. 1982. 697 F.2d 1172 (4th Cir.).

Yang, Jennifer Ann. 2004. "Marriage by Capture in the Hmong Culture: The Legal Issue of Cultural Rights versus Women's Rights." *Law and Society Review at UCSB* 3:38–49.

Yew, Lee Kuan. 2012. "Warning Bell for Developed Countries: Declining Birth Rates." *Forbes*, April 20. Available at http://www.forbes.com/forbes/2012/0507/current -events-population-global-declining-birth-rates-lee-kuan-yew.html.

Yick Wo v. Hopkins. 1886. 118 U.S. 536.

Zeleny, Jeff, and Carl Hulse. 2008. "Kennedy Chooses Obama, Spurning Plea by Clintons." *New York Times*, January 28. Available at https://www.nytimes .com/2008/01/28/us/politics/28kennedy.html.

Index

Judith A. Baer is Professor Emerita of Political Science at Texas A&M University. She is the author of *Our Lives before the Law: Constructing a Feminist Jurisprudence,* which won the 2000 Victoria Schuck Award from the American Political Science Association.